PREGNANCY,
BIRTH,
AND THE
EARLY MONTHS

THIRD EDITION

PREGNANCY, BIRTH,
AND THE
EARLY MONTHS

The Thinking Woman's Guide

RICHARD I. FEINBLOOM, M.D.

A Merloyd Lawrence Book

PERSEUS PUBLISHING
Cambridge, Massachusetts

Photo Credits:

pp. xiv, 230, 324   Marilyn Holt
pp. xxii, 50, 126, 222   Dorothy Littell Greco
p. 170   Janice Fullman
p. 274 Ulrike Welsch

Drawings by Kathleen Gebhart

Library of Congress Catalog Card Number: 00-105217
ISBN 0-7382-0181-2

Perseus Publishing is a member of the Perseus Books Group.

Find us on the World Wide Web at http://www.perseuspublishing.com

Perseus Publishing books are available at special discounts for bulk purchases in the U.S. by corporations, institutions, and other organizations. For more information, please contact the Special Markets Department at HarperCollins Publishers, 10 East 53rd Street, New York, NY 10022, or call 1-212-207-7528.

Text design by Jeff Williams
Set in 11-point Janson Text by Perseus Publishing Services

First printing, July 2000
3 4 5 6 7 8 9 10—03 02 01 00

To Joshua, Sarah, David,
and their mother,
Deborah

DISCLAIMER

This book is meant to educate and should not be used as an alternative to appropriate medical care. The author has exerted every effort to ensure that the information presented is accurate up to the minute of publication. However, in light of ongoing research and the constant flow of information, it is possible that new findings may invalidate some of the data presented here.

CONTENTS

2 SHAPING A HEALTHY PREGNANCY   51

INTRODUCTION TO THE
THIRD EDITION

In revising this book on pregnancy and infants, I was deeply impressed by how much health care for pregnant women had improved during the twentieth century and, indeed, in my own professional lifetime. Much of the accelerating progress in maternal and infant health care over the last twenty-five years has resulted from research, both basic and clinical. Basic research looks at how things work. Examples are explaining how genes direct the production of proteins or how drugs work. Clinical research looks at the results of treatments, such as whether a drug produces a desired effect. Clinical research related to pregnancy compares outcomes of a group of pregnant women who receive a promising treatment (drug, procedure, test) and outcomes of comparable groups who do not receive the treatment or who receive standard care. The groups have to be large enough to permit statistical analysis. This scientific method allows us to draw conclusions about what works and what doesn't, and the body of knowledge on maternity care is thereby increased. (Also see p. 5.)

As far as we have come in caring for pregnant women, we still have a long way to go. For example, although deaths of women during pregnancy, childbirth, and the postpartum period declined dramatically between 1930 and 1996 (from 670 to 7.5 per 100,000), since then the numbers have stopped dropping. The current rate is more than twice the target rate set by the federal government for the year 2000 under its Healthy People 2000 initiative. Black women are four times more likely than white women to die during pregnancy, birth, and the postpartum period. Among the explanations advanced to explain these figures is inadequate and unequal access to health care for all pregnant women. Many of the 43 million Americans without health insurance are women of childbearing age. (In my own state of California, as of the end of 1998, 1.7 million children, one of four in the state, did not have health insurance. Of these, 670,000 were children of working parents whose employers did not provide affordable dependent coverage and who did not qualify for federal or state aid.) An even more significant factor in the problem of inadequate care is ignorance. Important treatment questions remain unanswered. Among those relevant to a large number of pregnancies are how to prevent and treat preeclampsia (see p. 307) and how to prevent premature birth (see p. 309). Only research will solve these tough problems.

We now know enough to say with confidence that the progress that is about to unfold in basic research is stunning. I refer many times in this book to the breathtaking advances we can look forward to in the new millennium. When it comes to clinical research, women themselves are the key. Women have demonstrated a great willingness to help find better ways to deal with pregnancy and birth. This willingness depends on trust in the researchers. A great effort has been made by the medical profession and by the U.S. Department of Health and Human Services to sustain this trust. By law, protocols for research must meet stringent standards for safety, must be approved by the medical ethics committees of the institutions sponsoring the study, and must meet the guidelines of the funding organization. Protection of participants is the top priority. Efforts are also being made to bring studies sponsored by pharmaceutical houses through private physicians under the same exacting scrutiny.

Women can exert civic influence to promote research on pregnancy and childbirth. Most of the funding for research in the United States is provided by the National Institutes of Health (NIH). Women can influence the funding levels and priorities of the NIH through their elected officials as well as by joining the lobbying efforts of various women's groups. (See Appendix for information on the National Women's Health Network, The Boston Women's Health Book Collective, and other organizations.)

ACKNOWLEDGMENTS

I first became interested in the idea of writing about medical topics for the general reader during a one-hour, private meeting with Dr. Benjamin Spock. A session with this legendary physician-writer was part of a month-long course in child development offered in the first year of my pediatrics residency program at University Hospitals in Cleveland. The guiding light of this course was Dr. John Kennell, a leader in addressing the needs of parents and babies at the time of birth. John has inspired a generation of medical students and trainees in pediatrics at Case Western Reserve University and elsewhere. I cite his work in several places in the book.

After two years with the U.S. Army in Puerto Rico, I continued my formal education in pediatrics at the Boston Children's Hospital. There, my interest in the developmental needs of parents and children was reinforced by Dr. T. Berry Brazelton, who was then developing his neonatal behavior scale. We worked together on several projects, including arranging for parents to be able to sleep next to their children who were having overnight surgical ear, nose, and throat procedures. Dr. Joel Alpert, who preceded me as director of the Family Health Care Program, sponsored by Children's Hospital and the Harvard Medical School, was a further strong influence. In my years in Boston, still involved in teaching and research, I was a partner with family physician Stanley Sagov in the Family Practice Group. With midwives Peggy Spindel and Judy Luce, we integrated maternity care into the services offered—unique at the time for a family practice in our area. I am grateful to Stanley for having shared his considerable clinical experience and for his willingness to join me in critically examining and rethinking the approach to labor and delivery that was standard practice in the late 1970s.

Fortunately, I was at Children's at the time of the founding of its Health Education Department by Harriet Gibney. Long before today's proliferation of educational newsletters from medical institutions and web sites on topics of health care, Harriet envisioned putting the stores of knowledge of the staff (including speech therapists, nutritionists, and the like) of a distinguished medical facility into the hands of parents in a language they could understand and use. The department needed physician-writers and I needed an additional source of income. Through this matchup my writing career was born. My first project was the *Child Health Encyclopedia*, which was very well received in the United States and was translated into a number of foreign languages. This project required collaboration with many members of the hospital staff as well as editors John Durston and Philip Ward and had the full and necessary backing of the chairman of Pediatrics at the time, Dr. Charles Janeway, a beloved leader who brought out the best in people and professed that any child's having to be in a hospital represented a failure of our health-care system and level of scientific knowledge.

Skipping over years spent in various teaching, practice, and administrative settings, and several more books for the general reader, I now practice in San Francisco, as a member of the medical staff of The Permanente Medical Group (the physician component of Kaiser Permanente). Here I have gained new insights into the field of health education. At Kaiser, health education plays an important role in an integrated system of services. In the current edition of my book I have drawn on the excellent newsletters, geared to gestational age, sent to our pregnant patients and their families. These readable, concise, and attractive bulletins provide essential information and were developed by Kaiser's northern California regional programs in health education and perinatal care.

I again thank Elizabeth Noble, Jenny Fleming, and Peggy Spindel for their respective contributions on exercise, preparing children for birth, and the time after birth. I have carried forward their writings for the third edition with little change. I also express my appreciation to Jane Cutler, for tracking the popular media on the topic of pregnancy; to Archie Brodsky, for keeping me in touch with currents of change in maternity care occurring outside the medical establishment; and to Harold

Bursztajn, M.D., and Rob Hamm, Ph.D., for deepening my understanding of decisionmaking in pregnancy.

My special thanks go to Jenifer Cooke for her careful editing of the manuscript.

From the beginning, I have been lucky to have Merloyd Lawrence as my editor. Following the *Encyclopedia*, she has worked with me (and, in some cases, with my writing partners) on a succession of books on pregnancy and infancy and on one about medical decisionmaking. Merloyd is of the old school of editors who stay and grow with authors over years, even decades. I keep her high standards in mind as I write. Merloyd's special interests have been pregnancy and parenting. Through her efforts, many parents have been better informed about both.

PREGNANCY,
BIRTH,
AND THE
EARLY MONTHS

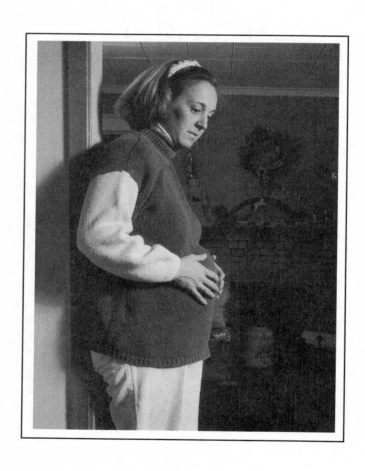

CHAPTER 1

Making Wise Decisions During Pregnancy

THE ABCS OF DECISIONMAKING

The first principle of good decisionmaking is to be informed. Know what your choices are, their pros and cons. If you can, do your homework before discussing issues with your doctor or midwife. Be at least as informed about your health care as you would be about buying a car or a computer. This book and others on pregnancy and birth, the Internet, and presentations in childbirth-education classes are sources of information for pregnant women.* (See Appendix for further reading and on-line browsing.)

The second principle is to attach numbers, when possible, to the odds of success (benefits) or failure (risks) of a particular choice. This will give you a more concrete idea of your chances and will help you choose more wisely. Figures are useful in weighing alternatives in medicine,

---

*In this book I generally refer to a pregnant woman as the *pregnant woman*, not as the mother, and to the baby before birth as the *fetus*, not as the baby, to avoid entangling myself with the divisive debate over abortion, in which the distinction between a fetus and a baby assumes great importance. As a physician I will stay with the medical definition of fetus. I do so fully aware that at some point in pregnancy every woman considers the fetus her "baby."

just as they are in the stock market and weather forecasts. For example, if the chance of rain is 10 percent, you might plan an outdoor picnic, but if the odds are as high as 33 percent (or one in three), you might make your arrangements for indoors. Knowing the numbers helps you decide.

Using the same example, as a check on the soundness of your decision, vary the prediction of rain up or down. You'll come to a number, say, a 25 percent chance of rain, for which either choice seems okay. Others may come to a different break point. At 25 percent you are indifferent to the choice and would accept making the decision by the toss of a coin. Make sure that the odds given in the forecast fall below or above your indifferent point.

Numbers, however, are only part of the decision. In deciding about a picnic, you are not only considering the odds of rain, but you are also factoring in the importance you attach to having to move from one site to another, from a rainy outdoors to a dry indoor area or from indoors to outside if the day proves sunny. You will take into account convenience, how many people are coming, logistics, and site (you will want to be close to shelter if you are outdoors and might for that advantage forgo a more attractive setting). In the language of formal decisionmaking theory your measure of importance is referred to as *value* and the product of value times the odds is called the *expected value*. The goal of the wise decisionmaker is to make choices with the highest expected value.

The third principle, therefore, is to examine your values. Make them *explicit*; then go back to the odds and recalculate the expected value. See if the result agrees with your initial, gut response.

Now you've made your choice, which you can think of as a conscious gamble (most casino or lottery gamblers are unaware of the odds). You are having a great time at the outdoor picnic, and rather suddenly, rain clouds appear, thunder rumbles, and it begins to pour. Everyone makes a mad dash for shelter. The question is, Did you make a mistake? My answer is an emphatic No, you did not. You made a responsible choice, and you had bad luck. Chance doesn't disappear simply because you were careful in weighing the risks and benefits and clarifying your values. After all, the weather forecaster (who, it turns out, is *always* right because he or she speaks only in odds) did not say it wouldn't rain, only that the odds were what they were. Even though you are justifiably disappointed, under these circumstances you are being unfair when you blame yourself. You may still learn from the experience, however. In the future, you might change your values and your indifferent point and arrive at a different choice.

As more choices become available in pregnancy, skills in decision-making take on increased importance. Let's look at one commonly faced choice, whether to have an amniocentesis (see p. 27) or chorionic-villus sampling (CVS) (see p. 29) to detect chromosomal abnormalities such as occur in Down syndrome. The definitive test for Down syndrome detects the abnormal chromosome in cells obtained from the amniotic fluid, by amniocentesis, or from the chorion, by CVS. However, these tests carry a 0.5 to 1.0 percent risk of causing an abortion. (Check the statistics of the doctor who would perform these tests for you.) It is thus possible that a normal fetus would be aborted while testing for an abnormal one. To determine whether this chance is worth taking, it is first essential to know your odds of having a fetus with Down syndrome. If they're substantially greater than the risk of abortion from the testing procedure, say, 10 percent, most women would want the test. If they're substantially lower, say, 0.1 percent, many women would just as soon take their chances.

What about our ability to define the odds for Down syndrome? It is good, improving, but still not perfect. To begin with, we can state the odds for each year of a woman's age (see Table 1.1), for example, 1 in 1,000 at age twenty-nine, 1 in 384 at age thirty-five, and 1 in 112 at age forty. We can refine these odds by using various serum markers (as a check on the soundness of your decision, see Expanded AFP, p. 24). Depending on the combination of tests used, our predictions can be as much as 75 percent accurate. Thus, a woman can know with this level of precision the risk of carrying a fetus with Down syndrome to term and weigh this risk against that of a procedure-caused abortion of what may be a normal fetus. Because 75 percent accuracy in prediction is the best we can do at this time, there is a 25 percent chance that a woman with no increased risk (by age and test results) will have an affected fetus. Whether a woman in this low-risk group wants to do nothing more or wants an amniocentesis or CVS will depend on the expected values she attaches to these alternatives.

For instance, let's say a woman is forty years old, had a hard time conceiving, is concerned this may be her last chance to bear a child and,

TABLE 1.1   Risk of Down Syndrome

Age of Woman	Chance of Down Syndrome
29	1 in 1000
35	1 in 384
36	1 in 307
37	1 in 242
38	1 in 189
40	1 in 112

Detection of Down syndrome by an expanded AFP screening program (blood screening test and followup diagnostic tests). Results are for every 100 women *who would deliver* a child with Down, according to woman's age.

age 35	AFP detects 71 and misses 29.
age 37	AFP detects 79 and misses 21.
age 39	AFP detects 87 and misses 13.

For women 35 years and under, 40% to 66% of cases are found.

Accuracy of expanded AFP and followup tests for other disorders:

> 97% of cases of anencephaly are found.
> 80% of the cases of open neural tube defects are found.
> 85% of the cases of abdominal wall defects are found.
> 50% or more of the cases of trisomy 18 are found.

NOTE: I have obtained these statistics from the California Department of Health Services, Genetics Disease Branch. Since new tests are being used in some centers and the populations being tested differ in their risks for defects, I recommend that you request current data, comparable to that presented here, from the center you are using.

based on her age as corrected by test results, has a 1 in 300 chance of having an affected fetus, which exceeds the risk of a procedure-related abortion. With these odds, the woman may take her chances and decline to find out more about the genetic makeup of the fetus. In contrast, a twenty-year-old woman facing the same odds might come to a different conclusion about her next step because most of her reproductive years still lie ahead.

Each of these women would have made a sound choice based on the risks and benefits and on her own values.

Just as it is important to know the odds, it is important to know how the data were derived. In this book I often refer to randomized control trials (RCTs) as the best way to assess the effects of a particular test, treatment, or practice. In an RCT everything about the group of patients receiving the test, treatment, or other procedure (the experimental group) and the group that is not (the control group) is supposed to match *except* for what is under study, for example, routine ultrasound, continuous electronic fetal monitoring, or episiotomy. Only in these cases can differences in outcomes (fewer fetal deaths or deep vaginal tears) be attributed to the treatment rather than to chance alone. If the groups differ, for example, if one group includes more women with a first pregnancy, this fact, rather than the treatment under study, may influence the outcome and thus invalidate the results. Generally, if the groups are large enough, minor differences among the women, such as differences in age, educational level, and weight, do not enter into statistical consideration because random assignment of the women should produce groups that are comparable in terms of these characteristics.

RCTs, particularly when used in the evaluation of drugs, can also facilitate identification of the contribution of the *placebo effect* to the outcome in question (relief of depression, lowering of blood pressure, etc.). The placebo effect accounts for the fact that many people improve when they believe that a pill will help them even if the pill is only a "sugar pill." The improvement is not imaginary; it's real. To prove drug efficacy there must be a statistically significant difference in the outcomes of the experimental and the control groups. In this way the contribution of the drug itself, and not of the action of taking a drug, can be determined.

One reason it can be difficult to conduct RCTs with pregnant women is that woman may not want to be assigned randomly to such groups as liberal or conservative use of episiotomy. Yet physicians are open to criticism for not insisting more often on RCTs before they adopt a new practice (as happened with routine continuous electronic fetal monitoring in labor [see p. 164] and with routine C-sections for babies in the breech [buttocks-down] position at term [see Breech Presentation, p. 277]). Further, once a practice is in place, it becomes more difficult to conduct a randomized control trial because patients will then be reluctant to take the chance of being in the control group and doctors will be reluctant to expose themselves to lawsuits for complications when they have deviated from "usual and customary" practice. As data from RCTs are not always available, we must make do with the best data we have, while recognizing its limitations.

BIRTH ATTENDANTS AND BIRTH SETTINGS

One of your first and most important decisions is the choice of a professional who will attend you during labor and delivery. This attendant can be a family doctor, an obstetrician, or a midwife. Before making your choice, consider what kind of labor and delivery best suits your needs and what type of continuity and attention you want during your prenatal visits.

As I discuss in Chapter 4, there are two major approaches to childbirth, what I call the *actively managed* and the *unhurried*. Others refer to these approaches as the medical model and natural childbirth. Generally, but with many exceptions, physicians, both obstetricians and family doctors, are educated (trained) to offer the actively managed approach, whereas midwives are educated to offer the unhurried approach. You need to match your attendant to the approach you want. Some physicians are expert in both approaches, and in some settings midwives are integral participants in the active-management approach. Many midwives continue their involvement when complications shift a labor from unhurried to actively managed. These practitioners will be discussed in more detail.

A decision that is basic to your approach to childbirth is *where* you want to labor and deliver. Possible sites include hospitals (used by the great majority of women), freestanding birthing centers (see p. 190), birthing centers in hospitals, and the home (see p. 191). Although not all physicians agree, I believe that safe, satisfying births can occur in all these settings.

Obstetricians and *family practitioners* are the two types of physicians who attend births. Both are board-certified specialists. Obstetricians are certified by the American College of Obstetrics and Gynecology (ACOG); family practitioners are certified by the American Board of Family Practice. (Some communities still have general practitioners— general physicians who have not been certified by the American Board of Family Practice—but their number is dwindling.)

One advantage of choosing an obstetrician is that obstetricians can deal with most complications of labor and delivery. For example, obstetricians can perform cesarean sections. Family doctors generally do not perform cesarean sections, nor do they usually handle complicated births; in these circumstances they call in an obstetrician to assist them. On the other hand, an advantage of choosing a family physician is that he or she can continue to care for the family after the baby is born. The family doctor's care is not limited to the pregnancy, but includes many other aspects of a family's medical needs. Thus, a family physician offers a family the opportunity for a more extensive and continuous doctor-patient relationship.

Fewer and fewer family doctors provide prenatal care or attend births. Depending on where you live, you may have to search for one who does. The American Academy of Family Physicians (see Appendix, p. 327) is a source of information on family doctors in your area.

When you interview (or otherwise gain information about) an obstetrician, find out what percentage of his or her deliveries are cesarean sections. Any figure over 15 percent or even 10 percent I would consider high unless the physician deals with a high-risk population. Otherwise, a high figure may suggest that the obstetrician's criteria for performing cesarean sections are too liberal and that he or she is too quick to cut. (See p. 213 on cesarean section.)

If you are planning an out-of-hospital birth, the issues to clarify are discussed in Chapter 4 (see pp. 189–193). If you are able to find a physician willing to attend a home or birthing-center childbirth, ask about the most serious problems she or he has encountered relating to the site of birth, how the physician dealt with these problems, and whether he or she would deal with them differently today. Openness about his or her practice and willingness to acknowledge errors are qualities generally associated with the best practitioners.

Nurse practitioners often work in physicians' offices and provide prenatal-care services. You may spend more time with the nurse practitioner than with the physician and will come to value the quality of this less-hurried time.

Midwives constitute the final category of professionals who attend births. They are specifically trained to deal with low-risk pregnancies and normal childbirth, and they apply nontechnological approaches to helping women with labor and delivery. Unlike many physicians, who are trained in the disease model of medicine, midwives do not view pregnancy as an illness or disease. By reputation, tradition, and long experience they are highly attuned to the needs of laboring women. They are women attending women; the term *midwife* means "with woman."

Nurse midwives are individuals who have both a nursing degree and midwifery training and who are licensed as such by the state in which they practice. Midwives attend births in hospitals and birthing centers, but their legal right to attend births at home is more restricted. In some states, midwives can open their own offices for independent private practice. Their styles of practice are influenced by the settings in which they function. The majority are women, and most belong to the American College of Nurse Midwives. (See Appendix for information on midwives' associations.)

Although the number of nurse midwives in the United States has increased, as has the percentage of births they attend (from 1.7 percent in 1980 to 9 percent in 1998—about one in ten), their presence in the United States remains slight compared with what it is in most other industrialized countries. In many countries midwives attend almost all women who are not considered at increased risk for complications and physicians attend the rest. In contrast, access to midwives by American women is limited, even for those women who know they want midwives as attendants.

Managed care, including HMOs, which has swept the U.S. healthcare scene in recent years, has had mixed effects on the relative positions of midwives and physicians. On the one hand, the push for lowering the costs of care has favored midwives. On the other, the designation of obstetrician-gynecologists as primary-care physicians (along with family doctors, internists, and pediatricians), a status based on reality, has reinforced their role as the major providers of obstetrical services because they are most often listed and paid for by health plans.

It would be naive not to acknowledge the impact of competing for a slice of the same pie on the relationship between midwives and physicians. Because the United States does not have a national health policy based on rational choices about the organization and distribution of services, professional organizations serving as lobbies for their members are left to slug it out in the marketplace and legislatures. In this contest, physicians, with their greater money and clout, have until now been largely successful in preserving their dominant position in the care of all pregnant women.

Midwifery is also practiced by *lay*, or *direct-entry*, *midwives*. Lay midwives are educated in several ways: some learn on the job, often at home births, as apprentices to experienced lay midwives; some attend accredited schools. In the 1970s many lay midwives worked and studied with family physicians, including me. Some states certify lay midwives and specify educational requirements; most do not. In many states lay midwives operate in a legal gray area. Some even prefer it this way and philosophically reject the notion that pregnancy is a medical problem subject to the state regulations that pertain to medical or nursing practice. Lay midwives attend births at home and in birthing centers. One such center was recently licensed in Oregon. They have contributed greatly, often against major opposition and legal harassment, to the proposition that normal pregnancy is the legitimate domain of women themselves. My personal experience with lay midwives has been very positive.

The relationship between nurse midwifery and lay midwifery is in flux. Whether the two groups of midwives will join ranks or continue their separate ways remains to be seen.

For more information on midwifery, I recommend the book *Midwifery and Childbirth in America* by Judith Rooks (see Appendix, p. 326).

Sources of information on choices within your community include friends who have had babies, doctors who can refer colleagues, local affiliates of the International Childbirth Education Association (ICEA) or La Leche League (although ICEA or La Leche League will not as organizations refer you directly to a doctor or midwife, their members will be willing to speak with you as individuals), the National Association of Parents and Professionals for Safe Alternatives in Childbirth (NAP-SAC), hospital departments of obstetrics (the chief of obstetrics may be able to match you to an appropriate doctor or midwife), the American College of Obstetricians and Gynecologists (ACOG), the American Academy of Family Physicians (AAFP), and nurses who work in maternity services. Most hospitals provide tours of their labor and delivery areas; while there, ask the guide about the styles of the doctors and, if the hospital has them on staff, midwives. The American College of Nurse Midwives (ACNM) will send you a listing of midwifery services in your area. A listing of freestanding birthing centers is available from the National Association of Childbearing Centers (NACC). The Mid-wives Alliance of North America, an organization of lay and nurse mid-wives that promotes midwifery and provides referrals, will also send you information. (See Appendix for addresses, web sites, and other re-sources.)

At the first appointment with the doctor, nurse practitioner, or mid-wife, indicate your preferences for labor and delivery. See whether you and the attendant are appropriately matched. Use the visit as an oppor-tunity to learn as well, taking advantage of the professional's experience and knowledge. Be open to having your point of view challenged. Con-sider having your partner or a friend with you on this first visit to sup-port you, provide an extra set of ears, and ask follow-up questions that might not occur to you.

Make a list of issues of concern to you. These may include the profes-sional's policy on intravenous fluids, anesthesia, episiotomy, labor posi-tion, and so on. Find out at what point in labor you can count on having the doctor or midwife with you, and clarify coverage arrangements. What happens if the person is away, for instance? In some large group practices the concept of "my doctor" is not even valid. Although a woman may see the same person more or less regularly at each prenatal visit, she will be attended during labor and delivery by whoever is on call. This may or may not matter to you, but if it does, you will want to find out right away.

Other Kinds of Support

Support in labor in addition to that provided by midwives and physi-cians, the primary birth attendants, is important and can take many forms: the *doula* (a Greek word meaning "a caregiving woman"), the maternity nursing aide of Holland (who participates in home births and stays on for a week after the baby is born), and labor coaches and com-panions. Studies in Latin America, Ireland, and the United States by doctors Marshall Klaus and John Kennell and psychotherapist Phyllis Klaus have shown that the participation of doulas in labor and delivery has very beneficial effects. Women who received support from doulas had a significant reduction in the length of labor, less use of Pitocin for labor stimulation, and fewer cesarean sections when compared with women who lacked continuous labor support. These findings confirm the great importance of psychological factors in having a positive labor experience and are consistent with similar favorable outcomes associated with care by midwives (see Chapter 4, p. 183).

In the United States doulas supplement the services of midwives and physicians. Because they are professionally trained and not emotionally involved with the woman, they serve a role different from that of a coach who is a friend or family member (usually the husband). Even the most highly motivated and prepared husband may find his physical and emotional resources depleted during the process of labor; at some point he may no longer be helpful to his wife and may even need some TLC for himself. Because the focus in labor must remain on the woman, consistent, predictable support for her is essential. I can't emphasize this point too strongly. Doulas are trained to provide just such support and to relieve husbands, friends, or other family members of this responsibility. For more information about this topic I recommend *Mothering the Mother*, written by Kennell and the Klauses (see Appendix, p. 326). Doulas are becoming more available, and there are now referral services in the United States and in Canada (see Appendix, p. 328).

Childbirth-education classes are offered by most hospitals, by local affiliates of ICEA, and by various home-birth organizations. Hospital classes generally support hospital policies and have an in-house quality about them appropriate for preparing families to have a baby in a particular institution. ICEA and home-birth classes take a somewhat more independent stance in their discussion of childbirth practice. Your reading and consultation with childbirth instructors and women who have attended different kinds of classes can help you choose an approach congenial to you.

La Leche League provides support for breast-feeding as well as for child care in general. Its members are available for individual consultation by phone or in person (often in your own home) about problems with nursing. Participation in this group can begin before the baby is born.

All these groups provide opportunities for expectant couples and single parents to meet others—one of the most useful functions the groups serve. For many of today's isolated families, the creation of community is an essential step in building confidence for birth and child care. See Appendix for the names and addresses of other support groups.

BEFORE YOU'RE PREGNANT DOS AND DON'TS

There are a number of steps you can take when you're planning a pregnancy. They are all discussed in greater detail elsewhere. Here they are presented in capsule form.

1. *Plan* your pregnancy. Know when you *could* become pregnant. Use a secure contraceptive to prevent pregnancy when you don't want to be pregnant. Without knowing that pregnancy is a distinct possibility for you, by the time you learn you're pregnant (several weeks at least after conception) valuable opportunities for prevention may have been lost, regrettably the case in over 50 percent of pregnancies. So begin preventive measures once you know you *could* conceive. The timeliness with which you can follow all the other points in this list depends on following this one recommendation.

2. Take a daily supplement of 400 milligrams of folic acid to prevent neural tube defects and other problems. (See Growth of the Fetus, p. 59, Nutrition and Weight Gain, p.87, and Expanded AFP, p. 24.) According to a survey in 1998, only 23 percent of pregnant women (many of whom did not know they were pregnant) were following this important recommendation. Use iodized salt or a vitamin with iodine for thyroid function.

3. Achieve your ideal body weight (see Obesity, p. 152, and Nutrition and Weight Gain, p. 87). Eat and exercise as if you were pregnant.

4. If you're taking drugs on a long-term basis for a chronic medical problem, consult your doctor about their safety for a fetus and consider alternatives as necessary (see p. 127). Check as well with your health-care provider about the safety of drugs prescribed for an acute illness during the prepregnancy period. Do the same for over-the-counter drugs. Remember, you will likely be pregnant for several weeks before you know it.

5. If you have a chronic medical problem, such as diabetes, tell your doctor you are planning a pregnancy and develop a safe strategy for handling your illness.

6. Avoid alcohol (see p. 143) and recreational drugs (see p. 145). (In addition to risks to the fetus, alcohol use actually decreases

your chances of becoming pregnant.) If you are a smoker, do whatever it takes to stop (see p. 142). Limit your caffeine use to one cup of coffee or one can of soda a day.

7. If you're not immune to rubella (German measles) (see p. 19), consult your provider about immunization. Continue using a contraceptive during the time of the immunization. The same recommendation may hold for varicella (chicken pox), but is not yet standard practice.

8. Read the section on genetics later in this chapter (p. 34) and collect and write down information about your and your partner's family history. Do any disorders run in your family? Pay particular attention to inherited disorders such as cystic fibrosis and to mental retardation. This information can help guide genetic counseling (see p. 47) and genetic testing of future parents. The fetuses of parents with mutated genes are at increased risk for the diseases such genes cause and are candidates for prenatal genetic testing. (Also see preimplantation genetic diagnosis, p. 44.)

9. If you have a cat, avoid changing its litter or wear gloves to do so. Avoid eating undercooked meat. (See Toxoplasmosis, p. 141)

10. If you are a caregiver for infants or toddlers, be sure to wash your hands thoroughly after changing diapers (see Cytomegalovirus, p. 135).

11. If you need an X ray, inform the staff administering the X ray that you could be pregnant. Expect that they will ask you anyway (see p. 146 on X rays).

12. Do not use a hot tub or sauna (see p. 150). It is also best not to use an electric blanket at the time of conception or during early pregnancy, as their use has been shown to increase the odds of spontaneous abortion by 75 percent.

13. If you are regularly exposed to organic solvents (usually in the form of cleaning solutions), protect yourself (and your fetus) by wearing a mask. (See Environmental Toxins, p. 147.)

14. Be sure your teeth and gums are in excellent shape. The last word is far from in, but there is mounting evidence that periodontal (gum) disease may be an important contributing factor to premature labor. (See Premature Labor, Birth, and Babies, p. 309.)

ROUTINE LABORATORY TESTS

Several laboratory tests are routinely performed as part of the early pregnancy assessment. Since most pregnant women will undergo these tests, it is good to have an idea of how the tests are taken and what their results are intended to reveal. I will first list these tests and briefly define them; then I will discuss them in greater detail. The specific tests you will have and the timing of the tests may vary. For the schedule of the tests used in our practice at Kaiser Permanente, which is representative of standard practice, see page 86.

1. Hematocrit and hemoglobin test: Done at about twenty weeks or earlier to detect anemia.
2. Urine test and urine culture: Test often repeated at all prenatal visits to check for diabetes, infection, and preeclampsia; culture often done at first visit to detect bacteria that can cause urinary tract infection without symptoms.
3. Blood glucose test: Usually done at twenty weeks to detect diabetes.
4. Syphilis test: Done selectively at an early visit to detect syphilis.
5. Blood type, Rh D factor test: Done by twenty weeks to identify fetuses at risk for blood-type incompatibility with the woman.
6. Rubella test: Done on an early visit to test immunity to this infection (German measles).
7. Pap test: Done at first pelvic exam to check cervix for cancer and infection.
8. Gonorrhea and chlamydia tests: Done at first pelvic exam to detect these two infections whether or not symptoms are present.
9. AIDS (HIV) test: Recommended on first visit to detect this infection whether or not symptoms are present.
10. Hepatitis B, blood test: Done on first visit to detect hepatitis B.
11. Expanded *AFP* test and fetal ultrasound: Done between fifteen and twenty weeks, ideally at sixteen to seventeen weeks to detect fetal malformations.

For newer test approaches, see page 25.

Blood Tests

The *hematocrit* is the percentage of a thin column of centrifuged blood occupied by red blood cells. The *hemoglobin test* is a reading of the concentration in the blood of the oxygen-carrying protein hemoglobin, which is contained within the red blood cells. Both tests can show whether anemia is present. One or both tests are usually repeated at thirty-six weeks' gestation.

Urine Test

A test for protein and sugar (glucose) in the urine is commonly done at every prenatal visit. Protein and glucose derived from the blood are normally present in the urine of nonpregnant women in minute quantities. Because blood flow to the kidneys is significantly increased in pregnancy, more blood is filtered and more protein and glucose pass into the urine. At some time during pregnancy, glucose will be detected in the urine of about one in six women. In a small number of these women diabetes, with its associated high blood-glucose levels, will be present. The presence of glucose in the urine warrants the testing of blood-glucose levels for diabetes.

Although it is common for some protein to be present in the urine during pregnancy, recorded as a trace amount on the test tape in common use, larger amounts raise a question about kidney disease or preeclampsia (see p. 307).

The urine test can also help detect urinary tract infection.

Blood-Glucose Test

A commonly performed test in prenatal care is measuring blood glucose following a glucose test meal. The purpose of this test is to detect diabetes, which it can do in the absence of symptoms or glucose in the urine. Recent studies have shown that the woman who has a normal fasting blood glucose (about 70 percent of all pregnant women) will also have a normal glucose challenge test. Only those with abnormal fasting glucose levels need to be tested further.

Syphilis Test

The serological test for syphilis, STS, detects syphilis even if the woman has no symptoms. The microorganism that causes syphilis can cross the placenta from the infected woman to the fetus with devastating results (see Syphilis, p. 141); treatment can prevent or ameliorate this complication. Treating the woman simultaneously treats the fetus.

The STS may be positive even when syphilis is not present (a *false positive*). Therefore, a positive STS must be confirmed by tests specific for syphilis. A false-positive test for syphilis warrants an investigation for, among other disorders, antiphospholipid syndrome, a cause of recurrent miscarriage (see p. 300) and other problems.

Blood Type, Rh D Status, and Tests for Antibodies Against Red Blood Cells

During pregnancy, particularly late in pregnancy and at birth, a small number of fetal cells, including blood cells, pass across the placenta into the woman's circulatory system. If the blood type of the fetus is the same as that of the woman, the woman accepts the cells without reacting to them. If the blood types differ, (incompatibility), the woman's immune system identifies the cells as foreign and produces antibodies to destroy them—the woman's immune system reacts to the gene-determined protein complexes on the outer wall of the fetus's red blood cells just as it does to other foreign proteins found on the cell surface of viruses, bacteria, and pollens. Alternatively, the woman may have preexisting antibodies that can react with her fetus's blood cells. In both cases the woman's antibodies eliminate fetal cells that have passed into her circulation. Furthermore, these antibodies freely cross the placenta into the fetal circulation, where they bind to the fetus's cells, causing them to be destroyed and removed from the fetus's circulatory system as well. The effects on the fetus, and, later, on the baby, range from mild, with no significant harm, to severe, with various degrees of jaundice (pp. 270–271), anemia, and even heart failure. Because of these possibilities and the opportunity to prevent, detect, and treat the most severe of these problems at an early stage, blood-typing of the pregnant woman is a routine pregnancy test.

The incompatibility of red cells that provokes an antibody response occurs most commonly in the case of an Rh D-negative woman with an Rh D-positive fetus. (What used to be called the Rh factor is now called Rh D. If our cells contain this surface protein, we are Rh D-positive. If we lack it, we are Rh D-negative.) About 15 percent of the population is Rh D-negative. Unless an Rh D-negative woman has previously been sensitized to Rh D-positive cells, for example, in a mismatched blood transfusion, she will not have antibodies to Rh D-positive cells at the beginning of her first pregnancy. Later in a first pregnancy with an Rh D-positive fetus many Rh D-negative women will become sensitized, but the quantity of the anti-Rh D antibody produced is too little or the antibody is produced too late in the pregnancy to destroy enough of the fetus's red cells to cause the fetus significant harm. Should the Rh D-negative woman carry an Rh D-positive fetus during a subsequent pregnancy, however, her renewed exposure to Rh D-positive cells would stimulate her already sensitized and primed immune system to produce far more of the antibody than was produced during her first pregnancy, which could jeopardize the fetus. For this reason, Rh D incompatibility in an unsensitized woman is a problem for pregnancies after the first one.

Rh D incompatibility is now almost entirely preventable through the use of a special gamma globulin called Rh D immunoglobulin. Rh D immunoglobulin is given to the Rh D-negative woman in time to attach to and eliminate Rh D-positive fetal cells in the maternal circulatory system before they are able to sensitize the woman. A first dose is usually given at twenty-eight weeks' gestation, and a second, larger dose is given within seventy-two hours of birth if testing shows that the baby is Rh D-positive. This one-two punch prevents virtually all Rh D-negative women from becoming sensitized and has almost completely prevented this once common and often difficult problem. The one exception to following this protocol for Rh D-negative women is when the father is known to be Rh D-negative. With two Rh D-negative parents, as will be discussed, the fetus will also be Rh D-negative and the conditions for sensitization are thus not present. Rh D immunoglobulin is also used to prevent sensitization of Rh D-negative women during other events associated with transfusion of fetal cells to the woman, such as amniocentesis, chorionic-villus sampling, abortion, and the turning of a breech before labor.

When an Rh D-negative woman who has been previously sensitized to Rh D-positive cells becomes pregnant, it is important to know the Rh D status of the fetus because Rh D-positive fetuses are at risk and need to be monitored for complications. The Rh D gene follows a recessive pattern of inheritance (see p. 35). A person who is Rh D-negative lacks both genes for Rh D. Thus a father who is negative will produce only negative fetuses, none of whom are at risk. On the other hand, a father who is Rh D-positive carries either one or two Rh D genes. Depending on the number of Rh D genes of the father, this pairing of partners will produce offspring who have a 50 or 100 percent chance of being Rh D-positive. In this case, defining the Rh D status of the fetus requires specific testing.

There are several ways to ascertain the Rh D status of the fetus. One is by gene analysis of fetal cells obtained by amniocentesis, as demonstrated by Phillip Bennett and his associates in 1993 at the Queen Charlotte's and Chelsea Hospital in London. Another, applicable later in pregnancy, involves obtaining fetal blood directly by needle puncture of the umbilical cord (see p. 162). The disadvantages of these approaches is that they entail some risks of their own and can actually cause transfusion of fetal blood into the woman's circulation, thereby adding to the problem of sensitization. (For this reason Rh D immunoglobulin is given after each of these procedures.) A new (and very exciting) approach, which has none of these disadvantages, was reported in 1998 by Y. M. Dennis Lo and colleagues in Hong Kong and Oxford. These researchers developed a technique to identify Rh D DNA of fetal origin in the woman's blood. The only risk is that of drawing blood.

If testing shows that the pregnant, sensitized, Rh D-negative woman is carrying an Rh D-positive fetus, who is therefore at risk, the well-being of the fetus is monitored through the rest of the pregnancy. Monitoring includes serial measurement of the level of the woman's Rh D antibody (an indicator of the amount of the antibody to which the fetus is exposed), fetal ultrasound (to evaluate the fetus's cardiovascular status), and measurement of the amount of bilirubin (the pigment derived from red blood cells, fetal in this case, that causes jaundice [see p. 270]) in the amniotic fluid. Treatment of the affected fetus and of the affected newborn are discussed elsewhere (see Treating the Fetus, p. 153, and Jaundice, p. 270).

The other important blood types are O, A, B, and AB. Compatibility of these types is crucial in blood transfusion, and type O also plays a role in the maternal-fetal relationship. Individuals with blood type O, and far less commonly, A and B, have naturally occurring antibodies against blood types A and B. Unlike D antibodies, A and B antibodies do not result from sensitization in pregnancy or under other circumstances. They are simply present. However, A, and, to a lesser degree, B antibodies do cross the placenta and can attach to and lead to the destruction of fetal red blood cells. The effects of this process are seen in the newborn as varying degrees of jaundice (see p. 270) or anemia, sometimes referred to as ABO disease. In general, the effects of ABO incompatibility on the fetus are much milder than those of Rh D incompatibility or of the rarer blood-type incompatibilities discussed next. Since anti-A and anti-B antibodies are present in the woman before pregnancy, there is no way similar to the use of Rh D immunoglobulin to prevent their formation. If ABO disease has occurred in one infant, there is an almost 90 percent chance that it will occur in siblings with the same blood type.

Some women have rare blood types that can be the basis of antibody production against the incompatible cells of their fetuses. Gamma globulin comparable to Rh D immunoglobulin is not available to prevent such sensitization. In this circumstance, the best one can do is to monitor and treat the fetus as with Rh D incompatibility. The antibody screening that is routine at the initial prenatal visit identifies women with so-called atypical antibodies that reflect rarer blood types.

Rubella Immunity Test

The *rubella antibody titer* identifies the adequacy of the mother's immunity to rubella (commonly known as German measles), a virus that can cross the placenta to infect the fetus, with varying harmful results, including deafness, cataracts, mental retardation, and heart defects. (See p. 140 for a discussion of congenital rubella syndrome.) Public-health policy in the United States promotes immunization of all girls prior to their childbearing years. The suspected exposure of a nonimmune woman during pregnancy to someone with rubella, rare because of near universal immunization, calls for monitoring the woman's antibody level to see whether it rises. A rising level indicates infection in the woman and possibly in the fetus. Infection in the woman raises the question of aborting the pregnancy, since there is at present no treatment for rubella in either the woman or the fetus.

Women who are not immune to rubella are encouraged to receive a rubella vaccine following the pregnancy to avoid problems in future pregnancies. They should receive the vaccine only when using effective birth control so that the vaccine virus cannot infect the fetus of an unsuspected pregnancy, although the risk to the fetus of vaccine virus is small.

Urine Culture

A significant number of pregnant women have bacteria in their urinary tracts without having any symptoms, so-called *asymptomatic bacteriuria*. These women are at increased risk for developing a symptomatic urinary tract infection (see p. 73) and, importantly, are at increased risk for premature labor (see p. 309). Treating these women with antibiotics can prevent clinical infection and help prevent preterm birth. Because asymptomatic infection can be identified with a urine culture, this test is commonly recommended during pregnancy. Standard urine tests (dipsticks with a test tape) can also reveal a urinary infection by a positive result on the color-coded site on the strip that measures an enzyme in white blood cells known as *leukocyte esterase*.

Pap Test

The Papanicolaou test of the cervix (Pap test, named after its inventor) is used to screen for cancer of the cervix by scraping cells from the cervix for microscopic study. Pregnant women are not more vulnerable to this disorder; testing in pregnancy simply takes advantage of the pelvic examination performed as part of the initial prenatal evaluation. The Pap test is repeated during the postpartum examination.

Gonorrhea and Chlamydia Tests

Gonorrhea is a common, bacterial, sexually transmitted disease, or *STD*. It causes vaginal and cervical infection (cervicitis), pelvic inflammatory disease *(PID)*, urethritis in both sexes, and throat infections with oral sex and can invade the blood and infect the body as a whole. In newborns, who are exposed in the birth canal, the eye can be infected with scarring and blindness a consequence. (See Preventing Eye Infection, p. 267.)

Chlamydia is another common bacterium implicated in a sexually acquired infection. It causes cervicitis, pelvic inflammatory disease, urethritis, and, in males, prostatitis. In newborns, who contract this germ in the vagina, chlamydia can infect the eye (conjunctivitis) and lungs (pneumonia).

Most women with gonorrhea or chlamydia have no symptoms. These woman are carriers and sources of transmission of the disease. Tests of the cervix in pregnancy for gonorrhea and chlamydia are performed usually at the same time as the Pap test in women considered at increased risk for these infections. Women with these bacteria are treated with antibiotics.

AIDS Test

AIDS (acquired immunodeficiency syndrome) is a major international public-health problem. AIDS is among the five leading causes of death in women of childbearing age in the United States and in children up to age five. New therapies may affect these figures. The problem is much more severe—shockingly so—in many developing nations, where most people cannot afford the currently available drugs and entire populations are being decimated. In some areas of sub-Saharan Africa as many as one in four people is infected.

One barrier to drug affordability has been the reluctance of U.S. pharmaceutical companies to waive their patent rights on anti-AIDS drugs so that these drugs can be produced more cheaply in impoverished countries. The situation is even more complex in such countries as South Africa, whose governments have opposed the use of certain antiviral drugs even though the companies making them have cut prices sharply. Distribution of drugs is another problem.

Testing of all pregnant women for infection with HIV (human immunodeficiency virus), which causes AIDS, is now recommended because of the growing effectiveness of drug treatment in prolonging the life and well-being of the woman and because drug treatment of the pregnant woman along with cesarean delivery has been shown to reduce the chances that the woman will pass the virus to the baby (known as *vertical transmission*).

The statistics are dramatic. Without treatment of the woman the rate of transmission to the fetus is 19 percent; this rate is reduced to 10.4 percent with elective C-section (C-section before the onset of labor). With drug treatment of the woman, the rate of transmission is 7.3 percent, reduced to 2.0 percent with elective C-section. (Viral transmission occurs primarily, but not exclusively, at the time of vaginal birth.) These figures do not take into account the quantity of the virus in the woman's blood or the degree of suppression of her immune system. These results must also be tempered with the risks to the woman associated with surgical delivery (see Cesarean Section, p. 213).

Although the details are still being worked out, because of the effectiveness of new drugs for the mother and the baby, women in certain stages of HIV infection can responsibly face the question of whether to embark on a pregnancy. They can also responsibly avoid infecting their male partners. Additionally, women with male partners who are HIV positive can avoid becoming infected through washing of sperm to rid it of the virus. Because of the complexities of these issues and the rapidity of research developments, I recommend that any woman who is HIV positive consult with an expert in HIV infection.

Without treatment, infection with HIV precedes the development of the clinical symptoms of AIDS by months to years. Thus, a woman can be infected but have no symptoms and nevertheless be capable of infecting others, including her fetus or baby. Transmission to the fetus and baby is higher in women in more advanced stages of infection (whose immune systems are more suppressed), whether or not they have symptoms. Transmission may also occur early in the woman's infection, as the virus spreads throughout her body before she has produced antibodies to it. Not all studies of transmission rates have differentiated the stages of infection of the women who were tested.

With the exception of the complications of AIDS itself, such as recurrent pneumonia, unusual infections, and, at the extreme, death, women infected with the AIDS virus do not have more problems than do noninfected women with their pregnancies. In addition, pregnancy does not appear to increase the severity of AIDS in the woman who has AIDS when she becomes pregnant.

When the baby of an HIV-infected woman is delivered vaginally, electronic fetal monitoring (see p. 164) is avoided because this technique requires rupturing the membranes and attaching an electrode to the fetal scalp, thereby increasing the chances of infecting the baby. The baby can also be infected through swallowing breast milk that contains the HIV virus, so breast-feeding is not recommended if the mother is HIV positive.

Because of the frequency of HIV infection in the general population, the very encouraging results of treatment for the woman, and the effectiveness in prevention of transmission of HIV to the baby, public-health authorities now recommend that *all* pregnant women, not just those at high risk, be tested for HIV infection. They should first be counseled about the risks and consequences of HIV transmission to the baby and of the effects of the virus on themselves.

Hepatitis B and C

Over 1.25 million Americans are infected with the hepatitis B virus. Most infected individuals have no symptoms of infection and are called asymptomatic carriers. Babies born of infected mothers, about 20,000 each year, are at risk for contracting the infection themselves. A minority become infected before birth as a result of passage of the virus across the placenta. The majority are infected during birth as a consequence of exposure to the virus present in the birth canal. Administering antihepatitis gamma globulin (antibodies) by a single injection to the baby at birth, along with the first of three doses of vaccine, is highly successful in preventing infection following exposure to the virus. However, this treatment will not arrest the progression of infection in babies infected before birth. Pregnant women are now routinely checked for hepatitis B.

Without treatment, a significant percentage of babies who are exposed to the virus during birth will become infected and develop liver disease—inflammation (hepatitis), scarring (cirrhosis), or cancer—and many will die. Because the vast majority of all exposed babies can be successfully treated before the virus has had the chance to infect them, it is now recommended that *all* pregnant women—not only those at high risk for infection—be tested for hepatitis B infection. The babies of women who test positive should be treated at birth as described.

The discussion of hepatitis B applies in part to hepatitis C, a viral infection whose great importance is slowly gaining public recognition. Hepatitis C infection occurs mainly in intravenous drug abusers and among people who engage in high-risk sexual behaviors. Hepatitis C is actually far more common than hepatitis B, infecting 2.7 million Americans—three times as many as are infected with HIV. Transmission of hepatitis C from mother to baby is far less common (occurring about 5 percent of the time) than is transmission of hepatitis B. Current drug treatment of hepatitis C is only moderately effective and is noncurative. There are few data about treatment in pregnancy. Vaccines are under development.

Expanded AFP Test

At this time there is no way to treat most fetuses with major birth or genetic defects that are incompatible with survival or will result in severe impairment. The thrust of early prenatal care, therefore, is to identify these fetuses for the purposes of therapeutic abortion. For women who choose to be tested, the process begins with considering the woman's age (the older she is, the greater the chance of a fetal genetic defect) and family history, proceeds to blood testing, as will be described, and, if needed, moves on to further diagnostic studies.

The blood tests currently used measure alpha-fetoprotein, estriol, and human chorionic gonadotropin. Taken together, they are often referred to as the *expanded AFP* test. The expanded AFP is abnormal in a fetus with open neural tube defects and other severe malformations. Open neural tube defects include *anencephaly*, failure of formation of the brain, and *meningomyelocele*, which consists of a defect in the vertebral column (*spina bifida*) through which protrudes a membranous sac composed of meninges (the cover surrounding the brain and spinal cord), cerebral spinal fluid, nerve roots, and malformed (dysplastic) spinal cord. Meningomyelocele is usually associated with hydrocephalus, a thinning and compressing of the brain from increased internal fluid pressure. These abnormalities can occur in as many as 1 in 500 pregnancies and are not related to the woman's age. Another major malformation detected by this test is failure of closure of the fetus's abdominal wall.

The expanded AFP is also abnormal when the fetus has certain dis-arrangèd chromosome patterns. The most common of these is *trisomy 21*, or *Down syndrome*, expressed in mental retardation and physical ab-normalities (see p. 46); the second most common such pattern is *trisomy 18*, expressed in severe mental retardation and death before birth or in early infancy. With chromosomal abnormalities, the woman's age is a risk factor; again, the older the woman, the greater the risk. (See Table 1.1.)

An abnormal expanded AFP for which no explanation in terms of early fetal abnormality is found by additional testing is also useful in identifying pregnancies at risk for other problems, such as growth failure (see p. 296), decreased amniotic-fluid volume (see p. 295), and malformations of the brain, heart, and limbs not apparent during sec-ond-trimester testing. These problems call for increased surveillance, usually by serial ultrasound studies, as the pregnancy proceeds.

Depending on the results of the expanded AFP a fetus is considered to be at low or high risk for an open neural tube or other defect, includ-ing trisomy 21. For fetuses considered at low risk, no further testing is undertaken, recognizing that a small percentage of affected fetuses will not be detected because of test limitations (see Table 1.1). For fetuses considered at high risk, and after the woman and her partner participate in genetic counseling, testing can proceed to a detailed ultrasound ex-amination (see p. 32); amniocentesis (p. 27) or chorionic-villus sam-pling (CVS) (p. 30); fetal chromosomal or gene analysis (p. 46); and measurement of amniotic fluid AFP and, in selected instances, of an-other chemical called acetylcholinesterase.

Also, depending on the results of the expanded AFP, and taking into account the woman's age, the fetus's risk for Down syndrome can be de-termined within a certain error factor related to limitations of the test (see Table 1.1). In fetuses considered at increased risk, the diagnostic studies described in connection with open neural tube defects are of-fered. (For further discussion of the decisionmaking process on this particular topic, see The ABCs of Decisionmaking, p. 1.)

Newer Statistics with Newer Test Approaches

The expanded AFP in the second trimester (between fourteen and twenty-two weeks) is the most common screening test now used.

However, it is likely that screening in the first trimester will become generally available in the future. Screening that combines a serum test (for serum pregnancy-associated plasma protein A) with ultrasound (checking the translucency of the fetal neck, which is increased in Down syndrome), has already been demonstrated to be effective in research settings. In the case of Down syndrome in particular, first-trimester screening (and testing of positives with CVS) will permit both earlier diagnosis (and abortion) (at ten to fourteen weeks) and more accurate diagnosis, with no more than 20 percent of affected fetuses missed (compared with an average of 25 to 40 percent of cases missed in women of all ages when relying on the expanded AFP test alone) and only 5 percent of normal fetuses identified as abnormal (false positives). Further, combining the results of these newer tests in both the first and second trimesters, as reported in 1999 by researchers at St. Bartholomew's Hospital in London, decreases the false-positive rate to 0.9 percent, thereby reducing the need for CVS or amniocentesis by four-fifths, with a similar reduction in the loss of unaffected fetuses. It is likely, however, that when the results of screening tests in the first trimester are abnormal, most women—placing a premium on earlier rather than later abortion—will want to proceed directly to CVS or early amniocentesis and not wait for the refined estimates that will become available later with the expanded AFP, even if the price is an increased risk of inadvertent aborting of a normal fetus. Obviously, each woman will have to weigh the risks and her values in deciding how to proceed.

Other Tests

Other tests are done in pregnancy when specific risks are suspected. Examples are the testing of couples of Ashkenazic Jewish background for Tay-Sachs disease (p. 40), testing women for chlamydia, and the testing for serum antibodies (immunity) to toxoplasmosis (see p. 141). Couples who are carriers of disease-causing genes that they do not want to pass on to their offspring can, if they can afford it, undergo preimplantation genetic diagnosis (see p. 44 in genetics section).

NONROUTINE BUT COMMON TESTS IN THE FIRST AND SECOND TRIMESTERS

Amniocentesis

Amniocentesis is the procedure of passing a needle through the abdominal wall into the uterus and amniotic cavity of a pregnant woman to obtain amniotic fluid for study. By means of amniocentesis it is possible to identify a fetus having certain genetic disorders (p. 34) and major malformations (see p. 24 on neural tube defects); to assess the maturity of the fetal lungs when preterm delivery is under consideration (see L/S Ratio, p. 163); and, in some cases, to provide medical treatment before birth (see Treating the Fetus, p. 153). Amniocentesis and chorionic-villus sampling, which will be discussed next, are integral parts of the testing program to identify severely disordered fetuses. The program also includes the family history (see p. 51), the woman's age (see p. 46 in genetics section regarding Down syndrome), and the expanded AFP test.

Amniocentesis for gene, chromosome disorders, and malformations is generally performed between fourteen and sixteen weeks, occasionally earlier. Before an amniocentesis, the uterus and fetus are examined with ultrasound to find the site of the placenta (to avoid puncturing it), to check for the presence of twins (each of whose sacs may need to be entered), and to verify the gestational age of the fetus. The woman's abdomen is washed with antiseptic solution and draped with sterile towels. The skin is numbed with a local anesthetic. Under ultrasonic guidance, to avoid injuring the fetus or the placenta, a hollow needle three to six inches long is passed into the uterus. Amniotic fluid is withdrawn through a syringe attached to the needle. Occasionally, no fluid is obtained after the first pass with the needle, and another attempt is made. If the second pass also fails, the usual policy is to stop and wait a week before trying again.

Women describe experiencing a uterine contraction at the time the needle is inserted. Following the procedure it is not unusual to have some cramping, along with a bruised feeling at the puncture site. One to two percent of women will have vaginal spotting of blood or leaking of fluid, which usually stops in two to three days.

When amniocentesis is performed for chromosomal and gene analysis, the amniotic fluid obtained is separated in a centrifuge into cell-rich and cell-free layers. The cell-free layer is subjected to biochemical tests and may be cultured for microorganisms. The cell-rich part, containing about 10 to 100 living cells, can be studied directly to determine the sex of the fetus, the presence of certain enzymes, and for gene analysis (see, for example, testing for Rh D DNA, p. 16). Because more cells are needed for chromosome analysis, the cells are cultured; in a few weeks the harvested cells can be studied biochemically and genetically. One of the more important recent advances in chromosome analysis is the technique known as FISH *(Fluorescence in Situ Hybridization)*, which allows identification of the most common chromosomal abnormalities in forty-eight to seventy-two hours. although FISH is dramatically more rapid than the ten to fourteen days needed for the standard amniotic cell culture, the latter is more complete in its analysis. A negative FISH does not exclude the possibility of an abnormality and must be followed by the standard culture performed on the same amniotic fluid. A positive FISH provides enough information for decisions about early termination. Because of its limitations and cost, FISH is generally used very selectively. Chromosomal tests with amniocentesis are 99.5 percent accurate.

In a low percentage of women, more than one amniocentesis must be done, either because of failure to obtain fluid on the first attempt or technical failure of the laboratory to process the sample. If the fluid contains blood, it may be unsuitable for certain analyses, and a new sample will have to be obtained.

Minor complications—uterine cramping, vaginal bleeding (from the uterus), and leaking of amniotic fluid through the vagina—occur in about 1 in 100 procedures. In the rare event that the fetus is pricked, the result can be a permanent skin dimple.

More serious complications also can occur. Even in the most experienced hands, amniocentesis appears to carry the risk of about one-half of 1 (0.5) percent for miscarriage (somewhere between 1 in 200 and 1 in 300), maternal bleeding at birth, or injury to the fetus. These risks must be balanced against those of having a fetus with an untreatable chromosomal disorder or major malformation.

Inadvertent puncturing of the placenta may lead to transfer of fetal red blood cells into the woman's circulation. If the woman's blood is Rh

D negative and the fetus's is Rh D positive, the possibility for sensitization of the woman exists with consequences for the fetus (see p. 16). Under these conditions, women are given Rh D immunoglobulin to prevent sensitization.

Several problems in chromosomal analysis may lead to no findings or to uncertain findings after amniocentesis. First, the cell culture may fail altogether, although few good laboratories have failure rates exceeding 5 percent. If cells from the woman have been shed into the amniotic fluid, these may grow out in the culture and be mistaken for those of the fetus. This problem occurs in about 1 to 2 per 1,000 studies. If male cells are grown from the fluid, they must of necessity be from the fetus; but if female cells grow, there is a possibility that they are those of the woman rather than those of the fetus. Accordingly, a separate chromosomal analysis of the woman's blood cells is recommended for comparison with the chromosomes of the cells grown from the amniotic fluid.

Laboratory errors are not completely avoidable, even in the best of hands, and can result in the woman's aborting a normal fetus or allowing an abnormal one to continue to term. The error rate for prenatal diagnosis, however, is remarkably low, ranging from 0.2 percent to 0.6 percent. For many couples, the waiting period—one and one-half to two weeks (which can be shortened, as mentioned, by FISH)—is a time of increased anxiety. For most, however, their risks and anxiety are well balanced by their peace of mind when certain very serious abnormalities of the developing fetus have been almost entirely ruled out.

Chorionic-Villus Sampling

Chorionic-villus sampling (CVS) is a painless procedure that can be performed in the hospital or a doctor's office as early as the fifth week of pregnancy. It is designed to detect chromosomal and gene abnormalities. Unlike amniocentesis, CVS is not useful in detecting open neural tube defects.

In the most common approach, a thin, hollow tube (catheter) is inserted into the uterus through the vagina, or, with fewer complications, through the abdominal wall, and guided by ultrasound or by hysteroscope (a fiberoptic viewing tube) into a position between the uterine lining and the *chorion*, a tissue layer that surrounds the embryo and later, the fetus, for the first two months of its development, and then develops into the placenta. A syringe attached to the tube sucks up several of the *chorionic villi*, projections of tissue that transfer oxygen, food, and waste between the mother's circulation and that of the embryo and are genetically identical with the embryo. Analysis of the cells of the villi thus reveals the genetic endowment of the fetus. Certain analyses can be done on the same day, including chromosome characterization, thereby enabling couples to avoid the anxiety of the wait for the results of amniocentesis (now much less of an issue with the advent of FISH). The risk of miscarriage with CVS is about 0.8 percent (between 0.5 percent and 1 percent, or, stated differently, 1 in 200 to 1 in 100). The risk of affecting the development of a fetal limb (arm or leg) is 0.2 percent if CVS is performed at less than ten weeks and 0.07 percent at over ten weeks.

Amniocentesis and Chorionic-Villus Sampling Compared

As previously mentioned, both CVS and amniocentesis are used for chromosome and gene testing of the fetus; their accuracy is comparable and over 99 percent. Of the two tests, only amniocentesis is also useful in detecting open neural tube defects and certain other major abnormalities. Although both tests aid in identifying a large number of severely impaired fetuses, neither successfully detects all fetuses with birth defects, major or minor. (See Major Birth Defects, p. 275.)

Until 1989 there were no randomized control studies that compared CVS with amniocentesis. Caution was therefore needed in interpreting the results of existing nonrandomized control studies. In one such study, important because of its size, reported in the March 9, 1989, issue of the *New England Journal of Medicine*, researchers compared 2,278 first-trimester CVSs with 671 amniocenteses performed at sixteen weeks of gestation. Successful cytogenetic diagnoses resulted from 97.8 percent of the CVSs and 99.4 percent of the amniocenteses; 0.8 percent of the women who had had a CVS later needed an amniocentesis to clarify an uncertain initial result. Other nonrandomized studies, not discussed here, have yielded similar findings, but there are differences in outcomes from one institution to another.

The first (and, at the time of this writing, only) randomized control study was reported in June 1991 in the *Lancet*. It involved 3,248 European women cared for in medical centers in several countries. The most significant finding was that women who had had an amniocentesis had 4.6 percent more babies who survived than women who had had a CVS; 91 percent of the women who had had an amniocentesis delivered a live baby, whereas 86 percent of those who had had a CVS delivered a live baby. This study suggests that even allowing for miscarriages CVS is slightly more likely to result in a fetal death sometime during the pregnancy than is amniocentesis. These are important findings because of the design and quality of the study, and they will allow parents to make more discriminating decisions. As found in other studies, about 1 percent of the CVSs had to be followed by amniocenteses to clarify uncertain chromosomal analyses. However, a 1992 multicenter study organized by Jefferson Medical College in Philadelphia (designed to look at a different question—the comparative safety of transcervical and transabdominal CVS) showed *no* differences in miscarriages after CVS compared with the best results following amniocentesis, underlining the importance of checking the statistics of the physician who will actually be doing the procedure. Since these studies were done, the risk of fetal limb defects with CVS has become known (see above) and must also be taken into account in any comparisons.

As previously mentioned, with CVS chromosome analysis is possible on the same day, whereas results after amniocentesis require up to two weeks (which can be shortened by FISH). On the other hand, an amniocentesis may have to be done after a CVS (about 1 percent of the time) because of uncertain results. Amniocentesis is easier for doctors to learn and is therefore more generally available than is CVS, which is performed at fewer specialized maternity centers. When it comes to your own care, as with all procedures related to pregnancy, I encourage you to ask about the individual outcome statistics of the physician or clinical service you are considering.

Analysis of a Woman's Blood for Fetal Cells and DNA

A still-experimental but promising diagnostic procedure in chromosomal and gene analysis is the study of trophoblasts (see Growth of the Fetus, p. 59) normally found circulating in a pregnant woman's blood but in very small numbers, which are readily obtained by venipuncture (drawing of blood from a vein, usually in the arm). Because trophoblasts have the same chromosomes and genes as the fetus, studying them (assuming that the technical details can be worked out) could provide the same genetic information as CVS or amniocentesis at far less risk, cost, and inconvenience.

A related technique is extracting fetal DNA from the woman's blood for analysis. This approach has been demonstrated to be feasible and less intrusive and risky than its alternatives in detecting Rh D-positive fetal red blood cells present in an Rh D-negative woman's blood, a finding of consequence for monitoring fetal health as the pregnancy proceeds (see Blood Type, Rh D Status, p. 16).

Ultrasound

Ultrasound (sonography) is a diagnostic technology that has had a major impact on maternity care and medical practice in general. It originated during World War II, when high-frequency sound waves were first used to detect enemy submarines. The echoes of sound waves beamed into the water were reflected back from any object encountered, to be heard by electronic sensors.

The use of sound waves in medicine follows the same principle. Intermittent, high-frequency (inaudible to the human ear) sound waves are generated by applying an alternating current to a device known as a transducer. A transmitting solution, such as mineral oil, is placed on the skin, and the transducer is applied. In its use in pregnancy, the transducer sends pulsations of sound through the mother's abdomen to the interior of the uterus. As the sound waves penetrate the various layers of tissue, some of the sound energy is reflected (echoed) back to the transducer. The transducer alternates rapidly between emitting (sending) and receiving (listening) states. In the listening state, the echoes received generate a small electrical voltage, which is amplified and displayed on a screen. Both the thickness and the consistency of various tissues—bone, heart, skin, and so on—can be seen in relation to nearby images. In this way, a two-dimensional (soon to be three-dimensional) picture of the fetus is produced as the transducer's position is changed. The echoes can also be converted into audible sounds, making it possible to "hear" the beating of the fetal heart.

Ultrasound can be used in several ways. It can measure the size of the fetus's body parts, such as the head, which is useful in dating a pregnancy, and it can follow the growth of the fetus. It can produce a cross-sectional picture, or slice, of the fetal body. A slice through the fetal abdomen can show the size and location of the organs inside. A slice through the brain can identify the ventricles (fluid-filled cavities), providing information about their normality or enlargement (*hydrocephalus*). Ultrasound can also be used to observe movements of fetal structures such as the beating of the heart, emptying of the bladder, movements of the chest, and sucking of the thumb. (See Fetal Biophysical Profile, p. 161.) More uses are yet to come.

The applications of prenatal ultrasound include the following:

1. Identifying an embryo or fetus to diagnose pregnancy
2. Monitoring the growth of the fetus
3. Determining whether a fetus has or has not been aborted (p. 53)
4. Verifying the existence of a tubal (ectopic) pregnancy (pp. 289–294)
5. Identifying multiple pregnancies and fetal position
6. Identifying fetal abnormalities such as meningomyelocele (p. 24), hydrocephalus (p. 275), and limb defects. More recently measuring the translucency of the fetal neck has proved useful in detecting Down syndrome. Some abnormalities are transient, occurring early in pregnancy and not later. A common transient abnormality is a small cyst (or cysts) within the brain known as a *choroid plexus cyst*. If the ultrasound is otherwise normal, these cysts may be significant in their rare association with trisomy 18 (see p. 46).
7. Locating the placenta and determining placental abnormalities (pp. 303–305 on placenta previa)
8. Measuring the amniotic fluid (see pp. 295–296 on hydramnios and oligohydramnios)
9. Guiding needle insertion in amniocentesis, chorionic-villus sampling, and fetal cord-blood sampling (see p. 162).
10. Measuring the fetal heart rate during prenatal visits (p. 159), stress and nonstress tests (pp. 160–161), and labor.
11. Treating the fetus before birth (pp. 153–156)

12. Measuring the pulsations of the fetal arteries in the umbilical cord as a test of fetal well-being (see p. 162).
13. Estimating the weight of the fetus to assess the safety of a vaginal birth after a previous cesarean birth.

The safety of ultrasound appears proven. To date there has been no evidence of fetal abnormalities related to its use, nor have changes been observed in living cells in tissue culture after exposure to the doses used in humans.

Although ultrasound examination is increasingly used in all pregnancies (including at Kaiser Permanente where I work), existing studies of performing a single ultrasound test or two tests, one early and one late, in pregnancies at low risk for fetal abnormality have not shown that outcomes for babies were improved. The studies showed that such routine testing led to earlier identification of twins, revision of the expected date of delivery, and earlier detection of fetuses with congenital malformations. In the case of severe malformation, earlier detection allowed for earlier abortion as an option. However, these studies used less powerful equipment than is now available. If they were repeated with today's technology and the increased knowledge we have of how to interpret ultrasound images, it is likely that significant benefits would be identified. There is now a strong general consensus, even without a controlled study, that one ultrasound in the second trimester should be routine.

The experience by parents-to-be of seeing ultrasound images of their babies has introduced a new graphic dimension into the fetal-parental relationship. New family albums often open with an ultrasound portrait. Utrasound images of the fetus with a beating heart and moving limbs have also fueled the claim of opponents of abortion that the fetus is a person from the time of conception.

GENETICS AND YOUR PREGNANCY

New Options from Genetic Science

Understanding how genes work and applying that understanding to the fields of medicine, agriculture, and animal husbandry must count as one of the greatest achievements of twentieth-century science. Hardly a day passes when some breakthrough, at times controversial, is not announced: cloning; production in the test tube of important hormones, such as human insulin; development of techniques to repair or better control the function of defective genes (including those that play a major role in cancer formation); the ongoing mapping of the estimated 70,000 human genes; introducing genes into vegetables to make them resistant to disease; genetic profiling of patients to determine which of several drug options will work best to treat various diseases; injecting the genes that direct blood-vessel growth into heart muscle that has blocked arteries; using DNA as a genetic fingerprint in criminal investigations or in genealogical research; and introducing genes of harmless protein constituents of disease-causing germs into vegetables and fruits that will induce and reinforce immunity against these germs each time a person eats these foods. This discussion, however, focuses primarily on advances in genetics that have applications in pregnancy. To understand these advances, you need to know the meaning of several technical words and understand several basic concepts. You should find the effort amply rewarding, for genetics is a subject that will affect us more and more in the years ahead.

The Austrian monk Gregor Mendel, the founder of modern genetic science, working in the city of Brno, Czechoslovakia, in the early 1860s, showed that the first generation of a crossing of two distinct varieties of any organism (yellow- and green-seeded peas in the case of Mendel's famous experiments) received a *dominant* hereditary unit from one parent and a *recessive* unit from the other. We now call these hereditary units *genes* and know that they occur in pairs in the nuclei of individual cells, each parent contributing one gene to the new generation. Since the landmark studies of James Watson and Francis Crick in the 1950s, we now know that genes are sequenced, or linked, in predictable order in the complex structure of a double helix (two intertwined coils or spirals), which is recognized microscopically with certain stains as a *chromosome*. Chromosomes and the genes that constitute them are made of the chemical *deoxyribonucleic acid*, or *DNA*. Although each cell is one-fifth the size of what the naked eye can see, each, remarkably, has six feet of DNA, tightly coiled, yet retrievable for use when the gene needs to be activated. If it were possible to line up all the DNA strands of one human infant in a single line, that line, defying our comprehension and even our imagination, would be long enough to make fifteen round-trips from the sun to Pluto, the most distant planet in our solar system.

Through a complex process not discussed here (but fascinating and well worth learning about) each gene is the blueprint, something like a computer code, for the assembly of a single protein from a specific sequence of amino acids. Most human diseases appear to result from too much, too little, or defective protein. At this time we know precisely which gene is defective in about 600 of the 3,500 single-gene diseases identified by study of family pedigrees. (Genetic centers now offer DNA tests for 30 to 40 of the more common inherited disorders, including cystic fibrosis.) Definitive treatment, that is, cure, of these diseases will lie in correcting the responsible genes. We are not at that point yet. For example, at this time we treat, quite effectively, genetically (as well as nutritionally) caused high levels of blood fats such as cholesterol with drugs to lower their production. Someday we may be able to correct the abnormal genes that make the proteins into which these excessive quantities of fat are incorporated.

As an example of putting to use what we already know, consider the production of human proteins for patients who cannot produce enough on their own. Many people with diabetes are unable to produce enough of the protein *insulin*. Until the field of genetic engineering came into its own, these patients had to rely on insulin extracted from the pancreases of cows or pigs; both had disadvantages. Making human insulin in large quantities became possible for the first time when the gene for insulin was spliced into the DNA strands of a common bacterium. As the bacterium reproduces in a vat of nutrients that support its multiplication, the inserted gene produces insulin in large quantities. This insulin is harvested, purified, packaged, and made available to people with diabetes.

Returning to the discussion of how genes from two parents are expressed, when the offspring has obtained a combination of a dominant gene from one side and a recessive gene from the other, the dominant gene always prevails. Individuals with this combination of a dominant and a recessive gene are said to be *heterozygous*, having two unlike genes for a particular characteristic. If they receive the same type of gene from both parents, they are said to be *homozygous*, whether the gene is dominant or recessive. For a recessive gene to be physically expressed, the offspring must be homozygous, having received that recessive gene from both parents. Recently, scientists have discovered that the same gene may function differently in an offspring, depending on whether it came from the father or from the mother.

Mendel's theories are usually expressed in symbols. Dominant genes are shown in capital letters (XX). Recessive genes are designated by the corresponding lowercase letters (xx). A pure dominant strain of yellow-seeded peas, for instance, is symbolized as YY. This genetic formula is known as the *genotype*. A pure recessive strain (for instance, of peas with green seeds) is shown by the genotype yy. When these two strains are crossed (YY by yy), all progeny will have the same genotype, Yy. You will see how this works if you think of the four possible combinations: the first Y combining with the first y to produce one Yy, and then with the second y to produce a second Yy; then the second Y combines with the first y to produce the third Yy, and with the second y for the fourth Yy. These are known as *heterozygous hybrids*, and they all have the same demonstrable characteristic known as the *phenotype*, which in this case is yellow seeds, since yellow (Y) is dominant over green (y). (Note that the letter *Y* is used here as an abbreviation for the phenotype "yellow." Later in the discussion Y will be used in a traditional way to refer to the male sex chromosome.) As discussed earlier, since genes determine proteins, we can now more accurately describe phenotypes as differences in proteins.

Genes That Cause Disease

All of us carry both dominant and recessive genes. These genes, often working in combination with other genes, control our individual characteristics, both those that are obvious, such as hair color, and those out of sight at the level of chemical molecules. A gene may cause a characteristic harmful to its bearer, in other words, a disease. The disease-causing gene may be either dominant or recessive, and it may be located on the sex chromosome or, more commonly, on an autosomal (nonsex) chromosome. An example of a dominant disease-causing gene is the gene that determines *retinoblastoma*, a cancer of the retina of the eye. Dominant conditions carried on the autosomal chromosomes (those not linked to sex) are the most frequent types of inherited disorders. Well over a thousand have been identified. The following are the criteria of a dominant gene:

1. The trait appears in each generation.
2. The trait is transmitted by an affected individual on average to half his or her children, regardless of sex.
3. Unaffected individuals do not transmit the trait to their children.
4. Males and females are equally likely to have the trait and to transmit it.

When a disease-determining gene is recessive, one recessive gene from each parent is required to produce the disease. The most common recessive genes are located on autosomes, but recessive genes can also be carried on the sex chromosomes. Many recessive genes are lethal; when one is matched with another, they produce a fertilized ovum so defective that it cannot survive. Such defective conceptions account for a significant percentage of spontaneous abortions (miscarriages) (see pp. 298–303).

A person who carries a recessive disease-causing gene and a normal dominant gene for the same characteristic is said to be a *carrier* of the gene or to be *heterozygous* for that gene. Most recessive disease-determining genes do not cause illness in the carrier. For example, the carrier for *sickle-cell anemia* usually has no problems, whereas the individual with two genes (homozygote) suffers from anemia and attacks of severe pain, the full-blown signs of the disease. However, in unusual circumstances of low oxygen, such as are found at high altitudes (in nonpressurized airplanes, for example), the carrier's blood cells can also undergo sickling (collapsing into the shape of a sickle) and cause pain. When oxygen levels return to normal, the carrier returns to normal as well. It is crucial to understand the difference between being a carrier of a disease and actually having the disease.

The characteristics of autosomal (non-sex-linked) recessive genes are as follows:

1. The condition determined by the gene appears only in siblings, not in parents.
2. On average, one-quarter of siblings will be affected, which is the same as saying that the risk of recurrence is one-fourth for each pregnancy.
3. Males and females are equally likely to be affected.
4. In the case of rare disorders, it is likely that the parents are blood relatives, which accounts in part for the occurrence of certain diseases in isolated and inbred groups.

An important point in understanding the role of both dominant and recessive genes in heredity is that the outcome in the offspring is determined *by chance*. In the example of retinoblastoma, involving a dominant gene, each child has a one in two (50 percent) chance of inheriting that gene and manifesting the disease. The same odds apply to each child, regardless of whether preceding siblings are affected. In one family, no children may be affected; in another, all children may be affected. But if we were to look at 100 children born of parents with this genetic setup, about 50 would have retinoblastoma. In the example of sickle-cell anemia, which involves a recessive gene, if two carriers have children, each child would have a one in four (25 percent) chance of being homozygous and having the disease. The fact that the first child was or was not affected does not alter the odds for the next child. Some families could have four affected children and some, none. Overall, in the population at large, one of every four children born to all carrier couples would have the disease.

Now that we are able to identify individual genes, we have learned that for some diseases inheritance may follow both dominant and recessive patterns. A good example of this dual pattern of inheritance is cystic fibrosis, a disease discussed below. In cystic fibrosis more than 750 mutations of a normal gene have been identified. The severity of disease varies according to the mutation present. Most patients with severe illness, usually apparent in infancy and early childhood, have two of the most common type of mutated gene, one from each parent. Theirs is a recessively inherited pattern. About 84 percent of patients with cystic fibrosis are in this category. Others, with a milder and later-appearing form of the disease, appear to have a different mutated gene and may require only one such gene, rather than two, to express their illness. Theirs is a dominantly inherited pattern.

The frequency of occurrence of recessive genes in a given human population varies according to the disease and the population. Some recessive genes are very common in certain groups. For example, the gene for sickle-cell anemia has an occurrence rate of 10 percent in African Americans; that is, one in ten African Americans carries the recessive gene for sickle-cell anemia. Therefore, a random pairing of any two African Americans has a 1 in 100 (or one-tenth of one-tenth) chance of bringing two carriers together. Each child of such a pairing has a one in four chance of being homozygous and having sickle-cell anemia.

Similarly, 1 in 30 Ashkenazic Jews (those of Eastern European descent) is a carrier of *Tay-Sachs disease*. A random pairing of any two individuals from this ethnic group has a 1 in 900 chance of uniting two carriers. Each child born of such a pairing has a 25 percent chance of being homozygous and having the disease.

Cystic fibrosis is a disease that involves an inability to adequately liquefy (hydrate) normal secretions in the lungs, intestines, and other parts of the body. Between 1 in 30 and 1 in 60 individuals in the general population is a carrier of the most common genes that cause cystic fibrosis. Thus, 1 in 900 to 3,600 random pairings is likely to bring two carriers together, with each offspring's having a 1 in 4 chance of being affected. Although this statistic holds for the majority of cases, more recent findings show that some genes for cystic fibrosis may follow a dominant pattern of inheritance.

The gene for *thalassemia* (or Cooley's anemia) occurs in about 1 in 12 to 1 in 30 people with ethnic origins in the Mediterranean basin (primarily Greeks and Italians), Africa, and Asia. Random pairings have a 1 in 144 to 1 in 900 chance of bringing together two carriers. Again, the chance for each one of the offspring to be affected is 1 in 4.

Phenylketonuria (PKU) is a recessively inherited disease that occurs in 1 in 10,000 births. It involves the accumulation of excess quantities of *phenylalanine*, an essential amino acid in the diet. This excess results from a genetically determined deficiency of the enzyme needed to process (metabolize) phenylalanine into another amino acid, *tyrosine*. The increased phenylalanine is toxic to the brains of infants and children and results in severe mental retardation. For this reason, newborns are routinely checked for PKU. Children with PKU are treated with a special diet that is markedly limited in phenylalanine and with required amounts of tyrosine. Women with phenylketonuria, who have been successfully treated as children and can as adults tolerate a normal dietary intake of phenylalanine, must resume the restricted diet when they become pregnant because the high concentrations of phenylalanine in their blood, passed through the placenta, can damage the fetus's brain.

Galactosemia is a recessively inherited disease that occurs in 1 in 100,000 births. This disorder involves the deficiency of an enzyme that converts galactose, a common milk sugar, into glucose, the sugar used by the body. The accumulation of galactose causes brain damage, liver disease, and cataracts. The treatment is a diet free of galactose. New-borns are routinely tested for galactosemia.

A relatively common recessively inherited disorder involves a deficiency of the plasma protein *alpha antitrypsin*. Low levels of this protein result in chronic lung disease (emphysema) and liver disease (cirrhosis). About 1 in 2,000 to 4,000 whites are affected and 10 to 20 percent of these have symptomatic liver disease.

When an abnormal gene is carried on a sex chromosome, most often the female sex chromosome, inheritance follows a different and more complicated pattern. The sex chromosomes are of two types, X and Y. The female has two X chromosomes; the male, an X and a Y. The father's sperm cells are equally divided between those carrying an X and those carrying a Y chromosome. The union of a Y-bearing sperm with the X of the mother produces a male (with some rare exceptions I will not go into here). The union of an X-bearing sperm with the X-bearing egg produces a female (again with rare exceptions). Thus it is the father who determines the sex of the baby.

The X chromosome is longer than the Y and contains more genes. In males, the genes on the X come from the mother only. If a recessive gene on that part of the X chromosome that is unopposed by the shorter Y chromosome is abnormal, there is no dominant gene to oppose it, and the male will be affected with the disease. In the female, the action of the sex chromosomes is more complex. One of the two X chromosomes that exist in every cell in her body (except the egg) will become inactivated early in fetal development. This happens on a chance basis. In other words, about half her cells will have an active X chromosome inherited from the mother; the other half, an active X chromosome inherited from the father. Therefore, in an *X-linked chromosomal disorder*, the female will be only partly afflicted. She will, however, be a carrier of the abnormal gene, capable of passing it on to her children. In summary, the characteristics of an X-linked recessive gene are as follows:

1. The incidence of disease is much higher in males than in females. If affected, females are rarely affected as seriously as are males.
2. The trait is never directly transmitted from fathers to sons.

3. The trait is passed from an affected male through all his daughters, and from her to half her sons.
4. The trait may be passed silently through a series of carrier females before manifesting itself in affected males.

Many of the *hemophilias* follow an X-linked recessive inheritance, with females as carriers who do not show symptoms and males who have the disease. On average, one-half the male offspring of a mother who carries the defective gene will have hemophilia. The other half, having received a maternal X chromosome that does not contain the abnormal gene, will be normal. On average, one-half the female offspring of such a mother will be carriers, like the mother, and the other half will be noncarriers. *X-linked dominant conditions* also occur, but are rare. Although it is correct to call asymptomatic females carriers, it is also true that these women may show some abnormalities of blood clotting on sophisticated testing, indicating that the gene involved has an effect although it is not sufficient to cause symptoms.

Another disorder that follows an X-linked chromosomal inheritance pattern, but one somewhat more complicated than the pattern described with hemophilia, is *fragile X syndrome*. The leading cause of inherited mental retardation, fragile X is so named because the tip of the X chromosome is partly or completely detached from the body of the chromosome. The gene that is normally located at the fragile X site is repeated hundreds of times in affected individuals and accounts for their abnormal development. The number of gene repetitions both in affected individuals and in carriers varies. In affected individuals this dose of the gene will determine the extent of the abnormalities, such as the degree of retardation. Based on chromosome studies, fragile X affects 1 in 2,000 males and 1 in 2,500 females, which means that it is *very* common.

At puberty some boys with a fragile X chromosome have, in addition to retardation, large testicles (three to four times the average size), prominent chins, large ears, and, often, enlarged heads. Girls may also demonstrate retardation and have unusual physical features, such as prominent ears, flat noses, and long and narrow faces. Fragile X may account for a certain percentage of other mental disorders, such as autism and schizophrenia, in addition to mental retardation and learning problems.

As mentioned, the extent to which the offspring of male and female carriers of the fragile X gene will be affected depends on the dose (or number of repetitions) of the gene they receive and from which parent. Such a transmission pattern is known as an X-linked dominant disorder with reduced penetrance. The word *penetrance* is used to indicate the extent or degree to which a gene is expressed phenotypically in off-spring. For non-sex-chromosome-linked recessive genes the penetrance is zero; carriers do not show signs of illness. In fragile X, penetrance is 80 percent in males and 30 percent in females. About 20 percent of males with the gene are themselves normal and are called transmitting males. If the transmitting father is the source of the gene, all his daughters will receive the gene, will themselves be unaffected, but will produce affected children of both sexes or carriers. The children of a mother who has mental retardation as a result of fragile X are more likely to have mental retardation than are the children of a carrier mother.

From this discussion you can see how complicated the topic of genetics has become since the days of Mendel. At the same time, the science of genetics has given parents more options. It is now possible to identify genes in cells both from adults and from fetuses (obtained by amniocentesis [see pp. 27–29] or chorionic-villus sampling [see pp. 29–30]). By testing parents who are at risk for being carriers, the risk for their fetus having the gene in question can be known. The at-risk fetus can then be checked for that gene (or genes). At present, treatment of affected fetuses is not available. Cure after birth of affected babies with abnormal genes is also experimental. Many parents abort fetuses destined to have serious diseases for which there is yet no cure. However, developments in gene therapy are moving rapidly, so stay tuned.

Gene testing is currently offered to parents at risk for various common recessive disorders, either because they are members of an ethnic group that has a high frequency of the disease, for example, Tay-Sachs disease, thalassemia, and sickle-cell anemia, or because they or another member of their family has the disease. Some common diseases, such as cystic fibrosis, involve such a large number of gene mutations that screening programs would be too complicated to make screening of all parents practical. Nonetheless, particular families at high risk can be tested.

Parents who know that they carry a gene that they do not want to pass on to their children may opt for a procedure of genetic testing known as *preimplantation genetic diagnosis (PGD)* of the embryo they produce. The procedure requires in vitro fertilization of the woman's egg with her partner's sperm in a petri dish. The embryo is subjected to genetic analysis when it consists of no more than sixteen cells. Only an embryo that does not have the mutated disease-causing gene in question is transplanted into the woman. Only several thousand PGDs have been performed worldwide. The limiting factor is cost— about $20,000 for each procedure (not so far paid for by health insurance plans).

Polygenic Inheritance

Many important characteristics (such as height, intelligence, and special aptitudes) are determined by several genes rather than by only one gene. These characteristics are said to be *polygenic* in origin. In predicting the outcome of mating when multiple genes are involved, we follow the Mendelian laws. But prediction rapidly becomes very complex as the number of possible combinations soars.

Most congenital abnormalities are polygenic. These include congenital heart disease, club foot, congenital dislocations of the hip, cleft lip and palate, and open neural tube defects. The last, and largest, group includes *meningocele* and *meningomyelocele* (see p. 24). Couples at risk for having children with these disorders may be identified through their family histories. Fetuses affected with certain of these malformations (open neural tube defects are prime examples) are identifiable through prenatal testing (see p. 24).

Mutations

Occasionally, genes undergo changes early in embryonic life, called *mutations*. Mutations are alterations in genes that produce permanent, transmissible characteristics in the offspring. For example, it is theoretically possible that a mutation could occur such that a couple with red hair (from families whose members all had red hair) would have a child with black hair. Some children of this child would receive genes for black hair also.

Mutations account for the spontaneous appearance of some well-recognized diseases for which no previous family history exists (neither parent possesses the abnormal gene). For example, a significant percentage of children with retinoblastoma (see p. 37) and with open neural tube defects (see p. 24) are the first ones in their families to manifest these usually inherited disorders.

Three types of genes appear to be more unstable than others and thus vulnerable to mutation: proto-oncogenes, which normally control cell growth; tumor-suppression genes, which normally restrain cell growth; and DNA repair genes, which normally correct abnormal sequences of DNA that arise. A mutated proto-oncogene is called an oncogene. It leads the cell to multiply more quickly. Cancers occur because of some combination of mutations of these three kinds of genes. One well-characterized tumor-suppression gene is known as the p53 tumor-suppression gene. It resides on the number 17 chromosome and produces a protein that controls cell growth by regulating other genes. It is a kind of master gene. In many cancers this gene is mutated, unleashing the cell to grow wildly, a characteristic of malignancies. Scientists now suspect that this gene mutates in response to environmental exposures, such as toxins in food. Viruses may be another stimulus for mutation. Further research offers possibilities for better understanding of triggering factors for gene mutation, for identifying people at risk for cancer (carriers of the gene), and for early identification of potentially treatable cancer. Testing for *breast cancer susceptibility genes* (BRCA) is now available. These genes are associated with a higher risk for breast and ovarian cancers. Testing should be offered to all women at increased risk for either type of cancer based on family history or ethnic background (in particular, Ashkenazic Jews).

Chromosomal Abnormalities

In ordinary cell division, each chromosome makes a copy of itself *(mitosis)*, with one copy going to each of the two cells produced by the division. Each cell thus receives exactly the same number and kind of chromosomes the parent cell had. In the formation of egg and sperm cells, however, a different and unique type of division occurs, called *meiosis*. In meiosis, each cell receives only half the number of chromosomes, one from each of the paired parental chromosomes. Human egg and sperm cells have twenty-three chromosomes each. When they combine, the new individual formed by their union has forty-six chromosomes, the characteristic number for the human species. (If the chromosomes were not halved before fertilization, they would double with each succeeding generation.)

For reasons not yet understood, on occasion in early embryonic cell division (see p. 45) the apportioning of chromosomes to the new cells is unequal, that is, the cells form with either an extra or a missing chromosome. This situation is called *nondisjunction*. Nondisjunction may result in abortion (miscarriage) or in the development of a fetus with a major chromosomal disorder, such as Down syndrome. Another derangement that occurs in cell division, again probably very early in embryonic life, is *translocation*, in which a segment of one chromosome detaches and joins with another chromosome. All resulting cells continue the same pattern. Egg and sperm cells with translocated chromosomes may, after fertilization, produce a defective fetus that is spontaneously aborted, an abnormal individual, for example, a person with Down syndrome, or an individual who is normal in appearance (phenotype) but who carries the same rearranged chromosomes as the parent. (A translocation with this latter outcome is known as a *balanced translocation* because the parent, although chromosomally abnormal, is phenotypically normal.) Three or more spontaneous abortions (miscarriages) or one spontaneous abortion and a malformed stillbirth or live birth are indications that a couple is at increased risk for having a translocation and should be studied for it (see pp. 298–302). As there are no treatments for chromosomal abnormalities, the best hope is for prevention, which will result from an understanding of the mechanism by which cells with abnormal chromosomes are formed.

The study of chromosomal conditions is called *cytogenetics*. In recent years knowledge in this field has exploded. Newer chemical methods of separating and staining enable geneticists to work from photographic prints of chromosomes, enlarged 3,000 to 4,000 times. The pairs of chromosomes are assigned numbers (from 1 through 22) according to the length and position of the *centromere*, the sharply constricted region that joins the halves of each pair.

The most common chromosomally determined disorder, which affects 1 in 1,000 pregnancies, is *Down syndrome* (formerly called mongolism), named for British physician J. Langdon Down. In Down syndrome nondisjunction results in three rather than the normal two number 21 chromosomes. Physical characteristics associated with Down syndrome are recognizable at birth. These include small size, floppiness, lax joints, and distinctive facial features. With growth, mental retardation and short stature become apparent.

One Down syndrome child in fifty has a translocation type of chromosomal abnormality, indicating that one of the child's parents has a *balanced translocation*. In this type of translocation, part of one of the number 21 chromosome pair has split off to join another chromosome.

Cytogenetic analysis of a child with Down syndrome is required to determine whether nondisjunction or translocation was involved. In cases of translocation, the parents and their close relatives should be checked to see whether they also have the translocation. Having the translocation places a parent at a much-increased risk for having a child with Down syndrome.

There are several other well-recognized chromosomally caused disorders. In *Klinefelter's syndrome*, males have an extra X chromosome; instead of being XY, they are XXY. The syndrome usually becomes manifest in adolescence, when the testes fail to develop and the breasts grow. Puberty may be delayed. The abnormal testes produce neither sperm nor testosterone, the male sex hormone. About 8 to 10 percent of these boys have (usually mild) mental retardation. Treatment consists of psychological counseling and the administration of sufficient male sex hormones to promote sexual development. Klinefelter's syndrome occurs in about 2 males per 1,000 in the population and is more common in the pregnancies of women over forty.

In *Turner's syndrome*, which affects females only, an X chromosome is missing, so that the individual has only one X instead of two. This disorder occurs in about 1 in 2,500 live female births and in about 5 percent of aborted fetuses. Individuals with Turner's syndrome fail to mature sexually at puberty because their ovaries do not develop.

Genetic Counseling

Genetic counseling involves both knowledge of the various patterns of inheritance discussed in this chapter and understanding of the principles of making decisions under conditions in which outcomes are uncertain, in particular, knowing the probabilities of outcomes and how they mesh with one's values (see p. 1).

Families come to questions involving genetics in several ways. When a baby with a congenital abnormality is born, or when there is a still-birth, parents understandably seek to find out the cause of the defect and the chances of recurrence. Recurrent miscarriages also raise the question of a genetic cause. Among those who should seek counseling are people in the following groups:

- Couples who already have a child with some serious defect, such as Down syndrome, open neural tube defect, congenital heart disease, a malformed limb, or mental retardation
- Couples with a family history of a genetic disease or mental retardation
- Couples who are blood relatives (first or second cousins)
- African Americans, Ashkenazic Jews, Italians, Greeks, and other ethnic groups at increased risk for carrying recessive genes that cause disease
- Women who are taking drugs known to cause fetal defects (see p. 130)
- Women who have had multiple X rays taken early in pregnancy
- Women who have had two or more of the following in any combination: stillbirths, deaths of newborn babies, miscarriages
- Women thirty-five years old or older
- Women whose routine prenatal tests detect a fetus at increased risk for a major malformation or genetic defect (see Expanded AFP, p. 24)
- Women and men at increased risk for breast cancer and women at increased risk for ovarian cancer (see p. 45). Ideally, a genetic history should be part of a health checkup *before* conception (see Before You're Pregnant Dos and Don'ts, p. 12, and Your History, p. 51). At the latest, it should be done early in pregnancy.

Genetic counseling needs to be highly respectful of the values of the woman and her partner. Not all people will make the same choices when presented with the same odds. One complaint raised by people with disabilities is that people without disabilities are ignorant about what it is like to live with a disability. People with disabilities, such as people with less-severe open neural tube defects (with resulting bladder problems and leg weakness), point out that they are able to lead vibrant, happy, fulfilled lives and feel stigmatized and demeaned by the attitude that fetuses with these defects should automatically be aborted. Some deaf parents point out that they want to have only deaf children because only then can full mutual understanding and closeness be achieved. (See reference to the World Institute on Disability in Appendix, p. 331.) On the other hand, the more severe forms of open neural tube defects (as well as fatal conditions such as Tay-Sachs disease) can have a profoundly negative effect on families.

Genetic-counseling services are located in most large medical centers and at all university teaching hospitals. Family physicians, pediatricians, and obstetricians are all good sources of information and referrals on genetic disorders. A registry of counseling centers is maintained by the March of Dimes (see Appendix).

The discussion of specific genetic disorders given in this chapter is far from exhaustive; only the more commonly encountered problems have been mentioned. (See Appendix for further reading.)

CHAPTER 2

Shaping a Healthy Pregnancy

YOUR HISTORY

During your first prenatal visit to your doctor, midwife, or nurse practitioner, you will be asked a lot of questions about your personal and family medical history. Often a health questionnaire is used. The information you provide will be important in reducing risks and promoting the health of both you and your baby.

Your general medical history will include a review of any drugs (prescribed or over-the-counter) you regularly take (see p. 127); any chronic illnesses that might affect or be affected by the pregnancy, such as recurrent herpes infection (see p. 138), heart disease, phenylketonuria (see p. 268), AIDS or HIV infection (see p. 21), hepatitis (see p. 138), phlebitis (blood clots of veins, usually in the legs; see p. 321, venous thromboembolism), or diabetes (see p. 288); and past surgical procedures, such as appendectomy, that could be important in evaluating symptoms that may arise, such as abdominal pain (see pp. 74–75).

Your health practices with regard to diet (see p. 87), exposure to cats (see p. 141 on toxoplasmosis), exercise (see p. 95), dental care (see p. 69), alcohol (see p. 143), tobacco (see p. 142), drugs (see p. 145), and seat-belt use (see p. 150) will all have a bearing on the pregnancy and should be reviewed. Ideally, women taking drugs for chronic illnesses will have a preliminary discussion about the safety of these drugs before they become pregnant (see Before You're Pregnant Dos and Don'ts, p. 12).

Your menstrual history, including menarche (age of first period), the interval between periods, and the date of your last period or of ovulation, if known, is useful in dating the pregnancy (see pp. 57–58).

Information on past pregnancies, including the gestational age of the baby, complications, the type of delivery (vaginal or C-section), the use of episiotomy (see p. 208) and oxytocin (see pp. 195–197), the weight and condition of the baby at birth and his or her current health, abortions (both spontaneous and induced; see p. 316), any difficulties becoming pregnant, and your experiences with care providers during the pregnancy and birth, including relations with doctors, midwives, hospitals, and birthing centers, are important data to share with your current care provider.

It will be useful for your doctor or midwife to know whether you and your partner planned to have a baby at this time and what impact the timing of this pregnancy has on your lives. Do you need professional assistance in resolving ambivalence about the pregnancy or in making the decision to continue or terminate it? Do the answers to these questions relate to the quality of your relationship in any way? Would you benefit from couples counseling or further discussion with your partner?

The family history takes on even greater significance in this era of rapidly improving prenatal diagnosis and treatment (see Genetics and Your Pregnancy, pp. 34–50, and Treating the Fetus, pp. 153–156). As discussed in the section on genetics, increased risk factors for a genetic disease may include age, racial and ethnic background, history of having produced a genetically abnormal child or a child with mental retardation (or such a history in either partner's family), recurrent abortions, and birth of a child with a major malformation or chronic illness. Family history also affects the risks for the woman during pregnancy. For example, a history of phlebitis and thromboembolus in family members raises the question of a hereditary abnormality in a blood-clotting protein for which the woman should be checked (see p. 321 on venous thromboembolism). Identification of this disorder allows for evaluation for preventive treatment.

It's also helpful to construct a family tree for each partner. The bottom of the tree has the children of the partners' generation, including those of their siblings. The tree flows upward through the partners and their siblings, their parents, grandparents, and so forth. List under each person's name any chronic illnesses, including mental retardation, and deaths with their causes if known.

Ideally, the elements of the history should be considered while pregnancy is still in the planning stage, as discussed previously in the section on genetics in Chapter 1.

PREGNANCY TESTS

A hormone indicating pregnancy can be detected in the blood of the pregnant woman as early as three days following fertilization and in the urine within one week. This hormone, known as human chorionic gonadotropin (HCG), is produced by the placenta (or, more precisely, by the trophoblast, the placenta's earlier form). Current tests for HCG done in medical laboratories or physicians' offices are over 98 percent accurate. Over-the-counter urine-pregnancy-test kits are somewhat less accurate, giving correct readings 85 to 95 percent of the time.

The level of HCG rises rapidly during early pregnancy, doubling every two days. The level peaks at ten weeks, then gradually declines to about one-half of peak levels, where it tends to remain. After an abortion or miscarriage the level falls off over the course of one week. Occasionally, if trophoblastic tissue has been left behind in the uterus, the hormone may be detectable for as long as several weeks. The level of HCG is markedly increased in hydatidiform mole (see p. 295).

Measurement of HCG can be helpful when a miscarriage or an ectopic pregnancy is suspected early on, before ultrasound can indicate the presence or viability of the embryo. The predicted rise in hormone level does not occur in pregnancies that are failing; the level may plateau or actually decline (see p. 303).

THE PHYSICAL EXAMINATION

A Chance to Learn

The physical examination is an opportunity for the woman to learn a great deal about her body. (See Figure 2.1.) If a woman chooses to include her partner, they both can learn more about her body. The exam

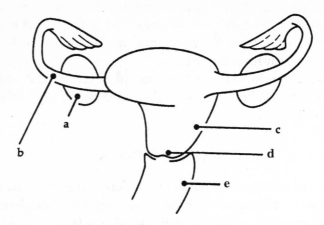

FIGURE 2.1   Female reproductive organs: (a) ovaries,
(b) fallopian tubes, (c) uterus, (d) cervix, (e) vagina

is also an opportunity for a woman and her doctor or midwife to build up mutual trust. The examination is clearly more than a simple checkup. You can add to the value of this experience in the following ways:

1. Read something about the female body and reproductive organs beforehand. Ask the doctor if he or she can supply any charts or other informational materials.
2. Ask questions if you do not understand something. Good, open communication is essential throughout the childbirth experience. Speak up if you feel pain.
3. Relax and participate in the examination. For the doctor or other attendant to feel the uterus and ovaries properly, the abdominal muscles must be relaxed. The examiner's hands, one in the vagina and the other on the lower abdomen, move toward each other to feel the structures in between. If the abdominal muscles are tense, the examination is hindered. You are an active participant in the examination. To help relax the abdominal and vaginal muscles you might try breathing in and out twice deeply, bearing down as though to push out a baby, then letting go of the buildup of muscle tension.

4. Ask for a mirror to see the cervix and other intravaginal structures. Many women have never seen a cervix, and this is an opportunity to understand its structure.

5. Bring your husband, partner, or a friend who will be of support later. If you plan to have your partner or a friend present at the delivery, this is a chance to involve that person from the start. Make clear to the doctor, nurse, or midwife that this person is an important member of the labor and delivery team.

Although the initial physical examination during pregnancy is a complete physical, from head to toe, its focus is on the reproductive system. The pelvic examination includes inspecting the labia; determining perineal muscle tone; inspecting the vagina and the cervix (see p. 66 on physical changes during pregnancy); taking cultures of the cervix for gonorrhea (see p. 137), chlamydia (see p. 134), and herpesvirus (see p. 138) in women considered at increased risk for these infections; taking a Pap test of the cervix (see p. 14); and feeling the uterus and ovaries.

The size of the uterus reflects the *gestational age* (the length of time the embryo or fetus is carried in the womb) and is recorded during early pregnancy in terms of weeks; for example, six to eight weeks' size (the uterus can first be felt to be enlarged at about six weeks' gestation). Later in pregnancy the size of the uterus is measured with a tape measure.

The Perineal Muscles

One part of the examination that requires collaboration between the examiner and the pregnant woman is the assessment of the perineal muscles. The perineum is the portion of the female body between the lower junction of the labia and the anus (see Figure 2.2). These muscles are used in childbirth, during intercourse, and in the stopping of urination. Since many women are unaware of the workings of these muscles, and relatively few exercise them regularly, their tone is apt to be weak. The examiner assesses the muscle tone by placing the fingers of the gloved hand onto the perineum just inside the entrance of the vagina and pressing down. The woman is then asked to tighten the muscles. The experienced examiner can determine whether tone is nonexistent, weak, average, or good. If your doctor or midwife does not check these muscles, you can do it yourself, using two fingers and pressing toward

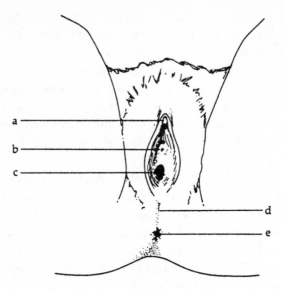

FIGURE 2.2   External female genitals: (a) clitoris, (b) urethra, (c) vagina, (d) perineum, (e) rectum

the spine. If your perineal tone is nonexistent, weak, or average, you should exercise these muscles. (My suggestion is to tighten and relax in units of five contractions, each lasting ten seconds, and to repeat the process ten times a day whether or not you are pregnant.)

Toning these muscles can help prevent tearing during birth and minimizes the need for an episiotomy. Good perineal tone can also enhance the sexual satisfaction of both partners in intercourse; women can increase their chances for and control over orgasm, and many men appreciate the gripping sensation they experience when the perineal muscles are tensed. Strong perineal muscles also prevent bladder sagging as women age (particularly if they have had children), and stress incontinence, the involuntary passage of urine during sneezing, coughing, laughing, or lifting. Perineal exercises, also known as *Kegel exercises* (after Arnold Kegel, the physician who first described them), have traditionally been a part of female hygiene in many preindustrial societies, passed on from mother to daughter as part of folk knowledge. (See also p. 103 on pelvic-floor exercises.) The effect on childbirth of having well-conditioned perineal muscles during childbirth has not been critically evaluated, although common sense would suggest its value.

Blood Pressure and Testing for Preeclampsia

Blood pressure is measured at each prenatal visit. An inflatable cuff is secured over the upper arm just above the elbow. A stethoscope is placed on the artery that passes under the crease at the elbow. The cuff is inflated to stop the pulse below the cuff and gradually deflated. The upper reading of the blood pressure, called the *systolic pressure* (*systole* refers to the contraction of the heart when blood is ejected with maximum force into the blood vessels), is the reading on the gauge when the pulse sounds first become audible. The lower reading, or *diastolic pressure* (*diastole* refers to the filling, noncontracted phase of the heart cycle), is the gauge reading when the pulse is no longer audible. The gauges are calibrated in millimeters of mercury. Thus, a pressure of 120 means that the pressure will balance or support a column of mercury 120 millimeters (about five inches) high in a thin tube. The systolic and diastolic readings are expressed as a fraction: the numerator is the systolic pressure, and the denominator is the diastolic pressure.

A pressure reading of 140/90 is regarded as the upper limit of normal. If either figure is higher, the blood pressure is considered too high (hypertension). Blood pressure varies in a predictable way during pregnancy. There is a normal dip of about five millimeters in the systolic and diastolic pressures during the first and second trimesters.

Blood-pressure determination is one of the most important serial measurements made in pregnancy. A blood-pressure reading over 140/90 occurring with protein in the urine after the twentieth week defines *preeclampsia*, a relatively common disorder with important risks for the woman and the fetus (see p. 307). Blood-pressure readings are also essential in monitoring women who are being treated for established hypertension whether or not it is complicated by preeclampsia.

Dating the Pregnancy

Many decisions about the growth of the fetus (see Intrauterine Growth Disturbance, p. 296) and the timing of delivery of a baby depend on accurate dating of the pregnancy (see Postdate Pregnancy, p. 306). Every effort must be made to determine gestational age by twenty weeks, beyond which dating becomes progressively less accurate.

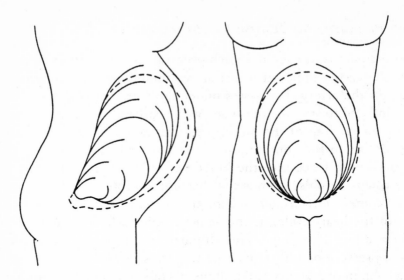

FIGURE 2.3   Growth of the uterus. Unbroken curve in middle is size of uterus at twenty-four weeks. Dotted line shows position of uterus after baby's head engages in the pelvis.

The date of the last menstrual period is the primary way of estimating when conception occurred (at roughly fourteen days before the next menstrual period is anticipated). Even better is the last date of ovulation, as determined by basal body temperature. Another milestone, but not a very accurate one, is the *quickening*, the moment when the woman first feels the fetus move, sometime between sixteen and twenty weeks. A woman's recognition of this sensation will vary, depending in part on whether she has had other pregnancies and is familiar with the sensation. Measurement of the size and the height of the uterus is a good dating method, particularly in first pregnancies (see Figure 2.3). Between eighteen and thirty weeks, the height of the uterus, measured in centimeters, correlates fairly well with the number of weeks of gestation, especially in first pregnancies. The fetus's heart can first be heard with a stethoscope between sixteen and nineteen weeks after conception, and by *Doppler ultrasound* by twelve weeks (see pp. 32–34).

With ultrasound, fetal heart movements can be visualized by six to seven weeks. The gestational sac is visible as early as five to six weeks. Between eight and twelve weeks, the distance between the head and buttocks of the fetus, the crown–rump distance, dates the gestational age very precisely. Between sixteen and twenty-six weeks, measurement of the diameter of the baby's head can date the pregnancy to within one and a half weeks of the gestational age with 95 percent confidence, a strong argument for routinely doing ultrasounds in pregnancy. Ultrasound researchers have also found that the length of the femur (thigh bone) of the fetus, measured during the second trimester, is 95 percent accurate to within six days of the fetal age. Other physical measurements are being studied for their correlation with gestational age.

GROWTH OF THE FETUS

The First Week

Egg and sperm cells meet during fertilization to form one cell with forty-six chromosomes. From this one cell, through cell growth, division, and differentiation, the fetus and placenta will eventually develop.

After fertilization, rapid cell division produces a hollow sphere with a blob of fifteen to twenty cells, the *blastocyst*. Most of these cells will differentiate into the tissues and organs of the body and placenta. Some will remain as genetically unchanged copies of the fertilized egg and form the future egg or sperm cells of the fetus, preserved for the life of the individual. After passing through the fallopian tube and reaching the uterus, the blastocyst continues to enlarge. In another three or four days it attaches to the surface of the uterus's lining in a process called *nidation* (meaning "nesting"). (For recent research breakthroughs in the growing of pluripotent cells removed from leftover embryos obtained by in vitro fertilization while in the blastocyst stage, and the opportunities for treating human diseases that may result, see New Contributions of the Fetus and Baby to Medicine in General on p. 156. For a discussion of preimplantation genetic diagnosis on in vitro fertilized embryos in the blastocyst stage, see p. 44.)

After seven days, the blastocyst, now composed of several hundred cells, invades the now-prepared lining of the uterus, known as the *decidua*, and gains a firm attachment to the woman. In the process, the sphere collapses like a cooling popover. The cells from the inside of the sphere form the germinal disk from which the fetus will develop. The rest of the cells compose the invading *trophoblast*, or primitive placenta. The trophoblast is unique, because it is the only human tissue that interphases with another immunologically separate individual, the woman, and escapes graft-host type rejection. Some cells from the trophoblast cross into the woman's blood and through special techniques can be identified as such. Because the trophoblast has the same genetic characteristics as the fetus, it is potentially useful in prenatal diagnosis (see p. 63).

The Second Week

Once the blastocyst is implanted, its trophoblast grows at an astounding rate, sending out fingerlike projections into the surrounding decidua. These projections become honeycombed, with walls and spaces. When the embryo is about two weeks old, maternal tissues are eroded to such an extent that the maternal blood vessels allow the woman's blood to rush into these trophoblastic spaces. Placental circulation is thus established, and the woman's blood begins to nourish the developing embryo.

The trophoblast also produces HCG (see p. 53), without which the entire lining of the womb, including the developing blastocyst, would be cast off. Tests used to detect pregnancy measure HCG in the woman's blood and urine.

The embryonic disk at this point is a double-layered plate, resembling an empty sandwich. The upper outer layer is called the *ectoderm*; from it the skin, hair, nails, and the entire nervous system will develop. The lower layer is the *endoderm*, which gives rise to the digestive tract, the respiratory system, and many of their accessory glands.

Between these two layers a third layer, the *mesoderm*, soon develops. The muscles and tissues lining the abdominal and pleural cavities derive from the mesoderm. Scattered between these three germinal layers are loose cells, called the *mesenchyme*. The mesenchyme does not belong to a single layer, but acts as a sort of loose packing tissue between layers. The mesenchyme gives rise to the heart, blood vessels, bones, and cartilage.

The Third Week

During the third week the oval germinal disk becomes pear-shaped, and then takes on the form of a violin. It also bends in the middle, so that it is no longer flat. Down the center of the ectodermal surface, which will become the baby's back, two parallel ridges form. A groove, or trench, between them, known as the *neural groove*, will form the central nervous system. The heart and blood vessels also begin to develop during the third week of embryonic life.

The Fourth Week

Very rapid changes take place within the body of the embryo during the fourth week. Shortly after the laying of foundations for the nervous and circulatory systems, the *gut*, or early digestive system, begins to form. By a process similar to the formation of the neural groove, the endoderm gives rise to the foregut in front and the hindgut in the tail region. A blind pouch in front pushes gradually forward, soon breaking through the undersurface of the head to form the mouth.

At four weeks and one-quarter-inch long, the embryo does not yet look like a fetus. It has a head and a tail, which can be distinguished readily. The neural groove has sealed over completely, and formation of the brain is progressing rapidly. (Failures of closure of parts of the neural groove result in the set of malformations known as open neural tube defects. See the discussion of prenatal diagnosis on p. 24 under Expanded AFP.) In the head, the beginnings of the eye and ear can be seen. A growing area called the mandibular process is beginning to form the face. The heart is now a large bulge on the underside of the embryo, already beating rhythmically.

Two Months

By two months the fetus, over an inch long, has assumed a reconizable human form. It has eyes, ears, and a nose. The hands have fingers, and the feet have toes. The head still looks too big for the body, which is potbellied because the liver is too large for the abdominal cavity. The sexual organs have begun to form.

Three Months

In the third month of development many different organs become more specialized. In the mouth, series of ten tooth buds appear in the upper and lower jaws. The most dramatic changes of the third month are seen in the sexual organs, especially those of males. Differentiation is more rapid in males than in females, and by the end of the third month, close inspection of the fetus will reveal whether it is male or female.

Four and Five Months

The changes occurring during the rest of pregnancy are much more subtle. Development is largely a matter of simple enlargement and maturation of the various organs. The four-month-old fetus, though tiny, looks like a baby in every respect, although the head is still relatively large and the legs relatively short. The skin is thin, red, and wrinkled.

From Six Months to Birth

By six months' gestational age, specialized structures in the fetus's skin are formed. On the head and sometimes over the back and shoulders there is a fine growth of hair, the color of which is unrelated to the color of the hair the child will have. Fingernails and toenails appear and grow slowly. At the time of birth they will project slightly at the tips of the fingers, and they will have to be trimmed in the first few days of life to keep the infant from scratching himself or herself. Oil glands appear in the skin and manufacture a greasy, sticky substance known as the *vernix caseosa*, which is like a salve or ointment coating the skin. By the end of the sixth month the fetus is fully developed; it needs only to grow in length, weight, and strength to face the demands of the world outside.

The pictures of the Swedish photographer Lennart Nilsson beautifully capture these stages of fetal development, as does the animated web site http://www.med.uc.edu/embryology/ (see Appendix, p.325).

Through research we continue to learn about the complex and wonderful aspects of fetal behavior. We now know, for example, that fetuses go through sleep-wake cycles (appreciated by women as periods of quiet and movement); they yawn and suck their thumbs; they are responsive to both light and sound. After birth, infants pay preferential attention to their own mothers' voices and to musical selections to which they were exposed in utero. Fetuses have a keen sense of hearing and need to be protected from noisy environments, as evidence now suggests that noise can stress them (see Protecting the Fetus, p. 127). Fetal sensitivity to sound is used in the nonstress test, a late-pregnancy measure of fetal well-being (see 158). A good source of information about the world of the fetus is the book *Your Amazing Newborn* by Marshall Klaus and Phyllis H. Klaus (see Appendix, p. 327).

The Placenta

The *placenta*, or afterbirth, plays a central role in pregnancy. It is a flat, circular structure about seven to eight inches in diameter and an inch in thickness and weighs roughly one pound. It is composed of millions of fingerlike projections, called *chorionic villi*, which are part of the fetal blood-vessel system and connect with the rest of the fetal blood vessels by way of the large umbilical veins and artery in the umbilical cord. In the body of the placenta, the villi are suspended in maternal blood and only a thin layer of cells covering the villi separates the maternal from the fetal circulations. Nutrients and oxygen pass from the woman to the fetus across this layer, and waste products from the fetus, including carbon dioxide, are returned to the woman's circulation for elimination. (The chorionic villi are used in prenatal diagnosis. See p. 29, chorionic-villus sampling.)

Fetal cells, usually in small numbers, also cross this fetal-maternal interphase in the placenta. These migrated cells, of various types, are important in several ways. Fetal red blood cells, (most commonly, Rh D-positive cells) can sensitize the pregnant woman who has a different blood type (most commonly, Rh D negative) to produce antibodies that bind to and destroy the fetal cells in both the woman's and the fetus's circulations (see Blood Type, Rh D Factor, p. 16). A similar process can occur with the fetus's platelets (the cells involved in blood clotting) if the type differs from that of the woman (see Platelet Disorders, 305).

Trophoblasts from within the placenta and of fetal origin are found in the woman's blood and can be analyzed for genetic characteristics. This process, still in the development stage, offers a way to obtain genetic information about the fetus without having to do the riskier procedures of chorionic-villus sampling or amniocentesis. A procedure already in clinical use is the extraction of DNA from fetal cells in the woman's circulation to identify the Rh D blood type of the fetus (see p. 16). Fetal

DNA obtained in this way will probably have widespread use. Fetal DNA has been isolated from the skin lesions of a common rash of the third trimester (polymorphic eruption of pregnancy; see p. 81, Skin Rashes), opening up a whole new area of research. Intriguingly, there is now evidence that some kinds of fetal cells can persist in the woman indefinitely, either without known ill effects or, as research now suggests, as a contributor to the development of autoimmune diseases, such as systemic sclerosis. (In autoimmune diseases—lupus erythematosis is the best-known example—the person produces antibodies against her or his own organs.)

Membranes, known as the *amniotic membranes*, which are thin, semi-transparent sheets of tissue, attach to the rim of the placenta and form a baglike, round dome that adheres to and conforms with the shape of the inner lining of the uterus. Tethered at the end of the umbilical cord, the fetus is suspended throughout pregnancy in the amniotic fluid within this rounded dome of membranes. Because of this fluid, it is practically impossible for the fetus to sustain injury from the outside.

The production of hormones is another important function of the placenta. Pregnancy places unique demands on the entire maternal organism; its special requirements must be met by adaptations that involve almost every organ system in the body. The size of the uterus and breasts and the volume of blood in the body must increase tremendously. To some extent, the pelvic joints loosen. Smooth muscles relax in the intestines and urinary tract and may contribute to such problems as constipation (see p. 76), heartburn (see p. 79), and urinary tract infection (see p. 73). These and many other adaptations are largely brought about by the action of the placental hormones on the woman's body. The placental hormones are also thought to be important in maintaining pregnancy and in initiating labor.

PHYSICAL CHANGES

Weight Gain and Growth of the Uterus

The most dramatic and obvious physical changes that occur with pregnancy are those related to the woman's shape and weight. A woman with an average pregnancy, who is carrying one fetus, has an overall pregnancy-related weight gain of 25 to 30 pounds. The fetus accounts for 7.5 pounds; the placenta and membranes, 1.4 pounds; the amniotic fluid, 1.8 pounds; increase in size of the uterus, 2.1 pounds; increase in maternal blood volume, 2.8 pounds; increase in breast size, 0.9 pounds; fluid in the skin and other tissues, 3.7 pounds; and maternal reserves, 7.4 pounds. (See pp. 87–95 for discussion of optimum weight gain.)

During pregnancy the capacity of the uterus increases 500- to 1,000-fold (see Figure 2.3) Its muscle cells stretch and thicken, and the elastic and fibrous tissues increase markedly, adding to the strength of the uterine wall. Its blood supply also increases. For the first few weeks of pregnancy, the normal pear shape of the uterus is maintained. As the fetus grows, the uterus becomes more globelike and, by the third month, spherical. Then it elongates more than it widens to assume an ovoid shape. After the third month the uterus is too large to be confined in the pelvis, so it rises into the abdomen. As it grows further, it comes in contact with the front wall of the abdomen, pushing the intestines to the side, and eventually it reaches almost to the level of the liver.

Weight gain in pregnancy begins slowly and picks up steadily later on. It is obviously correlated with the size of the uterus. About two pounds are gained during the first trimester; the other twenty-five or so pounds are gained during the second and third trimesters, with some leveling off during the last few weeks.

The growth in size of the uterus can be represented on a graph as a straight line that is directly proportional to the fetus's gestational age. This relationship holds primarily in first pregnancies and less so in later ones; it is especially accurate between the eighteenth and thirtieth weeks of gestation, again, more so in first pregnancies. A rule of thumb is that the number of weeks' gestational age equals the number of centimeters of uterine height. Uterine size is a good indicator of fetal growth.

Any abnormalities in the growth of the uterus need to be investigated. Smaller-than-predicted uterine growth over several months could be a result of *intrauterine growth disturbance* (pp. 296–297), *oligohydramnios* (see Hydramnios, pp. 295–296), the relatively uncommon condition of insufficient amniotic fluid, or both. Apparent excessive uterine growth could be explained by errors in dating the fetus (that is, the fetus is older than was thought); *hydramnios* (p. 295), an excess of amniotic fluid; multiple pregnancies; *hydatidiform mole* (p. 295); or, simply, a large fetus.

From the beginning of the second trimester the uterus contracts irregularly. Toward the end of pregnancy, women are able to perceive these contractions and report that they feel like menstrual cramps. During the last two weeks of pregnancy Braxton Hicks contractions (named for the physician who first described them) can occur as often as every ten to twenty minutes. They may be quite uncomfortable and account for false labor, or uterine contractions that are not accompanied by progressive dilatation of the cervix.

In some women a distinct bulge can be seen and felt in the midline of the abdomen between the two rectus muscles that run from the lower rib cage to the pubic bone. This bulge results from a spreading apart of these muscles, which deprives the midabdominal wall of one of its major supports. The gap between the muscles is bridged primarily by skin and *fascia*, which stretch relatively easily in response to the enlarging uterus. Treatment of this separation of the recti (also called a *diastasis recti*) is discussed in the section on prenatal exercise (pp. 95–112).

Cervix and Vagina

During pregnancy the cervix softens, enlarges, and turns a purplish red. The number of its mucous glands, and of the mucous glands in the vagina, markedly increases, as does the production of secretions. These glandular secretions account for the thick, white vaginal discharge that is common during pregnancy. Soon after conception the cervical canal is filled with a clump of thick mucus—the *mucous plug*—which is expelled during or shortly before labor. The mucous plug also serves as a barrier to the invasion of germs from the vagina.

The vaginal wall characteristically becomes duskier, softer, thicker, moister, and more elastic, all in preparation for the stretching it will undergo during delivery. The labia enlarge and turn a dusky blue.

Abdomen and Skin

By the third trimester, in about 50 percent of women, reddish, slightly depressed skin markings, called *striae gravidarum* ("lines of pregnancy"), are present on the skin of the abdomen and sometimes on the breasts and thighs. Their cause is unknown. After delivery these markings gradually change to silvery lines that shrink as the contracting abdominal and breast skin firms up. They are permanent *stretch marks* of pregnancy. There is no way to prevent or eliminate these scars; creams and ointments sold for this purpose are ineffective.

In many women, particularly women with dark hair and complexions, the skin of the midline of the abdomen becomes pigmented from the pubic bone to close to the tip of the breastbone. The dark line curves around the umbilicus. Neither the cause nor the significance of this line is known, and it rapidly disappears after delivery.

It is quite common in pregnancy for brown patches to appear on the woman's face and neck. These are known as *chloasma*, or the "mask of pregnancy," and usually disappear after the birth.

In white women in particular, tiny red spots commonly appear on the face, the neck, the upper chest, and arms. Each red dot consists of several tiny blood vessels branching from a central feeder, which can be seen with a magnifying glass. If pressure is gently applied to the center, for example, with the point of a pencil, the entire network is deprived of its blood supply and blanches. These *spider hemangiomas*, as they are sometimes called, are believed to be related to increased estrogen levels during pregnancy. Why some women have these spots and others do not is not understood, and their significance is not known. They disappear after giving birth. Another transient skin change is redness of the palms. Like the spiders, this redness is believed to be related to estrogen levels. Again, its significance is unknown, and the phenomenon vanishes after delivery.

Breasts and Preparation for Breast-Feeding

Women commonly experience tenderness and tingling of the breasts as one of the earliest signs of pregnancy. The breasts increase in size, often dramatically, and become lumpier as the milk-producing glands enlarge. Delicate blue veins appear beneath the skin and reflect the increased blood flow. The nipples enlarge and darken and are more erectile. Scattered through the *areola* (the dark circle around the nipple) are small bumps, which are enlarged sebaceous (oil) glands (also known as the glands of Montgomery). After the first few months, if the nipple is squeezed, *colostrum*, the thick, yellow fluid that comes in before the milk, will come out.

A woman who plans to breast-feed her baby should wear a nursing bra large enough to support her breasts during the last few months of pregnancy and during nursing. The bra can be worn day and night if her breasts are heavy or if she feels uncomfortable.

An inverted nipple can be identified by pressing the areola between the thumb and the forefinger. A normal nipple, or one that is simply flat, will protrude, whereas an inverted nipple will retract. Inverted nipples are uncommon, since most nipples that appear to be inverted are merely flat and will pose no difficulty for breast-feeding. Inverted nipples are best treated with breast shells (milk cups) during the days after birth. The cups can be worn under the bra between feedings, and a breast pump can be used to draw out the nipple before nursing. Breast shells must fit so that the nipples fit completely into the holes and the base of the cups does not irritate the skin. With the exception of treating inverted nipples, there is no evidence to support measures to toughen nipples by massage or application of creams.

Circulatory System

In pregnancy, blood volume increases about 45 percent. The two major components of the blood—the red cells and the plasma—do not contribute equally to this increase. The red blood cells increase by about 25 percent, whereas the plasma expands by 40 percent. As a result of this disproportionate increase, the hematocrit (the percentage of the blood made up of red blood cells) actually falls, since there are fewer red cells per unit volume of blood during pregnancy. Thus, the standards for defining anemia based on the hematocrit differ for pregnant and nonpregnant women. The predictable fall of the hematocrit begins between the sixth and eighth weeks of gestation.

During pregnancy the pulse rate at rest increases an average of ten to fifteen beats per minute. The volume of blood pumped by the heart increases significantly during the first trimester and even slightly more during the second and third trimesters. *Heart murmurs*, which reflect increased blood flow within the heart, are common in pregnancy. These flow murmurs must be distinguished from those related to heart-valve disorders, for which antibiotics against infection of the valves may be indicated during labor.

Respiratory System

Late in pregnancy many women experience some breathlessness, a result of compression of the lungs by the expanding uterus. Breathing becomes easier if the baby moves down into the birth canal before the onset of labor (see Lightening, pp. 78–79).

Urinary System

During pregnancy more blood flows through the kidneys. Even in women who are not pregnant, a small amount of protein and glucose is passed from the blood to the urine. As the amount of blood filtered increases, the amount of protein and glucose passed in the urine also increases, accounting for the common occurrence of measurable protein and glucose in the urine of pregnant women (see Urine Test, p. 15).

The urine-collecting system undergoes dilatation during pregnancy. The ureters, the muscular tubes that transport urine from the kidneys to the bladder, are relatively lax and dilated, in part a result of hormonal influences and in part a result of partial blockage of the lower ends of the ureters by pressure from the expanding uterus. The right ureter is subjected to further compression by the enlarging veins from the right ovary (which lie directly over the lower end of the right ureter) and by the weight of the uterus, which is usually rotated to the right. The dilatation of the ureters and relative stagnation of urine flow through them is believed to be a factor in the increased susceptibility of pregnant women to urinary tract infection (see pp. 73).

Gums and Teeth

Gums soften and thicken during pregnancy, probably in response to increased blood flow. Even with the mild irritation of toothbrushing, they may bleed very easily. A lump of thickened gum tissue (called a *pregnancy epulis*) may bleed vigorously when touched. Both the normal swelling of the gums and the pregnancy epulis disappear after delivery.

The increase in the size of the gums predisposes pregnant women to gingivitis, a gum inflammation that can weaken the supports of the teeth. For this reason, daily brushing, flossing, and regular dental cleanings and checkups are especially important for pregnant women (see

Before You're Pregnant Dos and Don'ts, p. 12). Contrary to folk belief, pregnancy creates no more long-term dental problems than those encountered in nonpregnant women, as long as the woman pays careful attention to diet and dental hygiene. However, dental health before and during pregnancy is taking on added importance as evidence mounts that periodontal (gum) disease may play a significant role in causing premature labor (see p. 309 on premature labor).

Psychological Issues

T. Berry Brazelton and Bertrand G. Cramer, in their book *The Earliest Relationship* (see Appendix), describe the emotional ups and downs, the mixed feelings, and the opportunities for growth provided by pregnancy. They describe the work of pregnancy as divided into three separate tasks, each associated with a stage in the development of the fetus.

In the first stage, parents adjust to the news of pregnancy, which is accompanied by changes in the woman's body but not yet by evidence of the existence of the fetus. In the second stage, the parents begin to recognize the fetus as a being who will eventually be separate from the woman. This recognition is confirmed at the moment of quickening, when the fetus first announces its physical presence. In the third and last stage, parents begin to experience the coming child as an individual, as the fetus contributes to its own *individuation* by distinctive motions, rhythms, and levels of activity.

In a book entitled *On Becoming a Family* (see Appendix), Brazelton writes about "a predictable kind of turmoil" in the last half of pregnancy, reflected in a series of questions parents-to-be ask of themselves: "Will I ever get to be a parent?" "Will I make it as a parent, or will I ruin my baby?" "If I get to be a parent, will I have to be like my parent? I certainly don't want to be like that!" As parents question themselves they wonder, "Have we made a mistake? Do we really want this baby?" And if there are such doubts, the question that follows is, "Could we already have damaged the baby by our being ambivalent?" Brazelton and his colleagues also found that parents-to-be rehearse for a damaged infant and as new parents are prepared to blame themselves if the baby is impaired in any way. This confusing swirl of emotions and mixed feelings is best understood as normal and represents a mobilization of energy to deal with the unprecedented challenge that lies ahead. At birth and thereafter this energy will flow into bonding with the baby.

Other psychological hurdles are more matter-of-fact. For some couples the change in the woman's body size and shape raises certain anxieties. For one, it is a public announcement of their sexual relationship, the only one allowed by society for an essentially private act. Some couples may feel embarrassed about publicizing what they have been up to.

Another anxiety has to do with a woman's self-image in light of accepted standards of beauty. The mass media decry obesity and portray slimness in the extreme as the only real kind of beauty. Being pregnant is often confused in many people's minds with being fat or unattractive. Because of the intense concern of women with weight and figure, the growing abdominal girth may touch a sensitive nerve. A woman may be concerned that she is no longer attractive to her partner, whereas a man may worry about whether he can still see his partner as beautiful.

Weight gain and increase in size are not the only factors in creating a sense of decreased attractiveness. Other bodily changes, such as large, sagging breasts, puffiness of the skin, stretch marks, swelling of the vulva, increased vaginal secretions, and tan spots on the face (p. 67) may contribute to a sense of loss of physical appeal.

Birth itself involves distortions of the female anatomy (bulging of the vulva, bleeding, stretching of tissues, and so on), which can be seen as inconsistent with views of a woman as a sexually attractive being. "How would a man ever want to sleep with a woman he's seen giving birth?"— a question asked by men and women alike—reflects this concern. Couples can use such fears and reservations about pregnancy as opportunities to acknowledge their concerns to each other, drawing closer through considering them together.

The deep emotions of pride and joy in being pregnant and in anticipation of having the baby generally override concerns that negatively affect the woman's self-image.

COMMON PROBLEMS

Morning Sickness

The queasiness very commonly experienced by women during early pregnancy, usually between four and fourteen weeks, may extend beyond the morning hours. The cause of this loss of appetite, nausea, and sometimes vomiting during the first trimester is not fully understood. Hormonal influences are believed to play a major role. There is no evidence to indicate that the decreased food intake associated with morning sickness is harmful to the fetus.

Measures that have proved helpful, more by experience than by systematic research, in relieving nausea are eating small, frequent meals, such as six per day; separating ingestion of liquids and solids by one-half hour; and eating a dry, unsalted cracker or biscuit before getting out of bed in the morning. The drug Bendectin, a combination of vitamin B6 and doxylamine, effectively treats nausea in pregnancy. Although the drug was approved by the U.S. Food and Drug Administration (FDA), after a rash of lawsuits, all unfounded, in the 1980s alleging that it caused birth defects, it was withdrawn by the manufacturer from the U.S. market. Bendectin is available in other countries, including Canada. Vitamin B6, which is available over-the-counter, has also been proved effective. The usual dose is 50 milligrams twice a day with a maximum daily dose of 200 milligrams. Also available without a prescription is Emetrol, taken in doses of one to two tablespoons on arising and repeated every three to four hours as needed. Several effective prescription drugs are also available.

Severe nausea and vomiting in early pregnancy suggest a hydatidiform mole (see p. 295). Causes unrelated to pregnancy also need to be considered. If other known causes of severe vomiting have been ruled out, the diagnosis of *hyperemesis gravidarum* may be considered. With this serious, though uncommon, disorder hospitalization is usually required to prevent sometimes life-threatening maternal illness. The cause is unknown, although psychological factors have been suggested, and hypnosis as a treatment has been effective in some cases. A 1991 controlled study involving fifty-nine women with severe nausea and vomiting, reported in the journal *Obstetrics and Gynecology*, showed that vitamin B6 taken by mouth effectively reduced and shortened symptoms.

Frequency of Urination

Among several causes of increased urination in pregnancy, the most important is decreased bladder capacity resulting from compression of the bladder by the growing uterus. Another factor that contributes to increased output of urine is the consumption of extra fluids, whether they are intended to relieve constipation or to assist in treating urinary tract infections. Frequency of urination may in itself reflect a urinary tract infection and should be watched. When there is doubt, a urine culture should be obtained (see p. 20).

Urinary Tract Infection

Urinary tract infection can be frequent and bothersome during pregnancy. The relative slowing of urine flow from the kidneys to the bladder during pregnancy is a factor that both predisposes a woman to urinary infection and interferes with its treatment.

Infection can involve the lower urinary tract (bladder and urethra), the upper tract (ureters and kidneys), or both. Upper-tract involvement is suggested by such symptoms as fever, chills, nausea, vomiting, and abdominal or flank pain. The signs of lower-tract infection (*cystitis*) are urgency and frequency of urination along with pain or burning (*dysuria*).

Symptoms and signs of upper urinary tract infection present the more serious problem. The evaluation of urinary complaints requires a urinalysis and urine culture. The presence of the typical symptoms described here and the presence of white blood cells along with bacteria in the urine argue for the diagnosis of urinary tract infection and the initiation of treatment.

The cornerstone of treatment for urinary tract infection is antibiotics, usually administered for ten days. Several-day, short-course antibiotic therapy for lower-tract urinary infections is effective for nonpregnant women and in asymptomatic infections during pregnancy. It has not been sufficiently studied with symptomatic bladder infections in pregnancy to be recommended yet. The treatment with antibiotics by mouth customarily recommended for lower-tract infections may not be adequate to treat upper-tract infections, and intravenous treatment may be needed, at least initially.

Silent urinary tract infection (*asymptomatic bacteriuria*) predisposes pregnant women to symptomatic infection. For this reason, urine cultures are part of routine prenatal testing (see p. 20). Positive results are treated with antibiotics. Both asymptomatic and symptomatic urinary tract infections may increase the risk for premature birth (see p. 309).

Pain in the Lower Abdomen and Thighs

Pain in the lower corners of the abdomen, especially on the right, is common in pregnancy and is believed to result from stretching of the uterine supports, especially the round ligaments. This pain, sometimes known as round ligament syndrome, usually occurs at about twenty weeks and must be distinguished from pain arising from appendicitis, cholecystitis (inflammation of the gallbladder), kidney stones, urinary tract infection, hernia, and other disorders. Pain that arises in the supporting structures of the uterus is related to position. It usually improves when a woman lies down, especially when she turns to the painful side. It is not normally associated with fever, loss of appetite, nausea, vomiting, diarrhea, or urinary symptoms. On physical examination, there are no signs of tenderness from pressure over the painful area, a response that is more common in the other conditions mentioned. Most women are able to accept stretching pain as long as they know it does not represent a threat to themselves or to the fetus.

Numbness or pain in the upper front thigh is believed to result from pressure of the uterus on the nerve that loops toward the thigh over the brim of the pelvic bone. The resulting discomfort is similar to that experienced when the "funny bone" in the arm is hit (also related to pressure on a nerve, in this case the ulnar nerve, which can be subjected to pressure as it crosses the inner part of the elbow). Numbness in the thigh can often be relieved by lying on the back or side, especially on the numb or painful side. This symptom does not usually persist after delivery.

Recognizing appendicitis in pregnancy can be tricky. First, loss of appetite, nausea, and vomiting are common in pregnancy, as they are in appendicitis. Second, the enlarging uterus can displace the appendix upward out of its usual position in the right lower part of the abdomen, confusing diagnosis. Third, some degree of elevation of the white blood cell count is common in pregnancy, as it is in appendicitis. A physician who suspects appendicitis must act decisively to make a diagnosis before the appendix ruptures. The safest approach is to err on the side of early operation if appendicitis is suspected.

Pain in the pelvic girdle late in pregnancy and a feeling of coming apart are related to the softening of the ligaments that hold the bones together, which allows the pelvis to give during birth. It is a counterpart to the molding of the baby's head, made possible by its open cranial sutures (see pp. 175–177). There is no specific treatment other than avoiding activities that can intensify the strain. Very rarely, the pubic bones actually do separate and require strapping for support.

Pain in the Upper Abdomen

Pain in the upper abdomen warrants a call to the doctor. There are several possible causes that need to be sorted out, including gallstones (see p. 294), heartburn (see p. 79), and preeclampsia (see p. 307).

Fibroids

Fibroids are benign (noncancerous) tumors of the uterus that become more common as a woman gets older. If present, fibroids commonly increase in size during pregnancy. Although they usually cause no symptoms, they can occasionally be mildly annoying or confuse a diagnosis. For example, a fibroid may suddenly increase in size and cause pain, usually because of bleeding within it. This complication resolves with time.

Fibroids may make the uterus appear larger than it is, leading to a mistake in estimating gestational age. A fibroid that impinges on the cavity of the uterus may be a factor in miscarriage. Fibroids that are strategically situated in the lower portion of the uterus may obstruct labor, but this is very rare. Generally, fibroids shrink markedly after delivery. During pregnancy they can be identified by ultrasound (see pp. 32–34).

Hair Loss

Hair loss, which results from premature cessation of growth in the hair follicles, is one of the more distressing developments of pregnancy, occurring after the birth. Fortunately, even though it may persist for up to one year, it is temporary. This conversion of the follicles from the growing (anagen) to the resting (telogen) state resembles normal hair-follicle behavior at the end of a normal growth cycle. Giving birth is one of the causes of a widespread premature conversion of hair follicles from the growing to the resting state. Diffuse hair shedding during combing may occur for three months after delivery. Should there be any question of this diagnosis, the shedding phenomenon can be duplicated by stroking the hair with a gentle tugging action. The hairs removed can be examined under a microscope, and, in the usual case, the follicles will be seen to be in a resting stage.

Constipation

Less frequent, harder stools that are difficult to pass are common in pregnancy. Factors involved include relaxation of the muscles of the intestine because of pregnancy hormones, pressure on and displacement of the large bowel by the expanding uterus, relaxation and stretching of the muscles of the abdominal wall, and the constipating effects of iron supplements. Hemorrhoids may intensify and be intensified by constipation.

Constipation can be corrected through increased fluid intake, increased fiber intake (raw fruit and vegetables, bran, psyllium seeds, and so on), and exercise (see Exercise and Relaxation, p. 95). Stool softeners, such as *dioctyl sodium sulfosuccinate*, can also help. If necessary, gentle laxatives can be used, for example, senna concentrate (Senekot), in a dose of one to four tablets at bedtime, or milk of magnesia, in a dose of two to four tablespoons followed by a glass of water.

Varicose Veins and Hemorrhoids

Varicose veins of the legs, rectum (hemorrhoids), and vulva are common in pregnancy, particularly in women whose relatives also have or had them, suggesting a familial susceptibility. The pressure of the pregnant uterus on the large vein (vena cava) that drains blood back from the pelvis and legs is a major factor in varicose veins in pregnancy.

Although some women complain of aching, the significance of varicosities of the legs is primarily cosmetic. They can be relieved by elevating the legs (keeping the legs outstretched in a horizontal position) and wearing elastic (support) stockings.

Hemorrhoids can bleed and form painful fissures. They are ameliorated by measures to prevent constipation (see previous discussion), sitz baths in warm water, lubricating creams, suppositories (witch hazel, Anusol), and avoidance of straining (having what the English some- times call an unhurried motion). Thrombosis (clotting) of an external hemorrhoid can be very painful. The clot can be removed under local anesthesia. If bleeding persists, if the hemorrhoids cannot be pushed back into the rectum, or if they become infected, hemorrhoidectomy (surgical removal of the hemorrhoids) may be required, although this procedure is very unusual in pregnancy. Tying off the hemorrhoids or injecting them with chemicals that collapse and scar them are preferred to surgery.

Varicosities of the vulva may be contained and relieved with counter- pressure by a foam-rubber pad held in place by a belt.

Although women can expect relief from varicosities of all kinds fol- lowing delivery, hemorrhoids may be more pronounced in labor and the immediate postpartum period. Because improvement normally oc- curs after delivery, surgical correction of varicosities, if considered at all, should be delayed if at all possible until the necessity for it becomes clear.

Dizziness (Light-headedness)

Light-headedness, especially when the woman stands up quickly after lying down for a while, is common during pregnancy. It results when not enough blood reaches the brain because the heart does not receive enough blood to pump. During pregnancy, when a woman stands, blood tends to pool in her legs and thus is less available to the heart. Given the time to adjust, the heart and arteries accommodate this redis- tribution of blood. The time needed varies. When light-headedness is a problem, it is a good idea to stand up slowly; if dizziness occurs, bend- ing forward or sitting down will relieve it. Dizziness that occurs while the woman is lying down is usually caused by pressure of the uterus on the great vein (inferior vena cava) that returns blood from the legs, pelvis, and abdomen to the heart. Lying on the left side usually allevi- ates the problem.

Leg Cramps

Painful spasms of the calf muscles, particularly at night, affect about half of pregnant women. The cause is not known. Physical measures to relieve a cramp include massage and stretching maneuvers to bend the foot upward at the ankle. When lying in bed, the woman should avoid pointing her toes straight down or under. Although often recommended, dietary change or calcium supplements have not been proven effective.

Backache

As pregnancy progresses, women compensate for the weight carried in the abdomen by hollowing out the lower (lumbar) spine so they can maintain the normal upright position of the upper torso. This forward bend of the lower spine, know as *lordosis*, stresses the muscles and ligaments of the lumbar back, a setup for backache. Wearing high heels further increases the lumbar curve. Preventive measures include wearing low-heeled or flat shoes, taking rest periods during the day, strengthening the abdominal muscles through pelvic tilting and curl-ups, and maintaining general body fitness (see Chapter 2).

Measures to treat backache include applying ice (in the acute stage), stretching toward the feet as far as is comfortable while sitting in a warm bath with legs outstretched, practicing relaxation techniques, resting more, placing pillows under the knees when in bed, and, least desirable, analgesic drug therapy with acetaminophen or, in the first and second trimesters only, aspirin and nonsteroidal anti-inflammatory drugs (NSAIDs), such as ibuprofen and naproxen. If these steps do not work or if the backache is incapacitating or associated with any combination of leg pain, weakness, and numbness, the health-care provider should be consulted.

Lightening

Lightening is the normal sensation women experience, particularly in first pregnancies, as the fetus (now almost a baby) drops during the latter weeks of pregnancy. Less stretching of the abdomen makes a woman feel lighter, hence the name. Lightening is accompanied by less shortness of breath, decreased pressure in the stomach, the feeling that the baby has dropped, increased pressure in the pelvis, increased backache, and more frequent urination. Descent of the fetus may also contribute to constipation, the initial appearance or aggravation of hemorrhoids and varicose veins of the legs, and swelling of the legs and feet. Nothing much can be done about lightening except to recognize what it represents and to bear with its associated, but temporary, discomforts.

Heartburn

Heartburn is a common problem in pregnancy and represents the backing up (reflux) of the acid contents of the stomach into the esophagus (food tube). Factors that contribute to heartburn are compression of the abdominal organs, including the stomach, by the enlarging uterus; the elevation of the stomach above the uterus; alterations in the action of the valve between the esophagus and the stomach; and hormone-induced loss of muscle tone in the esophagus and stomach.

Heartburn can be relieved by eating smaller quantities at a time, by avoiding lying down immediately after eating, and, if these measures fail, by using antacids at the end of each meal (see p. 129). If the symptoms come on when a woman lies down, the head of the bed can be raised six to eight inches by blocks beneath the bedposts to allow gravity to work against reflux.

Edema

Edema, or fluid accumulation in the tissues, is indicated by visible swelling and is normal in pregnancy. Edema of the feet and legs is very common in the third trimester and is related to hormonal effects on blood vessels and to increased venous pressure in the lower extremities from pressure of the uterus on the large collecting vein in the abdomen (inferior vena cava). When the uterus presses on the large veins that drain blood from the legs, backup of blood and the passage of protein-rich fluid from the vessels into the skin result. When the woman sits or stands in an upright position, the force of gravity also contributes to this phenomenon. Many women report that late in the day their rings are tight and their faces are puffy, showing fluid retention in the upper part of the body. Neither edema nor weight gain alone during the third trimester is predictive of increased fetal or maternal problems.

If edema is annoying, raising the legs will help. The best treatment is to lie down one or two times a day on the left side (to tip the uterus off the vena cava). In addition, the woman should avoid salty foods and eat more complex carbohydrates and proteins (fresh fruits and vegetables), and lean meats. Fluid, especially water, intake should be increased to eight to twelve glasses a day. Elastic hose will help reduce the swelling, but some women find these stockings too uncomfortable to be worth the bother. When edema is associated with *preeclampsia* (see pp. 307–309), protein is present in the urine and the blood pressure is elevated.

Vaginal Infection

Vaginal infection is common in pregnancy, and *Candida albicans* (a yeast) is the major culprit, causing an infection called *moniliasis*, or *monilia*. Symptoms of infection are itching, burning, and vaginal discharge. Examination of the vagina with a speculum reveals a yeast infection resembling cottage cheese. Microscopic study of a sample shows the characteristic branching structure of the budding yeast. Several effective antifungal drugs are used for local treatment. *Candida* in the vagina can be picked up by the baby during birth and infect his or her mouth, producing the condition known as *thrush* (p. 140).

Two other causes of vaginitis and vaginal discharge in pregnant (as well as nonpregnant) women are *Trichomonas*, a one-celled amoeba-like organism, and bacteria. Anaerobic (not requiring oxygen) bacterial infections are commonly referred to as bacterial vaginosis (BV). These vaginal infections may cause no symptoms and are diagnosed by microscopic examination and culture. Both are treated with *metronidazole* (common trade name, Flagyl), which is considered safe for the fetus after the first trimester.

Bacterial vaginosis has recently attracted attention because of its association with premature rupture of the membranes and premature labor (see p. 300). It is now recommended that women with a history of premature rupture of the membranes be checked for BV in subsequent pregnancies and treated if positive. A large study of treating BV in women without symptoms after sixteen weeks, which was reported in 2000, showed no decrease in premature labors.

Itching

Itching (pruritus) of the body, especially of the arms and legs, is a common and sometimes annoying symptom of the third trimester. It may be related to a rash (see the following section). When a rash is not present, the most common cause of itching is a partial blockage in the liver of the excretion of bile into the biliary system, including the gallbladder. Bile salts in greater quantities than usual spill into the blood and circulate throughout the body. In the skin these salts cause itching and mild jaundice, a yellow color that may also be seen subtly in the whites of the eyes. Over-the-counter anti-itch preparations can relieve mild symptoms. These include colloidal oatmeal for baths (Aveeno), cooling lotions (Sarno), and antihistamines (Benadryl, Chlor-Trimeton). If these measures are ineffective, a doctor can recommend various prescription medicines. This type of itching quickly resolves after birth.

Skin Rashes

Several rashes that appear in the third trimester are unique to pregnancy. One in about 200 women develops itchy, sometimes blotchy, red bumps or blisters on the abdomen, thighs, arms, and buttocks, which disappear after the baby is born. This rash is known as the *polymorphic eruption of pregnancy*, or PEP. There is no known treatment other than measures to lessen the itching (see previous section). In 1998, Selim Aractingi and his colleagues in the United Kingdom reported the isolation of fetal DNA in the skin lesions of PEP. The role of this DNA is unclear, but its presence is further suggestive evidence for the immediate and long-term impact of the fetus on the woman, a connection that appears ripe for further inquiry (see The Placenta, p. 63).

Another rash, less common than PEP, and also very itchy is called *prurigo gestationis*. It consists of small bumps, often distorted by scratching, located on the forearms and trunk. Its cause and treatment are unknown.

Fatigue

Even in the most physically fit women, fatigue is a common feature of pregnancy. Although psychological factors may play a role, it is likely that weariness has a still-unexplained physical basis. Pregnant women tire easily and need to rest and sleep. There is no treatment for this problem other than rest, especially rest that is not associated with guilt about being tired or shirking responsibilities. Most women experience fatigue more during some periods of the pregnancy than during others.

Some women are tired throughout their pregnancies, but others report having more energy than ever and experiencing no fatigue at all.

Headache

Headaches, whether resulting from migraine, tense scalp and neck muscles, or a mixture of both, can be treated much the same in pregnant women as in nonpregnant women. For pregnant women the emphasis is on nondrug treatments, such as massage, ice, avoidance of migraine triggers, and relaxation (see p. 107). A helpful technique is to stretch the neck while seated under a hot shower with the head and neck loosely dropping forward, hands clasped behind the head to allow the weight of the arms to pull the head gently down as it is turned from side to side to bring the tense neck muscles into the line of pull. Safe drugs to use for pain are presented on page 128.

When a woman has a headache that for her is unusual in its intensity or other characteristics, she should consult her health-care provider. Headaches are one of the symptoms of preeclampsia (see p. 307).

Insomnia

Difficulty in falling asleep and interrupted sleep are common in pregnancy, particularly in the third trimester. Known causes include kicking by the fetus, heartburn, frequent need to urinate, shortness of breath, difficulty in finding a position of comfort, and worry. For some of these factors there is not a lot that can be done but to grin and bear it. A pillow under the uterus for support can make a side position workable; a waterbed allows sleeping on the abdomen. For excessive worry, anxiety, or depression, all of which can disturb sleep, the pregnant woman should seek professional help.

A pregnant woman having trouble falling asleep can try the same measures used by nonpregnant women: eliminating caffeine-containing beverages; avoiding use of alcohol; not eating before bedtime; taking a warm shower; drinking a glass of warm milk. Relaxation techniques (see p. 107) can also help. If the woman doesn't fall asleep within about ten minutes, she should stop trying, get up, and leave the bedroom. TV is out (too stimulating), but reading a (preferably boring) book, with the lights turned low, is in. When drowsiness sets in, it is time to return to bed. If all else fails, a sedating antihistamine, such as diphenhydramine, is an option, after checking with the health-care provider about the dose.

Nosebleed

Nosebleeds appear to be more common in women who are pregnant than in those who are not. The best explanation offered is that the already very vascular inner lining of the nose (mucosa) becomes even more full of blood in pregnancy, presumably an effect of hormones. The vast majority of nosebleeds can be controlled by finger pressure along the outside of the nose sustained for five to ten minutes. For bleeding that won't stop, the woman should see her health-care provider or go to the nearest emergency room while continuing to maintain pressure.

Emotional Sensitivity

Many women report wide mood swings, forgetfulness, and unusual sensitivity to the surrounding emotional climate during pregnancy. For no apparent reason, or with only the slightest provocation, an otherwise well-composed woman will burst into tears. This heightened reactivity is no reason to avoid stress or to be treated with kid gloves. Knowing that emotionality is a normal feature of pregnancy should promote understanding by the woman and those around her that outbursts and withdrawals are normal and need not be taken too seriously.

LATER PRENATAL VISITS

Later in pregnancy the prenatal visits build on the important earlier steps of taking the initial history and performing the first physical examination and laboratory tests. These later visits offer expectant couples an opportunity to take a more active role if their professional attendants agree. Women can weigh themselves, for example, and can check their own urine for protein and glucose. Couples can learn to listen to the fetal heart with the fetoscope and feel the various parts of the fetus through the abdominal wall. They can keep their own records, plotting the growth of the uterus and the increase in weight over the course of the pregnancy. A woman can pay particular attention to the first feeling of fetal movement, recording the time and date, and she can note changes, especially decreases, in kicking, allowing for sleep periods toward the end of pregnancy. Decreases should be reported promptly to the nurse or doctor. (See Fetal Kick Count, p. 158.) Couples can come to the prenatal visits together and can even include their children (see pp. 120–122 on preparing children for childbirth). They can share their observations, fears, and pleasures with the doctor or midwife and can insist on fully understanding what is happening and what choices they have throughout the pregnancy.

It is possible for couples to lay claim to their own prenatal care just as they do to labor and delivery. The doctor or midwife then becomes a ready resource and a support, not merely a director of the birth. Obviously, parents-to-be need to decide if they want this kind of relationship and will accept the responsibilities it implies. Many people elect a less-active role for themselves or are in health-care settings in which no other option is available.

In uncomplicated pregnancies, after the initial examination, visits are traditionally scheduled every four weeks until the thirty-second week, then at thirty-four and thirty-six weeks, and weekly thereafter until birth—usually thirteen visits in all. A recent U.S. Public Health Service expert panel has recommended reducing this number for healthy women to nine for first pregnancies and seven for later ones.

The content of the visits depends on the stage of the pregnancy. Weighing in (p. 64), checking the urine for protein and glucose (p. 15), and measuring blood pressure (p. 86) are standard procedures. Maneuvers having to do with the uterus and baby obviously depend on the size of the uterus, which by the second trimester (twelfth week) has risen out of the pelvis into the abdomen. The height of the uterus is determined by stretching the measuring tape from the pubic bone up and over the uterus to its top (see Figure 2.3).

By sixteen to twenty weeks it is possible to hear the fetus's heartbeat with a stethoscope. Since the fetal heart sound transmits best through the fetus's back, the location of the loudest sounds indicates the position of the back. In normal, head-down (vertex) presentations, the heart tones are generally heard best below the woman's umbilicus; in breech presentations they are heard best above it. When the fetus's back is pointing forward, the tones are best heard in front of the abdomen.

When the fetus's back is pointed toward the woman's back (called the posterior position), its heart tones are apt to be loudest in the woman's flanks.

It is possible to hear the heartbeat by placing an ear directly on the abdomen. An extra-long tubing attached to the stethoscope will allow the pregnant woman to listen. An inexpensive, wooden listening device, shaped like a megaphone, may also be used. With an ear against its tip, the examiner places its base directly on the abdomen. These devices are available through the International Childbirth Education Association and its affiliates (see Appendix) and sometimes from doctors or midwives.

By normal adult standards, the heartbeat of the fetus is very fast, ranging from 120 to 150 beats per minute. It is sometimes faint and hard to hear, but this does not mean there is anything wrong. Since the sounds have to travel a variable distance through amniotic fluid, the wall of the uterus, and the fat, muscle, and skin of the woman's abdominal wall, it is easy for them to be muted.

With Doppler ultrasound (pp. 162–163), the fetal heartbeat can be detected as early as the twelfth week. The sounds heard through the ultrasound monitor are not those of the heart itself, but are machine-made sounds triggered by the movements of the heart, as sensed by the monitor from echoes of sound waves pulsed to the heart. The visual detection of fetal-heart movement by ultrasound imaging can occur as early as the sixth or seventh week of fetal life.

During the last trimester the examiner can feel the fetus through the abdominal and uterine walls. The firm pressure required to outline the fetus will not harm it. The woman can assist the examiner by letting her abdominal muscles relax completely; blowing air out and then letting go helps relax the abdomen. By feeling the location of the fetus's head and buttocks, the examiner can tell whether the fetus is head down (vertex), breech, or transverse (lying horizontally) (see pp. 277–283). Each position has implications for subsequent care in pregnancy. Palpation is also a reasonably good guide to the number of fetuses present (see p. 317 on twins). The fetus's size can be estimated as average, large, or small, a judgment useful in predicting its fit to the birth canal.

Physical examination can reveal whether the fetal head has descended into the pelvis. The examiner feels whether his or her fingers can get around the bottom of the head and come toward each other. If the fingers surround the head, it is still high in the abdomen; if not, it has descended into the pelvis. By differentiating between the lumpy hands and feet and the smooth back, and by the location of the heartbeat, the examiner can conclude whether the back is facing left, right, front, or back.

SCHEDULE AND CONTENTS OF PRENATAL VISITS

Here I present as representative of current practice the contents and timing of routine prenatal visits as we now conduct them at our branch of Kaiser Permanente. There may be variations in other settings. Further, some tests not regularly done at Kaiser might be done routinely in other populations because of the prevalence of certain diseases in those groups.

As soon as you know you are pregnant: meet with a trained health-education professional for orientation to prenatal care and to issues such as common problems, nutrition, and drugs in pregnancy. *Blood pressure and weight are determined at all visits*, as is the size (height) of the uterus once it can be felt.

Twelve weeks: first individual medical visit, pelvic exam, Pap test, cervical culture for gonorrhea and chlamydia; schedule expanded AFP test for fifteen to twenty (ideally sixteen to seventeen) weeks.

Eighteen weeks: review results of expanded AFP and next step if any; check fetus's growth and heartbeat (done at all subsequent visits); determine whether more specialized attention may be needed because of risk factors.

Twenty to twenty-four weeks: arrange for ultrasound and tests for anemia, diabetes, and Rh D factor.

Twenty-eight to thirty-two weeks: review results of ultrasound and lab tests, and take indicated action if any. Review and revise if necessary the estimated delivery date; Review record of fetal heart kicks.

Thirty-six to forty weeks: review record of fetal heart kicks; pelvic exam may be done to check on fetal position and status of cervix; discuss labor signs and when to go to the hospital or birthing center.

NUTRITION AND WEIGHT GAIN

A good diet is a cornerstone of a healthy pregnancy, necessary to create a healthy baby and to sustain the woman through pregnancy, delivery, and nursing. Nutritional needs of women increase during pregnancy and nursing because the woman is really eating for two. The best available advice on diet can be summarized as follows:

1. Follow the guidelines in Table 2.1 and consider the recommendations based on the new food groups described later in this chapter.
2. Gain a minimum of twenty-five pounds (unless you are overweight to start), but do not allow yourself to become overweight.
3. Gain weight gradually and steadily.
4. Do not attempt to lose weight during pregnancy (even obese women should gain weight).
5. Do not restrict your intake of salt (sodium); use iodized salt to optimize thyroid function.

The best recommendation based on the evidence available at this time is that underweight women should gain twenty-six to thirty-five pounds, normal-weight women between thirty and thirty-seven pounds, and overweight women no more than fifteen pounds. As discussed on page 152 (Obesity), a pregnancy is safer for the woman and the fetus when the woman's weight going into pregnancy is normal, a fact worth considering when you are planning a pregnancy. Another point is that women will weigh, on average, six pounds more after the postpartum period than they did when they first became pregnant. Many women do not return to their prepregnancy weight unless they make a special effort. For a large number of women, pregnancy is the first step in a pattern of weight gain, which increases with subsequent pregnancies. Be aware of this risk and watch your weight, diet, and exercise during and after pregnancy. Extra pounds gained are hard to lose. Notice during prenatal visits where your weight plots out from month to month on the graph of weight gain that is a part of many prenatal charts. If your pattern of weight gain starts to move up and off the normal curve, stop and ask why. If it is important to you to return to your

TABLE 2.1 Daily Food Guide

What Is a Serving?	Recommended Servings You Need Every Day	Write in the Number of Servings You Ate Today
Bread, pasta, rice tortillas, cereal, oatmeal	7 or more	
1 slice bread 1 tortilla 3/4 cup dry cereal 1/2 cup hot cereal, cooked rice, noodles, pasta 6 crackers		
Vegetables	3 or more	
1 cup raw or 1/2 cup cooked vegetables 1 cup green salad 3/4 cup vegetable juice		
Fruits	2 or more	
1 medium piece fresh fruit 1/2 cup chopped, canned, or cooked fruit 3/4 cup orange or other fruit juice		
Milk, yogurt, or cheese	3 or more	
1 cup low-fat or nonfat milk or yogurt 1 cup of low-fat or nonfat frozen milk or frozen yogurt 1 1/2 oz. of low-fat cheese 2 cups cottage cheese		
Meat, turkey, chicken, fish, eggs, dry beans	2 or more	
3 oz. lean meat, fish, or poultry 1 cup cooked beans, lentils, or tofu 2 eggs 4 Tbs. peanut or almond butter (nonhardened, nonhydrogenated)		

TABLE 2.1 *(continued)*

Choose High-Vitamin Foods

You can get the extra calcium, iron, and folate that you and your baby need to be healthy if you eat some of these foods every day.

Calcium-rich foods

- Dairy products (milk, cheese, yogurt)
- tofu (calcium fortified)
- canned fish with bones (salmon, sardines)
- almonds
- broccoli
- green leafy vegetables (spinach, bok choy; mustard, turnip, beet, and dandelion greens; collards, kale, chard)
- corn tortillas
- orange juice fortified with calcium

Iron-rich foods

Try to eat iron-rich foods in combination with foods or juices high in vitamin C such as oranges, pineapple, broccoli, or strawberries. Vitamin C helps your body absorb the iron.

- beef, chicken, or turkey
- liver or other organ meets
- oysters
- tofu
- green leafy vegetables (spinach, bok choy; mustard, turnip, beet, and dandelion greens; collards, kale, chard)
- dry beans
- iron-fortified cereals
- raisins and dried fruits

Folate-rich foods

- dark green, leafy vegetables (like spinach or greens)
- broccoli
- asparagus
- liver
- fortified breakfast cereals
- oranges and orange juice
- peanuts and almonds

prepregnancy weight after your baby is born, eat carefully and exercise so that you will return to your desired weight within weeks.

The Daily Food Guide is adapted by me from the one recommended in our practice at Kaiser Permanente.

Fats

Fats are important in the diet and should supply between 20 and 30 percent of calories. Although fats do contain more calories, gram per gram, than other food components, reducing fat in the diet to the vanishing point with reduced-fat foods in an attempt to control weight, a major public preoccupation, can backfire—often people consume even more calories to achieve satiety. No matter what anyone tells you, *it's the calories that count.* Marked restriction of fat in the diet has paradoxically contributed to obesity.

The type of fat consumed is as important to health as is the overall amount. Foods containing trans fats should be limited. Trans fats result when liquid vegetable oils are hydrogenated to harden them. They are present in margarines and in many packaged, prepared foods, such as refrigerated biscuit dough, ready-to-eat cake frosting, cheese crackers, chocolate chip cookies, doughnuts, french fries, graham crackers, microwave popcorn, pound cake, snack crackers, and taco shells. Read the labels. You will probably not see the term *trans fat* as such (regrettably, not a food-labeling requirement), but you may see the word *hydrogenated* in such phrases as "partially hydrogenated soybean oil." Or, when you subtract individual fats (saturated, polyunsaturated, and monounsaturated) listed on a label from the total amount of fat given, there may be some quantity of fat unaccounted for. Many fast foods, such as doughnuts and french fries, which contain high levels of trans fats, are exempt from labeling requirements and can be advertised as cholesterol free and cooked in vegetable oil. Trans fats are worse than saturated fats in negative effects on the blood-fat profile (cholesterol level, etc.) and as contributors to coronary artery disease. A promising exception in margarine products, although data on safety in pregnancy are lacking, is Benecol, popular in Finland since 1995; its key ingredient, sitostanol, derived from pine trees, appears to reduce blood-cholesterol levels. A similar product derived from soybeans is Take Control. Whether these margarines have an effect on reducing coronary artery disease is not known. Also not yet known are the long-term effects, positive or negative, of the plant fats (sterols) contained in these products.

A healthy diet should emphasize fats that are oils at room temperature, including canola, safflower, olive, and corn oils. The diet should include fish at least twice a week (salmon—deep-sea is healthiest—and mackerel are among the most beneficial because they contain high levels of omega-3 fatty acids, which have a positive effect on body fats), and should minimize saturated fats found in red meats. Recent data show that eating one egg a day, or an egg several times a week, is not harmful.

A gram of fat has the same number of calories whether it comes from peanuts, meat, or olive oil. Gram for gram, fat has the most calories of all food components, so quantity of fat as well as quality is important.

For further information on fat in the diet, check the following web sites: www.amhrt.org (the American Heart Association), www.nhlbi. nih.gov (the National Heart, Lung and Blood Institute), and www.heartinfo.org (the Heart Information Network).

Sugar

Sugar is added to many foods, and average consumption is increasing, a factor in obesity. It is difficult to tell from labeling, which lists total sugar, how much is from the food itself, how much is added, and how the total compares to recommendations. Clues to added sugar are mention of corn syrup and fructose in the list of ingredients. Also, don't be fooled by the claim of "all-natural sweeteners."

Grains

A healthy diet during pregnancy should emphasize whole grains. Most of us eat very refined products most of the time. Studies suggest that eating whole grains can reduce the risk for heart disease, minimize the chances of developing the most common type of diabetes, and prevent several types of intestinal disorders. A whole cereal kernel—including oats, rye, barley, and wheat—contains all three parts of the kernel, including the *bran*, which is rich in fiber (a good preventive for constipation) and B vitamins; the carbohydrate- (and calory-) rich *core*, or *endosperm*; and the *germ* (as in *wheat germ*), also rich in B vitamins and other important nutrients. To find whole-grain products, look for the word *whole* as part of the first ingredient on the label. A product that lists enriched or wheat flour is a refined product, missing some of the key elements found in whole grains. If you're not used to whole-grain breads and cereals, add them to your diet gradually, as they can cause intestinal cramps and constipation at first.

The Virtues of Soy

Tofu and other soy preparations (including soy milk) may be as close to perfect foods as any. They are complete proteins, containing all the amino acids the body needs but cannot manufacture itself. Like other legumes (members of the bean family), they have no cholesterol, contain healthy forms of fat (mono- and polyunsaturated fats and omega–3 fatty acids), and are rich in fiber. Soy has the additional advantage of being rich in naturally occurring chemicals called isoflavones, which, in conjunction with other components of soy, lower blood cholesterol. Isoflavones may also help prevent the damage that narrows blood vessels in the process of atherosclerosis, may hinder the clotting of blood that leads to heart attacks, and may even play a role in preventing breast cancer. Apparently isoflavones are beneficial only when consumed as part of soy, not as purified supplements. Processing greatly affects the amount of isoflavones present in a soy product. For example, one ounce of soy isolate contains sixty milligrams of isoflavones; one-half cup of soy flour, fifty milligrams; one cup of soy milk, thirty to forty milligrams; and soy sauce and oil, none. (For more information, call the soy hot line, 1-800-TALK SOY, or visit the web site http://www.soy-foods.com.)

A note of caution comes from a recent study in the United Kingdom, which showed that boys whose mothers ate an exclusively soy-based vegetarian diet during pregnancy were five times as likely as others to have hypospadius, an abnormality of the penis in which the opening occurs on the lower shaft instead of on the tip. So, pending further studies, it's best to use soy to meet just *part* of protein needs.

Folic Acid

The vitamin folic acid deserves special mention. A daily intake of 0.4 milligrams taken from the time of conception through the first three months protects against fetal neural tube defects (see p. 24) and possibly against certain heart defects, cleft palate, and prematurity. If a fetus in a previous pregnancy has had a neural tube defect, the recommended daily dose of folic acid is ten times greater, 4.0 milligrams. Because women do not usually know for several weeks that they are pregnant, this vitamin should be taken at the protective dose when pregnancy is being planned in order to gain the full benefit from it.

The average diet supplies 0.05 to 0.5 milligrams of folate, the salt form of folic acid, daily, mainly from meat and dark green, leafy vegetables. Since January 1998 all enriched cereal grains sold in the United States must by law contain 0.14 milligrams of folate per 100 grams of cereal. Considering that dietary folate is only about one-half as bioavailable (usable by the body) as supplementary folic acid, it is easy to see why a supplement is required to reach 400 milligrams a day.

Vitamin Supplement

With the exception of folic acid, other nutrients for the fetus can be obtained by eating a well-balanced diet as described. The extra folic acid can be obtained from a supplement containing this vitamin alone or in combination with other vitamins, even though a combination is excessive. Taking quantities of vitamins greater than the daily requirements for pregnancy and lactation serves no purpose and should not be done. Megadoses (much more than the recommended daily amount) of some vitamins have been reported to damage the fetus.

Inadequate dietary iodine has recently received attention as a cause of underfunctioning of the woman's thyroid gland, resulting in less maternal thyroid hormone available for the fetus and greater risk for impaired fetal-brain development. Factors in decreased iodine intake include reduced use of iodized salt and reduced fortification of animal feeds and bread with iodine. Corrective measures include, in addition to reversing these trends, adding iodine to prenatal vitamins and other foods. Whether testing pregnant women for thyroid hormone would be useful is not yet known.

Iron Supplement

The question of whether iron supplements are necessary in pregnancy has not been evaluated with a randomized control study (see Table 2.1 for iron-rich foods). Despite the lack of evidence in favor of iron supplements, it is common practice to include iron in the prenatal vitamins recommended in pregnancy. My opinion is that this practice is unnecessary.

Herbs in Pregnancy

(See p. 128.)

Food Preparation

To prevent infection of yourself and the fetus by food-borne bacteria (see, for example, Listeriosis, p. 140), follow these rules:

1. Fully cook meat, poultry, and seafood. Eat cooked food immediately. Avoid undercooked foods. Avoid cold, ready-to-eat seafood and cold leftovers. Do not eat pate and raw egg dishes. Heat processed meats (bologna, hot dogs, salami, sausages) to steaming.
2. Use only pasteurized milk and avoid soft cheeses (for example, camembert, brie, feta cheese, and blue cheese).
3. Thoroughly wash fresh fruits and raw vegetables.

PREGNANCY AND A PLANT-BASED DIET

Pregnancy is an excellent time to consider in a fresh and thoughtful way what you eat. There is mounting evidence that a grain-based diet, with less animal (meat, fish, dairy, eggs, and poultry) protein and fat will help prevent heart and blood-vessel disease, high blood pressure, kidney disease, osteoporosis, obesity, and even some cancers. Although recognizing that the U.S. government has recently revised its dietary recommendations based on this new evidence, many experts on nutrition believe that the government is too strongly influenced by the meat and dairy industries and that these changes do not go far enough. Reducing the fat in hamburgers in our kitchens and in fast-food restaurants—a step in the right direction taken several years ago and, regrettably, reversed—still doesn't get at the crux of the problem, namely, the hamburger itself.

Apart from the considerable direct health benefits for individuals, a shift toward a diet that includes less meat and more reduced-fat dairy products will have highly beneficial ecological and economic effects. For example, a meat-based diet requires the continual creation of new farmland, raising of more cattle, clearing of forests, costly and inefficient use of crops and water, and heavier use of fossil fuels in food production and processing. Environmental effects, although counteracted in some instances by new farming methods, range from increased soil erosion and water pollution to increased levels of greenhouse gases in the atmosphere. The Physicians Committee for Responsible Medicine (see Appendix), a national, nonprofit organization of physicians and consumers, has been actively addressing these problems and has promoted a new four food groups.

The new four food groups are (1) whole grains, (2) legumes, (3) fruits, and (4) vegetables. A healthy diet—meeting dietary needs for calcium, protein, iron, and vitamins—includes a variety of foods from each of these groups. Other foods, including nuts, sweets, dairy products, meats, and oils, are options; it isn't necessary to include them in the diet. If you do consume them, use small quantities and select those with the healthiest kinds of fats (see p. 90). During pregnancy, be sure to include a moderate amount of non–plant-based proteins (see discussion in The Virtues of Soy, p. 92).*

EXERCISE AND RELAXATION

As in the case of eating right, pregnancy offers a wonderful opportunity to develop habits that will work for a lifetime. The purpose of prenatal exercise is to improve muscle strength and stretch tight muscles, since muscles are frequently tensed and shortened, as well as weak. Many common discomforts of pregnancy—backache, varicose veins, cramps, constipation, breathlessness, heartburn, postural discomfort—may be prevented or alleviated through a balanced program of exercise and relaxation. Also, a woman in good physical condition can withstand the

---

*This information on new food groups was adapted from information supplied by the Physicians Committee for Responsible Medicine (PCRM), a national, nonprofit organization of physicians and consumers. PCRM promotes an optimal diet for prevention of disease.

rigors of a long or hard labor, as well as the exertion needed to care for the new baby, better than a woman who is out of shape. But conditioning takes time to develop, and the sooner a pregnant woman begins exercising, the better.

In addition to strengthening and stretching muscles, prenatal exercise provides several benefits that may enhance the birth experience. Women who exercise regularly throughout pregnancy claim heightened body awareness, confidence in their physiological functions, and knowledge of how these functions are affected by the changes brought on by pregnancy. A woman who learns to trust her body can better trust her uterus and let go during labor, and will feel comfortable enough after birth to bond with her baby. After delivery, the physical fitness skills learned during pregnancy should be continued as an integral part of a healthy lifestyle. The exercises described here can be done in an exercise class or on your own. Don't feel guilty if, for whatever reason, you can't participate in an exercise program. Look on exercise as an enhancement, but not a crucial aspect of the care you give yourself.

Choosing an Exercise Class

Although the obstetrics and gynecology section of the American Physical Therapy Association has an increasing number of registered physical therapists who are trained to support women in achieving good musculoskeletal care during the childbearing years, in many communities there are no such therapists. Often, no exercise classes are available, either. Health spas, fitness centers, yoga classes, and dance schools offer prenatal or postpartum exercises, but these vary greatly in quality. Unfortunately, many of these programs neglect the muscles of the pelvic floor and reflect little understanding of the physiological changes of pregnancy. However, as long as a woman listens to her body and does nothing that causes strain or pain, she can usually reap the benefits and avoid the hazards of any reasonably good exercise program. With increasing consumer demand, more quality exercise classes should become available, so women should make their preferences known. If no classes are available, the exercises that follow should be of help.

Exercise classes for pregnant women and their partners may be held separately or as part of general childbirth-education classes. In either case, they provide contact with other childbearing couples. In addition to gaining group support, couples in these classes can learn about other resources early in their pregnancies, when they may still be open to making choices and changes in their birth arrangements.

The ideal exercise class has a small number of participants who can be individually evaluated and supervised, rather than trained as a group to follow the leader. The instructor explains the rationale for each position and movement, along with the role of the muscles in pregnancy, birth, and afterward. The best classes present the exercises in a broad context, coordinated with breathing, relaxation, and psychological preparation for birth.

General Principles

A suggested exercise session lasts for one and one-half hours and consists of roughly equal proportions of calisthenics, stretching, and relaxation. Aerobic exercises, such as walking, swimming, dancing, and cycling, can be done for recreation. The exercises here need be done only a few times each session to be beneficial, but they must be performed slowly and properly. Jerking and straining should be avoided. The goal is increased body awareness and comfort, not training for the Olympics. Quivering muscles or sudden jerky movements that bypass a weak muscle group indicate that the exercise is too difficult and should be modified. Once an exercise is mastered and is no longer taxing, it is advisable to make it more challenging by changing the position of the body or the leverage of the limbs, instead of merely doing it more times.

Breathing must be coordinated at all times with exercise movement. A good rule of thumb is to exhale during exertion. Another is to breathe in through your nose and out through your mouth (with your lips slightly parted). For example, when doing a curl-up for strengthening the abdominal muscles (to be discussed), fill your lungs by inhaling through your nose while your head, neck, and upper back are flat on the surface (floor or mat). As soon as your lungs are full, immediately begin exhaling through your pursed lips while elevating your head, neck, and upper chest. Then inhale again. When you reach the curled-up position and as soon as your lungs are full, exhale as you lower yourself back to the surface. To increase the time in the curled-position, lengthen the time of your breathing in and out. Straining while holding the breath in the throat has an undesirable effect on the circulation of blood, especially in pregnant women. It limits the return of blood to the heart; hence, less blood is pumped from the heart to the lungs to receive oxygen, and then out into the body. Since less oxygenated blood can reach the woman's tissues, including the placenta, less oxygen is available to the fetus. Exhaling during exertion not only prevents such negative cardiovascular effects, but also avoids strain on the pelvic-floor and abdominal muscles. In fact, exhaling during exertion actually improves the return of blood to the heart, as positive pressure is maintained in the abdomen relative to that in the chest. This principle is even more important during the pushing stage of labor.

A woman should become conscious of the natural expansion of the chest and abdomen during inspiration and their contraction during exhalation. Strange as it may seem, not everyone breathes in the most efficient way. Many people contract their abdominal muscles during inspiration and expand them during expiration rather than the reverse, and this needs to be pointed out to them. Tightening the abdominal muscles on exhalation is a good preliminary exercise that demonstrates the role of these muscles in forced exhalation; the abdominal muscles can be strengthened only during exhalation.

Although exercise programs can be expanded beyond the basic principles and movements discussed here, it is important to focus on the muscles most stressed in childbearing—the muscles of the abdomen and the pelvic floor. In most woman, both are weak. Typically, the abdominal muscles are rarely exercised, although they are quite visible, and most women sit or stand and rarely use the perineal muscles by squatting. During pregnancy, these muscles must meet the demands of increased weight gain, changes in the center of gravity, and support for the enlarging uterus, as well as meet the challenge of the expulsive phase of labor.

Abdominal and Back Muscle Exercise

The muscles of the abdominal wall provide much of the support for the spine and thus play an important role in the health of the back. Together with the *gluteus maximus* muscles—the major muscles of the buttocks—the abdominals control the angle of the pelvis in relation to the spine, which affects stability and stress of the lower back. The common view is that backache is due to weakness of the back muscles, but back muscles are more likely to be too tight than too weak. Thus, it is the abdominal muscles that need emphasis in back-care programs.

The abdominal muscles run from the lower edge of the ribs in front and on the sides to the rim of the pelvis. You can feel them if you lie on your back, knees bent, and raise your head and shoulders. Move your hand around over your abdomen from your ribs to your pelvis and feel the firmness over the entire area. The abdominals actually consist of several sets of muscles arranged in layers:

The *recti*, which run straight down the center of the abdomen and consist of two bundles about three inches in width, one on each side of the midline, separated by about an inch and a half of tough, fibrous tissue.

The *obliques*, two layers of muscles that run diagonally, one on each side of the body, from the ribs to the pelvis, crisscrossing in opposite directions.

The *transversus*, which is wrapped around horizontally.

During pregnancy the growing uterus stretches the abdominals from a straight line between the pelvis and ribs to an expanding curve between upper and lower attachments. Therefore, it makes sense to begin abdominal strengthening exercises as early as possible.

The curl-up is the basic exercise for the abdominal muscles. A curl-up is a modified sit-up, done to a maximum of forty-five degrees off the surface, with knees bent and the back of the waist flat on the surface used. To exercise all abdominal muscles adequately, curl-ups should be done in both straight and diagonal directions.

For a diagonal curl-up, twist one shoulder toward the opposite knee, alternating shoulders on successive curl-ups. Lie flat after each curl-up. Repeat the exercise up to fifty times, but stop if it starts to hurt.

The work of the abdominals can be progressively increased by changing the position of the arms as follows:

1. In the initial position, the arms reach toward the knees, assisting the movement (60 percent abdominal-muscle effort).
2. The next progression involves a neutral position, with arms folded across the chest (80 percent effort).

3. Finally, the arms are clasped behind the head to increase the leverage (100 percent effort).

Each woman begins at the appropriate level and progresses at her own pace. The physical changes that occur in later pregnancy make the more advanced curl-ups (2 and 3) too difficult.

It is important to check regularly through pregnancy for any separation of the rectus muscles from the stretching of the fibrous band that unites them like a central seam. Such a separation is called a *diastasis recti*. This condition is usually observed after the fifth month, but may be seen earlier in women who have retained it from a previous pregnancy. Many women notice the bulging in the midline of the abdominal wall as they get up off the floor after exercising or as they get out of bed or the bath. Although diastasis recti is painless, it may lead to postural backache because of abdominal wall weakness.

To check for diastasis, lie on your back with knees bent. Raise your head (which activates the rectus muscles), allowing your hands to reach toward your knees. You or your exercise coach can then check the width of the soft area between the tense rectus-muscle bundles. If three or more fingers can be placed between the contracted rectus muscles, diastasis recti is present. With this degree of separation, the bulging can usually be seen as well as felt.

A woman with a diastasis should avoid strenuous work with the abdominal muscles, as in double leg-raising exercises on the back (described later) and heavy lifting or straining. She should also be careful, when arising from the floor or bed, first to roll on one side and then push herself into a sitting position with her arms. It is usually not possible to close the gap of a diastasis during pregnancy because of the progressive and continuous stretching of the abdominal wall by the enlarging uterus. However, couples can be reassured that it is possible to bring these muscles together again with exercises after birth. The presence of diastasis recti requires that a woman's exercise program be modified only with regard to curl-ups; the other essential exercises are still suitable. If the rectus muscles cannot stay parallel when the head only is raised, it makes no sense to increase the load by bringing the shoulders off the floor as well. Furthermore, the oblique abdominal muscles contract when the shoulders curl forward. Because they attach to the sheath covering the rectus muscles, their action will lead to further strain and muscle imbalance, which can increase the diastasis.

To perform the modified curl-up, the woman with diastasis recti lies on her back with knees bent and hands crossed at the area of the gap to support the muscles. She performs head raises only, taking care that the abdominal wall is pulled *in* as the breath is exhaled, in order not to increase the bulging. She should do the exercises frequently for a short time, following the same program postpartum. After a few days postpartum, the woman can evaluate the gap while performing a modified curl-up without hand support. If the diastasis persists, she should continue the modified curl-ups. If the muscles are parallel at the midline, she can slowly increase the curling up by bringing the shoulders off the floor, but only little by little. Too rapid progression can lead to reseparation.

Note the difference between curl-ups and sit-ups. Sit-ups involve lying flat on the floor with legs extended and straight, and then sitting up. With curl-ups, the knees are bent to stabilize the lower back (lumbar spine). The movement is limited to the abdominals and is never more than about forty-five-degrees forward flexion off the surface. A sit-up, which involves a ninety-degree movement, is performed primarily by the hip flexor muscles, which run from the front of the upper thighbones to the lower spine and pelvis. When these muscles contract, they pull the spine and the thighs closer together and hollow the spine—just the effect that should be avoided. The abdominal muscles, on the other hand, roll the body forward as the ribs approach the pelvis without straining the lower spine. In the early part of a sit-up, the abdominals do most of the work; the second half of a sit-up hardly exercises the abdominals at all and may actually conceal weak abdominal muscles, as is typically seen in a person who jerks quickly through the first phase of the movement. Keeping the legs straight and, as is sometimes done in sit-ups, fixing the feet with external force (as, for example, by tucking them under a horizontal bar) further encourages use of the hip flexor muscles and thus increases lumbar strain. *Avoid sit-ups at all times.* Conversely, bending the knees minimizes use of the hip flexors and brings the abdominals into full play. The American College of Obstetricians and Gynecologists guidelines (see Table 2.2) recommend against the supine (on-the-back) position for resting or sleeping after the fourth month. Not all experts agree.

Pelvic Tilting and Bridging

Pelvic-tilting movements focus on the lower part of the abdominal wall and can be done in many positions. The action is to decrease the curve of the lower spine (the small of the back) by squeezing the buttocks tightly together and pulling in the abdominal muscles, thus rotating the pelvis to the back (posteriorly). Like curl-ups, pelvic-tilting exercises can be done progressively in three different positions while lying on the back.

1. The knees are bent, the feet flat on the floor.
2. With heels sliding along the floor, the legs are extended as far as possible while the pelvic tilt is maintained. With practice and increasing muscle strength and control, the tilt will be possible with the legs fully extended.
3. Finally, with the tilt maintained, the legs and thighs are bent and brought over the waist. Then the thighs and legs are simultaneously and gradually lowered and extended to the point at which the pelvic tilt is maximally stressed, yet maintained. Usually this point occurs before the thighs are lowered forty-five degrees. Many women will be able to lower the legs as far as forty-five degrees only after considerable practice. In late pregnancy this maneuver is difficult for many women. Do not perform this exercise if diastasis recti is present.

There is a difference between leg lowering as described and double leg raising, with which it is often confused. In double leg raising, the woman lies on her back with her legs outstretched and perfectly straight. She then lifts the stiffened legs together from the surface upward. The problem with double leg raising is that during the most difficult initial part of the movement, the pelvic tilt is out of control because the hip flexors, not the abdominals, do the work. As with a seesaw, the short lever of the pelvis rises before the longer lever of the outstretched legs. This exercise can cause much discomfort and aggravation of back pain. The point is not simply to raise or lower the legs. You must be able to maintain the pelvic tilt and protect the lumbar spine while the muscles that do so are challenged and thereby strengthened. *Double leg raising should be eliminated from any exercise program, especially one designed for pregnant women.*

Basic pelvic tilting can also be done in sitting, standing, kneeling, side-lying, and hands-and-knees positions. In the hands-and-knees position, the work of maintaining the pelvic tilt can be increased by extending first one arm, then one leg, then opposite arms and legs together. In this exercise, the abdominal and gluteal muscles hold the pelvis in line with the spine against gravity and the leverage of the different arm and leg positions. This is also a good position for the woman with a diastasis who cannot do curl-ups. The hands-and-knees position relieves backache and pressure from the uterus, and the progressive exercises mentioned improve balance and strengthen the arms and shoulders.

Bridging is the act of raising the buttocks off the floor. It helps improve the pelvic tilt by strengthening the gluteal muscles, which pull the pelvis down in conjunction with the upward movement of the abdominals. Bridging is done lying on the back, preferably with the legs straight at the knees and with the heels resting on a low table or footstool. The buttocks are lifted from the floor to form a bridge with the body. If this exercise is done with the knees bent, the woman must be taught to feel the difference between gluteal contractions and the leverage exerted by the hamstrings, which run from below the knee to the sitting bones of the pelvis. The closer the heels are to the buttocks, the more substitution occurs with the hamstrings, which can extend the hips when the knees are bent and thereby reduce the value of the exercise. Bridging should be done with the pelvis tilted back and buttocks held as firm as possible. A further progression is to straighten alternate knees while in the bridge, and then to move the extended leg from side to side, keeping the thighs parallel throughout.

Pelvic-Floor Exercises

The importance of the muscular and fascial layers that make up the pelvic floor cannot be overemphasized. Particularly important is the *pubococcygeus* muscle, which runs from the coccyx (tailbone, or tip of the spine), encircles the vagina and rectum, and attaches to the pubic bones at their point of joining. In Western cultures, the muscles of the pelvic floor are typically not exercised, and many women are unaware of them. The three main functions of the pelvic floor are

1. To support the pelvic abdominal organs and the increasing weight of the uterus in pregnancy
2. To provide sphincter control of the anus and urethra
3. To enhance sexual response, since healthy muscles grip and massage the penis during intercourse and vigorously contract during orgasm to provide increased satisfaction to the woman and her partner

Structural changes in the pelvic floor, such as laxity and various degrees of sagging of the uterus, bladder, or rectum, are common in Western society, particularly in women who have borne children. Functional changes, such as urinary-stress incontinence (the leakage of urine with coughing, sneezing, or straining), lack of sexual satisfaction for either partner, and incomplete emptying of bowels or bladder, are also very common. Many women believe that stress incontinence and falling-out feelings are normal consequences of pregnancy, since many of their friends have the same symptoms. Smoking, obesity, and chronic chest conditions, which all cause increases in intra-abdominal pressure, aggravate pelvic-floor dysfunction. Although softening of tissues related to hormonal and blood-supply changes and some descent of the pelvic floor are normal during pregnancy, adequate urinary control can be expected to be maintained throughout.

Healthy pelvic-floor muscles can help facilitate the safe progress of the baby during the second stage of labor. Well-exercised muscles with an enhanced blood supply can better withstand stretching before their fibers become underoxygenated or stretched to the point of tearing. Arnold Kegel, a pioneer in studying the pelvic floor, has shown that during the crowning of the baby's head, a strong pubococcygeus muscle remains protected by the pubic bones, whereas a thin, fibrous, unexercised muscle is dragged down with the fetal head and is more likely to be injured.

There are problems in learning to contract the pubococcygeus, because the action is internal and out of sight and no bones are involved in the movement. Many women are unaware of the pubococcygeus and cannot contract it in isolation from other muscle groups. Typically, when asked to tighten this muscle, women contract other muscles, such as the muscles of the buttocks or inner thighs. Since vaginal examinations are not performed during exercise or childbirth classes, it is essential for the woman, perhaps with the aid of illustrations, to locate this muscle herself.

A woman can become aware of this muscle while urinating simply by stopping in midstream several times and paying attention to the muscles used to do so. A woman who cannot do this will need to reeducate this muscle. The muscle can also be identified and evaluated during the prenatal physical examination (see p. 53). Inserting one or more fingers into the vagina, while at the same time trying to squeeze, is another way for a woman to identify this muscle.

Once a woman has identified the correct muscle, she tightens the anal and vaginal sphincters, thereby also raising the perineum (the region between the lower end of the vagina and the anus). Useful analogies to this action are the rising of an elevator and the drawing up of a hammock. The muscular contractions must be done slowly enough to recruit as many muscle fibers as possible. Contract-relax exercises (also known as Kegeling) can be done at any time. In particular, the pelvic floor should be braced during such exertions as sneezing, coughing, or lifting.

Research has shown that the pelvic floor readily fatigues with exercise and that the average woman cannot make more than a few contractions of consistent strength. Similarly, holding a contraction for more than ten seconds is beyond the ability of most unconditioned women. The exercise should be done little and often—just three or four contractions in a series, followed by a rest interval. A total of about fifty should be done daily before, during, and after pregnancy. Sexual intercourse is another opportunity for the practice and improvement of pelvic-floor control and has the advantage of feedback from the woman's partner. Pelvic-floor exercises can be done anywhere, anytime. They should become as routine as brushing the teeth.

In societies in which squatting is common, the pelvic floor is always being strengthened because it must support all the internal organs when in the squatting position. Squatting also strengthens the muscles of the thighs and promotes safe lifting habits by avoiding bending at the waist. Squatting is a useful exercise in pregnancy, and the squatting position is also recognized as useful during childbirth both in terms of effective pushing and in maximizing the space in the birth canal. (See Position in Labor and Delivery, p. 204, and Breech Presentation, p. 277.)

Stretching Exercises

For health and well-being, flexibility is as important as strength. The muscle groups that are tight are typically the hamstrings, calf muscles, inner thighs, hip flexors (muscles that bend the thigh toward the abdomen), and back extensors (muscles that straighten out the back, as in a position of attention). Yoga exercises are particularly suited to enhance flexibility (see Appendix).

The hamstrings can be stretched by standing with one leg elevated on a chair or table, by long sitting (knees straight, legs outstretched), and by lying on the back and lifting *one* straight leg at a time. (Avoid double leg raising, as described previously.) In pregnancy these positions are preferable to bending forward, which usually involves rounding of the back and excessive pressure on the spinal disks (the structures that act as shock absorbers between the individual vertebrae). In stretching the hamstrings it is important to bend at the hips rather than to bend the spine.

Calf stretching can be done kneeling on one knee (runner's stretch) with the foot of the forward leg firmly applied to the floor as weight is shifted progressively forward; or by standing with one foot in front of the other, keeping the knee of the rear leg straight with its foot planted squarely on the floor as the forward knee is bent. The hip flexors can also be stretched in the half-kneeling position (the position runners assume at the starting line), one foot in front of the other, with the weight transferred onto the forward foot until a pull is felt in the opposite groin.

The back can be stretched in a tailor-sitting position (knees bent, ankles crossed, and legs allowed to fall apart). The trunk is then bent forward to bring the head toward the floor. A modified back stretch can also be done in a half-tailor-sitting position (one leg outstretched and one leg bent) with the trunk bent to either side. Sitting with the legs extended (long sit) and holding the back at a ninety-degree angle (without leaning on the arms) is an excellent stretch and postural exercise. The lower back can also be buttressed against a wall and the exercise made more difficult by raising the arms while keeping contact with the wall.

The adductor muscles (which pull the thighs inward toward each other and contract to hold an object between the knees) can be stretched while sitting on the floor with the soles of the feet together, allowing the force of gravity to let the thighs fall apart. The pelvic-clock exercise, arching the pelvis around like the hands of a clock, of Moshe Feldenkrais can also be done in this position and increases pelvic awareness. This maneuver involves sitting on the floor with the soles of the feet together and rotating the pelvis round and round, first clockwise, then counterclockwise.

Aerobic Exercise

Aerobic exercise refers to activities that increase the pumping of blood by the heart and the movement of air in and out of the lungs and includes any combination of walking, skipping, jumping, jogging, and dancing, using backward, forward, and sideways directions for variety. Other aerobic activities are running, cross-country skiing, brisk walking, and non-weight-bearing activities such as swimming and cycling. Warming up and cooling down, including stretching before and after aerobic exercise, are particularly important to prevent injury and are often overlooked. Women can continue with their favorite sports, listening to their bodies for signs about what to do and how much, as the pregnancy progresses and after delivery. Table 2.2 contains guidelines for planning appropriate aerobic activities.

Relaxation

An ability to relax is a great asset during childbirth, when actively being is as important as doing. For one thing, relaxation during labor allows the woman to conserve energy. Giving birth involves using the forces that push the baby down the birth canal as well as reducing the forces that oppose this descent. Tightening up increases resistance; opening up decreases it. In a sense, a pregnant woman allows her baby to be born simply by yielding to the forces pushing the baby out. Letting go through increased awareness of the body is a skill that can be learned and practiced.

Sheila Kitzinger, noted British childbirth educator, has described the "puppet-string" approach to relaxation. In a comfortable lying position, with plenty of pillows, the woman imagines various parts of her body attached to strings operated by a puppeteer. The puppeteer can pull the strings straight up or at various angles and can pull them in any combi-

TABLE 2.2 Exercise Guidelines for Pregnancy and Following Birth

1. Regular exercise (at least three times per week) is preferable to intermittent activity.
2. Avoid vigorous exercise in hot, humid weather. Stay well hydrated before, during, and after exercise. Wear light clothing that "breathes."
3. Ballistic movements (jerky, bouncy motions) should be avoided. Exercise on a wooden floor or a tightly carpeted surface to reduce shock and provide a sure footing.
4. Avoid deep flexion or extension of joints because they are looser in pregnancy and more vulnerable to trauma. For the same reason, avoid jumping, jarring motions or rapid changes in direction.
5. Vigorous exercise should be preceded by a 5-minute period of muscle warm-up. This can be accomplished by slow walking or stationary cycling with low resistance.
6. Follow vigorous exercise with a period of gradually declining activity that includes gentle, stationary stretching. Because connective-tissue laxity increases the risk of joint injury, stretches should not be pushed to the point of maximum resistance.
7. Measure heart rate at times of peak activity. Do not exceed 140-150 beats per minute unless in consultation with your physician.
8. Take care to rise from the floor gradually to avoid orthostatic hypotension. Continue some form of activity involving the legs for a brief period.
9. Drink liquids liberally before and after exercise to prevent dehydration. If necessary, activity should be interrupted to replenish fluids.
10. Women who have led sedentary lifestyles should begin with physical activity of very low intensity and advance activity levels very gradually.
11. Stop activity if any unusual symptoms appear. Consult your physician.

Pregnancy Only

1. Do not let your heart rate exceed 140-150 beats per minute.
2. Do not exercise strenuously for more than 15 minutes. Limit total time to 45 minutes and stop before you're worn out. You should be able to carry on a conversation at all times.
3. Avoid contact sports, scuba diving, and high altitude exercise (unless you are specially conditioned for thin air). Otherwise, there are no restrictions on what you can do safely, but take it easier than when not pregnant.
4. Strength training with light weights and frequent repetitions are okay.
5. After the fourth month don't do exercises while lying flat on your back.
6. Avoid exercises that require holding your breath and bearing down (thereby markedly increasing pressure in the abdomen.)
7. In the second half of pregnancy, swimming is by far the ideal exercise. It takes the weight off you while you work out.
8. Limit your use of saunas and whirlpools to a few minutes at a time.

nation; for example, the right shoulder and the right index finger can move together, or the right shoulder can move with the left knee, and so forth. A woman can activate the strings herself, or she can ask her partner to do so and to let her know which strings are being pulled. After an imaginary string has been pulled, the woman allows the muscle to relax and the body part involved to sink back into a resting state.

The method of relaxation based on Stanislavsky acting techniques uses imagined activities. In a relaxed sitting or lying position, with eyes closed, the woman gets in touch with various parts of her body by imagining them engaged in activities such as chewing sticky taffy, walking barefoot on sharp pebbles at the beach, kneading dough, following an airplane overhead to the distant horizon, tasting a sour lemon, and so forth. She does not actually make these movements, but does them in her mind.

Although there are many relaxation techniques, relaxation cannot really be taught. People learn how to relax *indirectly*. Childbirth classes often include training for conscious release, yet the receptors that control muscle tension do not reach a conscious level in the brain, so conscious release is not physiologically possible. The most effective body-work approach to relaxing a muscle is to tighten the muscle that has the opposite action. Examples of this approach include dragging down the shoulders for tense and elevated shoulder muscles; fingers long, to extend overactive finger flexors; and dragging down the jaw, for tension in the face. As you do these exercises, note which muscles are tense and which are relaxed. Then let go of the tense muscles to permit maximum movement in the intended direction. In actively dropping your jaw you can become aware of relaxation in the muscles of your cheeks.

Mental relaxation must be encouraged along with physical release. These skills form the basis of yoga and meditation programs. Focusing on the natural rhythms of breathing will quiet the mind and facilitate relaxation of the body. Controlling the breath, on the other hand, requires effort, diminishes awareness of the body, and impairs relaxation. Couples can experience these phenomena for themselves by alternating controlling breathing with simple observation of it (see next section).

The passive state of mental relaxation can also be obtained by repeating the number "one" or any other word silently, or by using a mantra, as in meditation. The procedure, adapted from Herbert Benson's *Relaxation Response*, is as follows (note that this exercise does not work well after a heavy meal):

1. On an empty stomach, in a quiet environment, select a comfortable chair, sit in a relaxed position, and close your eyes. Place your feet comfortably on the floor, and rest your head against the wall or back of the chair.

2. Deeply relax all your muscles, from your feet to your face-toes, ankles, calves, thighs, lower torso, chest, shoulders, neck, head. If this is hard, try tensing each part and then relaxing it. Squeeze your fists and arm muscles. Then let them relax and hang loosely at your side, on the arms of the chair, or in your lap. Repeat with your feet and legs, squeezing them first and then letting them loose.

3. Breathe normally through your nose. Pay attention to your breathing and to the air moving through your nose. Do not overbreathe. As you breathe out, say "one," or another word silently to yourself. Rather than focusing on breathing, some people find it easier to imagine a pleasant scene.

4. When other thoughts and feelings float into your mind, just let them be. Do not push them away, but do not pay attention to them either. Be indifferent; adopt an "oh, well" attitude. If a reminder (to do something, for example) comes into your mind, open your eyes, get up, write it down, sit back down, and start again from the beginning.

5. Continue for ten to twenty minutes. Open your eyes to check the time, but do not use an alarm. If you have done the exercise for too short a time, close your eyes and go back to it. Then sit quietly for several minutes, at first with your eyes closed and then with them open.

6. Do this exercise daily. Do not expect immediate results, and do not expect any results unless you do the exercise on a regular basis. Some people prefer doing the relaxation exercise at the beginning of the day, others at the end of the day. Some do it at both the beginning and the end of each day. Once you have practiced the exercise and feel comfortable with it, you can also use it at times of particular stress.

Breathing in Labor

As part of a changing emphasis in childbirth education, many practitioners are reevaluating traditional psychoprophylactic breathing techniques, such as the Lamaze and Bradley methods. This rethinking recognizes that each woman's labor is different and that women, left to themselves and encouraged to experiment, are capable of finding the laboring position and breathing patterns that work best for them.

Increasingly, controlled patterns of breathing are coming to be considered excessively rigid. This view in no way minimizes their historical importance as a reaction to the totally anesthetized childbirth practiced in the early twentieth century, nor does it deny the continuing appeal of these methods to women who want consciously to control pain in childbirth. All too often, however, women become preoccupied with fixed patterns of breathing that do not respond to the needs of the body. Breathing normally, and in response to internal cues, may be more beneficial. The purposeful alteration of breathing, with the goal of pain control through distraction, consumes energy and limits feeling and awareness. Women who have had a normal childbirth often report that lack of energy, rather than unbearable pain, is their most common difficulty during labor. This lack of energy may result from anxiety and tension and may be exacerbated, rather than helped, by the distraction techniques and breathing interventions that have been taught by childbirth educators.

Shallow chest breathing does not permit sufficient fresh air to enter or sufficient stale air to leave the lungs for adequate gas exchange to occur in the tiny air sacs. If this type of breathing becomes rapid, dizziness and light-headedness (symptoms of hyperventilation) may occur as the woman accelerates her breathing to stay on top of her intensifying contractions. Hyperventilation also leads to chemical changes in the blood that decrease its oxygen-carrying capacity and change its acidity. Both effects are undesirable for the fetus.

Although women are commonly taught to achieve an inverse relationship between the speed and depth of respiration (the slower, the deeper; the faster, the more shallow), research has shown that as the breathing rate increases, women in labor do not naturally decrease the amount of air they breathe in and out with each breath. The rate of breathing is the only practical guide for couples. It should not exceed twenty breaths per minute, and, to stay within optimum limits, it should be much less.

Traditionally, women have been told after full cervical dilatation to "breathe in, hold your breath, and push!"—an effort that results in a forced expulsive effort against a closed glottis. This approach is now being reconsidered. The closed-pressure system formed after even five seconds of forced breath retention leads to increased pressure inside the chest, reduced return of blood to the heart and lungs, and a reduction of the amount of blood pumped by the heart through the body, including the placenta. Thus, blood flow to the fetus can be impaired. Holding the breath also results in reflex tensing of the pelvic floor, which increases resistance to the baby's descent—just the opposite of what is desired.

A more beneficial approach, according to recent thinking, is to push with lips pursed to let air out gently during bearing down—in effect, to breathe the baby out. Furthermore, women need to bear down only to the extent that such pushing brings a feeling of relief. They should follow their body's internal cues.

The birthing center at Pithiviers, France, directed by renowned obstetrician Michel Odent, works on the assumption that women know how to give birth if left alone. No formal prenatal instruction is given. Instead, women come to the center about a week before their due date and learn what they need from other women who have just given birth. They spend much time singing around the piano. When they go into labor, they are free to assume any comfortable position, and many labor and give birth in a warm pool (see Water Birth, p. 193). The reported results are excellent.

My opinion is that preparation for labor and delivery, including breathing techniques, should be kept simple, with emphasis on natural events and normal physiology. If childbirth can be seen as an involuntary process that needs only to be allowed to unfold, rather than to be controlled, the laboring woman will be better able to direct her energy within, instead of dissipating it by attempting to put her mind outside her body. Each woman should strive to find her own way, fully recognizing that women already know how to have babies if left to themselves.

GUIDELINES FOR WORK

(See Table 2.3 on page 114.)

SEX DURING PREGNANCY

Although pregnancy can be a profoundly sexual experience, sexual feelings during pregnancy may fluctuate widely, from intense passion to no interest whatsoever. For example, in early pregnancy, a woman experiencing morning sickness is not likely to be interested in intercourse with her partner. Several studies indicate a decrease in desire in the third trimester as well. Yet at certain times during pregnancy, some women experience an increased desire for genital sex.

The dramatic changes in a woman's body that are part of a normal pregnancy run counter to some of society's most cherished ideals of beauty. In American society, which tends not to acknowledge and respect the sexuality of the pregnant woman, these changes are thought of as anything but sexual turn-ons. Couples would do well to concentrate on their own positive feelings toward each other, deemphasizing any stereotyped negative feelings toward sexuality, pregnancy, and sex and pregnancy.

Intercourse is perfectly permissible during pregnancy, although adjustments in position and penetration will have to be made to accommodate the woman's expanding abdomen. The man-on-top position is too uncomfortable for late pregnancy; a side-by-side or sitting position is preferable. After the baby has dropped, rear-entry positions are particularly comfortable, with the woman kneeling, crouching, or lying. Lots of pillows can be used for support, to keep weight off the abdomen. Pillows and more pillows are to intercourse during pregnancy what a rocking chair is to breast-feeding.

Kitzinger has pointed out that in advanced pregnancy, it may be better for the man to ejaculate and withdraw just before a woman comes to orgasm. An erect penis in a heavily pregnant woman may prevent her from making the kind of pelvic movements that will bring on orgasm. In pregnancy, as at other times, the man should be aware that the clitoris can be overstimulated. A good general rule is that, once the clitoris has become swollen, the man should ask the woman when she wants penetration.

During pregnancy, many couples prefer to express sexual feelings in ways other than intercourse—cuddling, showering together, massage, or caresses that lead to orgasm. The sensitivity of a woman's breasts and nipples often markedly increases in pregnancy. Breasts can become the focus of erotic arousal, but need to be handled gently. Pregnancy offers couples the opportunity to explore new forms of sexual expression, which can be continued after the birth. The topic of lovemaking during pregnancy has inspired much recent interest and several books (see Appendix).

TABLE 2.3   When to Terminate Various Levels of Work During a Normal, Uncomplicated Pregnancy

Job Function	May Work to (weeks)
Secretarial, light clerical, professional, managerial	40
Seated; light tasks (prolonged or intermittent)	40
Standing	
Prolonged (more than 4 hrs)	24
Intermittent (more than 30 min/hr)	32
Intermittent (less than 30 min/hr)	40
Stooping and bending below knee level	
Repetitive (more than 10 times/hr)	20
Intermittent (between 2–10 times/hr)	28
Intermittent (less than 2 times /hr)	40
Climbing Vertical ladders and poles	
Repetitive (more than 4 times/8 hr shift)	28
Intermittent (less than 4 times /8 hr shift)	28
Stairs	
Repetitive (more than 4 times/8 hr shift)	28
Intermittent (less than 4 times /8 hr shift)	40
Lifting	
Repetitive	
More than 50 lbs	20
25 to 50 lbs	24
Less than 25 lbs	40
Intermittent	
More than 50 lbs	30
25 to 50 lbs	40
Less than 25 lbs	40

SOURCE: Adapted from AMA Council on Scientific Affairs: Effects of Pregnancy on Work Performance; 1988; with permission of the American Medical Association.

Pioneering childbirth researcher Niles Newton identified eleven points of comparison between undisturbed childbirth and sexual excitement.

1. Change in breathing
2. Tendency to make vocal noises
3. Facial expression reminiscent of an athlete under great strain

4. Rhythmic contraction of the upper segment of the uterus
5. Loosening of the mucous plug from the opening of the cervix
6. Periodic contractions of the uterus
7. Use of a position in which the woman's legs are drawn up and spread apart (a dated observation, as women do not necessarily give birth or have intercourse in this position)
8. A tendency to become uninhibited
9. Unusual muscular strength
10. A tendency to be unaware of the world, and a sudden return to alert awareness after climax (orgasm) or birth
11. A feeling of joy and well-being following the orgasm or birth

Obviously, the degree to which a couple can experience labor and delivery in such sexual terms will depend on the setting in which birth takes place and how it is conducted. Relaxation and a sense of security are important factors.

Common fears regarding intercourse and orgasm during pregnancy relate to precipitation of an abortion (miscarriage), initiation of premature labor, and causing harm to the fetus in some way. There is no evidence that intercourse causes miscarriages, although it may be the precipitating factor in a pregnancy that is destined to abort (see p. 301). Although there is some evidence that intercourse and orgasm may trigger the onset of labor, research findings are divided on this question; the consensus is that intercourse is not a factor in premature labor. There is no evidence that intercourse harms the fetus.

If certain conditions are present or suspected, intercourse during late pregnancy is best avoided.

1. Broken amniotic sac, allowing communication between the uterus and vagina and thus increasing the chances of infection of both the uterus and the fetus (see Preterm Rupture of the Membranes, p. 313, and Premature Rupture of the Membranes at Term, p. 314)
2. Premature labor
3. Placenta previa (pp. 303–304)
4. Impaired well-being of the fetus for example, if the infant is suspected of having intrauterine growth disturbance (see pp. 296–297)

HAVING A BABY LATER IN LIFE

The number of American women over the age of thirty-five who are having children is steadily increasing as more women postpone parenthood because of career choices. Women over thirty-five and their fetuses do face special problems. However, data from the Royal Victoria Hospital in Canada (reported by Ruth Fretts and her colleagues) show that if serious genetic problems and birth defects are eliminated by genetic testing and therapeutic abortion (see p. 316) and if the women are treated properly for chronic illnesses such as diabetes and hypertension, 994 of 1,000 babies will be born alive to older women compared with 997 in 1,000 for younger women, a difference of 3 per 1,000. With modern treatment the difference in maternal mortality based on age, once significant, can be largely eliminated. Thus the news for older pregnant women is very encouraging.

Problems remain, some of them without ready answers. Older pregnant women are more likely to have placenta previa or placental abruption (see p. 303) and to require cesarean sections. Fetuses of older women are at increased risk for miscarriage (see p. 298), fetal defects, premature birth (see p. 309), and stillbirth (see p. 284). Because older women are more likely than younger women to have a chronic illness, such as hypertension, that requires treatment, decisions about drugs safest for the fetus (see Drugs Taken During Pregnancy, p. 127) will have to be made, preferably before conception. (Also see Before You're Pregnant Dos and Don'ts, p. 12.)

CHILDREN AND BIRTH

As more parents want to make birth a family-centered experience, whether in the hospital, in the birthing room, or at home, there is an increased focus on preparing older children for the birth and arrival of a new sibling. Some parents choose to include an older child during labor and delivery; many do not. In any case, thoughtful preparation of the older child is important.

Many parents who have been through the experience of preparing an older child for the arrival of a sibling emphasize three points.

1. The key to success in preparation is the attitude of the parents; if the child is to be unafraid, enthusiastic, and excited about the birth, the parents must be that way, too.
2. The bonding that takes place after birth should occur not only between the parents and the newborn but between the older child and the new sibling as well.
3. Children participate to the degree to which they are comfortable. They should not be forced or pressured to do more than they want to do; and they should be permitted as much or as little involvement as they can comfortably handle.

Conveying the Unfolding of Pregnancy and the Time of Birth

Parents should tell their child about the expected baby as soon as they are sure the woman is pregnant. Many parents say their child needed the nine months to prepare as much as they did. Even though time is a difficult concept for small children, they seem able to grasp it if it is linked to their own experiences. Some parents use the signs of the seasons to convey the passage of time. If, for example, the baby is due in June, a parent may say something like, "First there will be fall, when the leaves turn pretty colors; then winter, when the trees are bare and it is cold and snow is on the ground; then spring, when the crocuses peep above the ground and the willows turn yellow; then the forsythia, then the lilacs, . . . and then our baby will be born when the roses bloom." Of course, the age of the child will be a factor in trying to convey time this way; but this pattern can be understood by children as young as two and a half years, who may memorize and repeat the sequence.

One mother said she used pictures showing the month-by-month changes in the uterus and fetus to make up a time line for the wall of her daughter's room. Sources of pictures for such a time line include the illustrated booklets given out by many physicians and midwives, sets of posters available in stores, and illustrations copied from picture books on pregnancy (see Appendix). By adding the appropriate picture to the time line each month, the child gets a clear sense of the progression of the pregnancy from the pictures as well as from his or her mother's increasing girth. Another kind of time line is a series of photographs of the mother, perhaps taken by the child, showing the changing configuration of her body throughout the pregnancy.

Another idea that works particularly well for children between ages two and eight is to make a special calendar they can use to count down to the due date, beginning at about thirty-eight weeks. (We suggest having the calendar run at least two weeks beyond the due date in case the baby arrives late.) Each day on the calendar is a small movable door or window that opens to reveal a picture or surprise, preferably related to new life—such as a baby animal toy, a toy robin's egg, or seeds.

Family Celebrations and Activities

Family celebrations—holidays, birthdays, festivals—can be used to convey passage of time before the birth of the baby. Some religious and ethnic groups have holidays with strong associations for children. For Christians, Christmas, with its focus on baby Jesus, is the time to celebrate babies in general, first anticipating their coming, then marveling at their birth, and finally rejoicing in their arrival. Repeating Christmas traditions that center on the birth of a baby (such as the calendar just described, which is similar to an Advent calendar, candles around the house, or familiar music) helps young children get into the spirit of the event and makes it real for them. The same can be achieved with birthday customs already followed in the family—cake and candles, presents, singing, and retelling family members' memories of past birthdays. Children of all ages, and adults too, love to hear the story of their birth. Retelling and rehearing their own beginnings helps them prepare for another birth in the family.

Many parents have found that focusing attention on a pet helps a child understand that another being needs care and space of its own and has a will of its own, and that its needs must be respected. Parents can take their children to visit younger animals in pet shops, in children's zoos, or in the homes of friends to let them experience new lives. With pets, children can learn, over a period of time, that care is a never-ending circle of love and attention. Of course, contact with human babies is even more to the point.

The idea of a nickname may come from the child when he or she refers to the baby during the pregnancy. If not, parents can suggest one, realizing it may not catch on. One eighteen-month-old had a beloved doll she called "Wolly." When she saw her mother's belly growing, she transferred the name to the baby inside. She would talk to "Wolly" and pat her mother's stomach. The nickname did not stick after little sister Katy's birth, but it did help the toddler relate to her new sibling during the pregnancy.

Often it helps to talk about the baby as a special gift to the whole family, to be cared for by everyone, just as the older child was a special gift to the parents. The older child may then more easily appreciate the idea of preparing gifts for when the baby is born (receiving blankets, quilts, decorated T-shirts, mobiles, special songs). Children can participate in making these gifts. Families who enjoy music together can make up or choose a particular song to welcome the new baby. They can rehearse it together before the baby comes so that it becomes a kind of theme song in the home for many days, or even years, after the birth.

Preparing an Older Child for the Events Surrounding Childbirth

Depending on the policies of the caregiver and the developmental level and interest of the child, older children may be included in visits to the midwife or doctor. Parents can explain that these people will be present to help with the birth of the baby. As the pregnancy advances, children usually enjoy listening to the heartbeat and feeling the fetus kick and move around. If at all possible, children should be included in visits to the hospital to meet the doctor or to look through the nursery window. If a home birth is planned, parents should explain to an older child that the woman might have to go to the hospital for help.

Parents may want to bring a child to some childbirth classes. Classes that use slides and pictures of births are particularly useful, depending on the interests and age of the child. Birth movies can give a child who will be attending a home birth a real sense of the sights and sounds of birth. Children can meet the midwife, nurse, or labor coach. Class leaders can suggest well-illustrated, informative books on birth and the arrival of a new baby, as can libraries and bookstores (see Appendix).

Visits to friends who have new babies, especially those whose pregnancies the child may have followed, are helpful. Contact with babies gives children a better idea of what newborns are like—how tiny and helpless they are and how gentle and loving one must be with them. Children often enjoy watching and imitating the exercises a woman does in preparation for birth, including relaxation and breathing techniques.

Depending on the age and temperament of the child, parents may want to discuss any fears he or she has about the birth, for example, what happens if the baby does not breathe right away. It is important to be alert to the child's questions and observations and to be aware of the deeper meanings they convey. Children at any age can have distorted ideas of birth, and by listening, parents will have a good chance to correct them.

Including a Sibling at the Birth

If you plan to have children present at the actual birth, assuming this is an option at the site you have chosen for labor and delivery, you need to do extra preparation. Talk about the hard work of pushing the baby out, and the concentration and patience it takes to have a baby. Show them the different positions you might assume, and let them hear the kinds of sounds you might make. One family played a tape of their first labor to their older child—the sounds of his own birth—to accustom him to the sounds he would here.

Don't forget to talk about blood—the good blood—and its purpose and value when the baby is born. Talk about how a baby looks when it first comes out of the mother and about the importance of the placenta to the baby.

Give the child a task. Four- and five-year-olds can give you ice chips and orange juice, for example. Older children can help time contractions, wipe your face with a washcloth, hold your hand, breathe along with you, hold a flashlight (at a home birth), and so forth. Although most children want to feel useful at a birth, expect that they may also need to be out of the room for a while. Make them as aware as possible before the birth that they can choose to be there or not and that whatever they choose is all right with you.

Identify a caretaker for the child. Unless children are well into their teens, most will need someone at the birth who is there solely for them.

Explain that while Mommy is having the baby, she won't be able to give him or her the same kind of attention and care that she normally does. For this reason, this other familiar and loved person will be there. The person you choose for the caretaker role should be comfortable with birth in the setting you have chosen. Consider having this person join you at several childbirth classes and show him or her the books about pregnancy and birth that you particularly like. Also, this "birth-sitter" should understand that if the child does not want to be present at the birth, that is fine, and his or her job is to stay with the child.

Define the father's role at the birth. Will he be the caretaker for the child and leave others to support the mother, or does he want to be primarily involved with her? The child should know in advance what role the father will play.

A surprise bag of goodies, suitable to the age of the child, will keep most children interested and peaceful during what might be a long labor. For young children, these small treats are often the most exciting part. Their interest will alternate between the items in the bag and aspects of the labor and delivery.

Parents who have included their older children in a birth say that it does not eliminate sibling rivalry. But, as one parent reported, "There seems to be a deep reservoir of trust and love from the older to the younger," because, as her three-year-old said to the baby, "I saw you born."

Given the chance, children have a wonderful capacity to respond to an experience in ways that adults find difficult to imagine. One four-year-old was overheard describing to a friend of the same age the recent birth at which she was present: "Mommy cried, the baby cried, and there was blood, but it was good blood."

Following the Birth

After the birth, when the mother first sees her older child at the hospital or at home, she should reassure him or her that she is fine, physically tired, perhaps, but in no way hurt or unrecognizable. She is still the same person, still the child's mother. Birth is such a dramatic happening that a young child, particularly a child under age six, may feel that the world has turned upside down. The child should see his or her mother behaving normally again—walking, talking, and laughing—especially if the child was present at birth and witnessed his or her mother assuming strange positions and making odd, possibly frightening, noises.

The mother should make time during the days following birth for some quiet cuddling and spending time with the older child alone, perhaps when her partner or friend is with the baby. Depending on the child's age and temperament, he or she may ask for a lot of this kind of physical reassurance immediately or may act reserved and reject the mother's attention. Sometimes this diffidence comes from a feeling of awe toward the mother and the new baby, and sometimes from a feeling of anger and a fear of rejection. Such withdrawal is a common reaction, particularly in children aged five to eight.

Children need time to integrate the experience of birth, just as parents do. If parents continue to show that they love and care for the older child as well as for the new baby, then the child can share affection and positive feelings toward his or her mother and the new baby at his or her own pace. Older children, as well as parents, need time to bond with the newborn. They should have as much freedom as possible within the limits of safety for the infant to explore, touch, kiss, and handle the new sibling. With a younger child, parents may have to make it very clear from the beginning that they will not allow the baby to be hurt or even pressed too firmly. A parent can demonstrate touch to the child by encouraging him or her to hug the baby gently; touch the baby's hair, hands, and feet; and even hold the baby. Each day special playtime for the newborn and the sibling should be set aside.

A festive birthday party for the newborn can be a long-remembered highlight for siblings. Older children can help in the preparations, such as making and decorating the cake. The party is the time for the special song or for a version of "Happy Birthday." If the celebration includes champagne, children can have their own small glasses with juice or soda, so they can join in the toasts. Children love to receive and give gifts, and gift giving can express love within the family. Gifts to the older child from the parents, the new baby, and others, and gifts from the older child to the new brother or sister are all appropriate. For preschool children, well-chosen books are particularly fitting. For children who like dolls, they are especially appropriate gifts. A special area where the child can care for the doll can be set up with replicas of the equipment used in caring for the real baby—changing table, diapers, and bottles. Items can be added over time to keep the child's interest.

A big jar filled with packets of nutritious snacks (raisins, nuts, sesame sticks) that are especially for the older sibling can head off difficulties with the older child during nursing times (a La Leche League suggestion). The child can have his or her own snack at nursing time and sit with mother and baby. The child might enjoy decorating the jar and putting his or her name on it. The jar should be one the child can open and should be kept within reach.

Bath time can be a delightful opportunity to include the older child. Newborns love water, and it seems to have a soothing and pleasurable effect on children of all ages, whether they need to be scrubbed or not. With adult supervision, the older child can support the baby in the water and feel very useful and trusted. Time spent touching and caressing during the bath and immediately after can teach lessons in gentleness and care. After the bath, a little warm oil can be massaged into the baby's skin.

A picture sign can teach a small child about the importance of not disturbing a sleeping infant. The sign can depict each member of the family engaged in quiet activity while the baby is sleeping. When the baby needs to sleep, the older child can hang the sign on the baby's door. The child will quickly learn about a baby's need to sleep without being disturbed.

Older children will probably experience jealousy toward the baby and long for the good old days when they had their mother all to themselves. It is important that children understand and eventually accept that the baby is here to stay, but it is equally important that both parents take time to do things individually or together with older children. If there is more than one older child, parents need to make sure that whoever was the baby before does not get dropped by the older siblings in favor of the new arrival. Parents may need to talk about this with the older children before the birth. Even if the father is the primary caretaker for the older child during the few weeks following birth, it is important for the mother to spend time with the child as well. After those first few weeks, even if a woman is busy nursing the baby full time, there will always be some brief periods when the sleeping baby can be left with another adult while the mother takes the older child on one of those favorite trips to the library, park, or ice-cream parlor. There should be special time each day at home for the older child to read, talk, cuddle, and play with the mother while the baby sleeps.

"Growth of the Fetus" is adapted from Boston Children's Medical Center, *Pregnancy, Birth and the Newborn Baby* (New York: Dell, 1972). Reprinted by permission.

"Exercise and Relaxation" was written with the help of Elizabeth Noble, P.T., founder of the Maternal and Child Health Center, Cambridge, Massachusetts, and the OB-GYN section of the American Physical Therapy Association. It is adapted from Stanley E. Sagov, Richard I. Feinbloom, Peggy Spindel, and Archie Brodsky, *Home Birth: A Practitioner's Guide to Birth Outside the Hospital* (Rockville, Md.: Aspen Systems Corporation, 1984).

"Children and Birth" is adapted from *Children at Birth*, a nonpublished essay used for prenatal classes, with the kind permission of Jenifer M. Fleming.

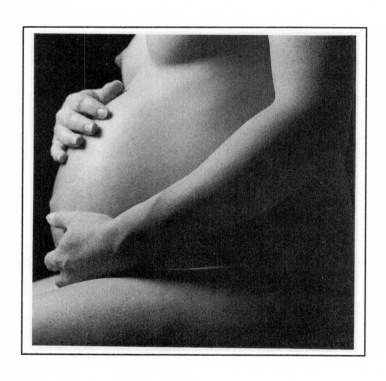

CHAPTER 3

Caring for the Baby-to-Be

PROTECTING THE FETUS

Although the fetus is remarkably well protected from harm from the outside environment, there is an expanding body of knowledge about what can be injurious. In this section I present what is known about the effects of drugs, herbal medicines, vaccines, infections in the woman, addictive substances, environmental hazards, and obesity on pregnancy.

Drugs Taken During Pregnancy

Table 3.1 lists the conditions for which pregnant women are most likely to need drugs and the drugs that can safely be used to treat those conditions. Drugs listed as alternatives are safe, but less commonly used. Table 3.2 lists drugs that are known to be harmful to the fetus. Although several well-known trade names are given, most drugs are identified by their generic names, which are likely to be unfamiliar to most people. If you know the trade name of a drug, for example, Tylenol (acetaminophen), you can ask your pharmacist or physician for the generic name, check it yourself on the label or package insert, or look it up under its trade name in one of the books or Internet sites about drugs written for the general reader. (Knowing the generic name for over-the-counter drugs will allow you to shop for a drug at the best price.)

TABLE 3.1 Selected Drugs That Can Be Used Safely in Pregnancy

CONDITION

Acne
Drugs of choice: Topical erythromycin, clindamycin, benzoyl peroxide
Alternative: Systemic erythromycin, topical tretinoin (vitamin A acid) *See* Table 3.2
re: systemic retinoids.

Allergic rhinitis (hay fever)
Drugs of choice: Topical: glucocorticoids, cromolyn, decongestants: xylometazoline, oxymetazoline, naphazoline, phenylephrine (nose sprays); systemic: diphenhydramine (Benadryl), dimenhydrinate, tripelennamine, astemizole

Anxiety reducing drugs: See Table 3.2 for conditions of safe use

Asthma
Drugs of choice: Inhaled: albuterol (Ventolin, Proventil), cortisone sprays; systemic: prednisone (a common cortisone preparation)

Constipation
Drugs of choice: Docusate sodium or calcium, glycerin, sorbitol, lactulose, mineral oil, magnesium hydroxide
Alternative: Bisacodyl, phenolphthalein

Cough
Drugs of choice: Diphenhydramine, codeine, dextromethorphan

Depression
Drugs of choice: Tricyclic antidepressant drugs (e.g., Elavil), fluoxetine (Prozac)
Alternative drugs: Lithium
Comment: When lithium is used in the first trimester, fetal echocardiography and ultrasonography are recommended because of a small risk of cardiovascular defects.

Diabetes
Drugs of choice: Insulin (human)
Alternative drugs: Insulin (beef or pork)
Comment: Avoid orally taken drugs that lower blood glucose (hypoglycemic drugs.)

Headache, tension type
Drugs of choice: Acetaminophen
Alternative drugs: Aspirin and nonsteroidal anti-inflammatory drugs (e.g., ibuprofen), benzodiazepines
Comment: Aspirin and nonsteroidal anti-inflammatory drugs should be avoided in the third trimester).

Headache, migraine type
Drugs of choice: Acetaminophen, codeine, dimenhydrinate
Alternative drugs: Beta-adrenergic-receptor antagonists (e.g, Inderal [propranolol]) and tricyclic antidepressants (both to prevent attacks)

TABLE 3.1 *(continued)*

Hypertension

Drugs of choice: Labetalol, methyldopa
Alternative drugs: Other beta-adrenergic-receptor antagonists, prazosin, hydralazine
Comment: Angiotensin-coverting-enzyme (A.C.E.) inhibitors should be avoided because of risk of severe kidney damage to the fetus.

Infections

Drugs of choice: Amoxicillin, cephalosporins, erythromycin; sulfonamides, trimethoprim
Comment: sulfonamides (commonly combined with trimethoprim, e.g., Septra, Bactrim) used late in pregnancy can contribute to jaundice in the newborn (See p. 269) by displacing bilirubin from binding sites on albumin.
Alternative drugs: clindamycin, nitrofurantoin, metronidazole
Comment: Avoid metronidazole in the first trimester.

Itching

Drugs of choice: Topical: moisturizing creams or lotions, aluminum acetate, zinc oxide cream or ointment, calamine lotion, glucocorticoids (cortisone creams and ointments); systemic: hydroxyzine, diphenhydramine, glucocorticoids (e.g., prednisone), astemizole
Alternative drugs: Topical: local anesthetics

Mania (and bipolar affective disorders)

Drugs of choice: Lithium (See comments under Depression), chlorpromazine, haloperidol
Alternative drugs: For depressive episodes: tricyclic antidepressant drugs, fluoxetine, valproic acid (Also see Table 3.2)
Comment: If lithium is used in the first trimester, fetal echocardiography and ultrasonography are recommended because of small risk of heart defects; valproic acid may be given when neural tube closure is complete following the first trimester). Regarding valproic acid: *also see* Table 3.2.

Nausea, vomiting, motion sickness

Drugs of choice: Diclectin (doxylamine plus pyridoxine) This drug is available in Canada and elsewhere but not the U.S. (see discussion of its non- availability on p. 71, Morning Sickness)
Alternative drugs: chlorpromazine, metaclopramide (in third trimester), diphenhydramine, dimenhydrinate, meclizine, cyclizine

Peptic ulcer, heart burn, and dyspepsia

Drugs of choice: Antacids, magnesium hydroxide, aluminum hydroxide, calcium carbonate, ranitidine
Alternative drugs: Sucralfate, bismuth subsalicylate

Sleeping pills: See Table 3.2 for conditions of safe use.

Thrombophlebitis, deep-vein thrombosis

Drugs of choice: Heparin, antifibrinolytic drugs, streptokinase

130

TABLE 3.2   Drugs with Proven Harmful Effects on Fetal Development

Angiotensin-convering-enzyme inhibitors: prolonged kidney failure in newborns, decreased mineralization of the skull, kidney growth failure

Anticholinergic drugs: newborn meconium ileus (a condition of sticky, thick stools, which are hard to pass and block the intestine)

Antithyroid drugs *(propylthiouracil and methimazole)*: fetal and newborn goiter and hypothyroidism

Carbamezapine: neural tube defects (See p. 29)

Cocaine (See p. 145)

Danazol and other androgenic drugs: masculinization of female fetuses.

Alcohol (See p. 143)

Hypoglycemic drugs *(used in diabetes)*: neonatal hypoglycemia (low blood sugar)

Lithium: heart malformation *(See Table 3.1 re monitoring for.)*

Marijuana *(See p. 145)*

Misoprostol: Weakness of facial and eye muscles due to underdevelopment of the nerves which control them (known as the *Moebius sequence*). Other birth defects are sometimes associated.

Nonsteroidal anti-inflammatory drugs *(includes aspirin, ibuprofen, and naproxen, with possible exception of sulindac)*: constriction of the ductus arteriosis (an artery in the fetus that connects the main artery to the lungs with the main artery to the rest of the body, allowing blood returning from the body to the heart to mix with blood pumped from the left side of the heart. In the fetus very little blood is pumped to the lungs whose air spaces are fluid filled. The ductus normally closes off shortly after birth to allow blood to flow into the lungs), and severe inflammation of the intestine (necrotizing enterocolitis)—see recommendations for safe use in Table 3.1.

Nicotine and other components of tobacco *(See p. 142)*

Phenytoin: growth retardation, central nervous system malformations

Psychoactive drugs *(e.g., barbiturates, opiods such as codeine and meperidine; and benzodiazepines [drugs used for anxiety and insomnia of which Valium is the best known])*: newborn drug withdrawal syndrome when these drugs are taken late in pregnancy

Systemic retinoids *(isoretinoin and etretinate, used mainly for severe acne)*: malformations of many body systems

Tetracycline: malformations of teeth and bone

Valproic acid: neural tube defects in about 2% of first trimester exposures. Testing of exposed fetuses for these defects *(See p. 29)* is almost 100% effective.

TABLE 3.2   *(continued)*

Tables 3.1 and 3.2 are adapted from the article "Drugs in Pregnancy" by Gideon Koren, M.D., Anne Pastuszak, M.Sc., and Shinya Ito, M.D. of the University of Toronto which was published in the April 16, 1998 issue of *The New England Journal of Medicine*. The perspective of the authors also informed my discussion of this topic.

These tables do not list caffeine, discussed on page 145, and oral contraceptives (birth-control pills), which a woman may have taken before she knew she was pregnant (see Before You're Pregnant Dos and Don'ts, p. 12). Oral contraceptives have not been shown to harm the fetus.

A drug that is *topical* is applied to the skin; one that is *systemic* is taken into the body orally, by injection, or rectally.

Herbal Medicines

In the United States, herbal medicines, legally called dietary supplements, are widely used (a $12-billion market in 1997 and growing by more than 10 percent a year). No rigorously obtained data are available to answer questions about the safety of these supplements during pregnancy or breast-feeding. Two publications may be of some help to the consumer: the *Physicians' Desk Reference for Herbal Medicines* and an English-language edition of *The Complete German Commission E Monographs: Therapeutic Guide to Herbal Medicines* (see Appendix). The latter contains no references to scientific studies. (See Appendix for additional references.)

Drugs (medicines) marketed to the public in the United States must be approved by the Food and Drug Administration (FDA) for efficacy and safety. Herbs are exempt from this scrutiny and approval as long as they are not called drugs or medicines and no claim is made regarding health benefits. Manufacturers can make claims for effects on the structure and function of the body, however.

Studies of herbs carried out in other countries, mainly Germany, suggest a health-promoting role for more than 200 plant products. The standard for herbs set by the German government is that of "reasonable certainty" of effectiveness and safety, a lower standard than that required of drugs. I have not reviewed the German reports and do not know whether they address the question of use during pregnancy and nursing. If they do, however, I can say that they cite no scientific studies to support their recommendations.

Even though more studies, some using a randomized control design, are now being done on herbs and other alternative treatments (see p. 282 on turning fetuses in the breech position by stimulating an acupuncture site on the toe through a process called *moxibustion*), manufacturers of herbs in the United States are not obligated to prove that their products work or are safe and have shown no interest in doing so. To the contrary, to quote from the November 13, 1998, feature article on herbs in *Time* magazine, "But ever since Republican senator Orrin Hatch of Utah rammed through the 1994 Dietary Supplement Health and Education Act—with the enthusiastic support of a supplement industry largely based in his state—herbs and other supplements have been all but exempt from federal oversight." This act was passed over the strong objection of the FDA.

Under current U.S. law, consumers have no guarantee that an herbal product contains what the label says it contains or that it is free of contaminants. The best advice is to buy only from well-known, reputable companies. The question of safety during pregnancy and breast-feeding remains unanswered.

Sources of Information.   In the Appendix I have listed sources of information on drugs available to the public. Your birth attendant and genetic counseling services (see Appendix) are additional resources. Good books for the public are lacking. The widely used *Physicians Desk Reference* (PDR) is a problematic source of information because it is so cautious in its disclaimers (for example, "Use in pregnancy is not recommended unless the potential benefits justify the potential risks to the fetus.") that it labels no drug safe for use in pregnancy. The PDR intends to correct this shortcoming in future editions. Most often, women's anxiety about how drugs will affect their pregnancy relates to drugs they used before they knew they were pregnant. This concern can be prevented by following the recommendations in Before You're Pregnant Dos and Don'ts (p. 12).

Vaccines

There are two types of vaccines: those containing dead or parts of dead microorganisms (e.g., diphtheria) or their toxins (e.g., tetanus toxoid), and those containing modified, living microorganisms (e.g., altered viruses that cause measles, rubella [German measles], mumps, polio, and chicken pox [varicella]). All vaccines are designed to stimulate the immune system to produce antibodies against a microbe or its toxins without making the person sick; living microbes used in vaccines are modified so that infection by them doesn't cause illness. The components of the germ (bacteria or virus) that stimulate the immune system to produce antibodies are called *antigens.*

Live-virus vaccines are generally not given during pregnancy to avoid the risk of infecting the fetus. Of these vaccines, only the polio vaccine can be given with relative safety during pregnancy, and its use is recommended only during polio epidemics in which the risk of contracting paralytic polio clearly outweighs the risk of any complication associated with taking the vaccine. Fortunately, because of near universal immunization of the population, such epidemics have not occurred in the United States for over forty years.

The rubella vaccine currently used can infect the fetus in a minority of exposures, but to date no cases of congenital rubella syndrome (see pp. 140–141) have been reported after its use. The risk from vaccination within three months of conception appears to be so small as to be almost negligible. Thus the inadvertent use of rubella vaccine in a pregnant woman should not in itself be a reason for therapeutic abortion, even though the final decision is an individual matter (see Genetic Counseling, p. 47). The safest policy is for pregnant women to avoid rubella immunization and for nonpregnant women not to become pregnant for three months following immunization. Women whose blood-antibody levels show that they are not immune to rubella (less and less common now that most girls are immunized) should receive the vaccine before they become pregnant or after delivery.

Killed vaccines, which contain no living microorganisms, can be used safely after the first trimester. Examples are tetanus toxoid, killed polio vaccine, and influenza vaccine (during the flu season). Influenza vaccine should also be used during the flu season in the first trimester in women with chronic diseases like asthma who might not be able to contend with an attack of influenza.

The field of immunization is rapidly evolving with new types of vaccines based on genetic engineering. The genes that code for (direct the assembly of) antigens contained in germs are extracted and introduced into new, harmless delivery systems, such as modified viruses and everyday fruits and vegetables. Vaccines against strep throat, flu, the germs that cause ear infections in children, and even cancer are examples of possible future developments.

Infections

The fetus is generally well protected from infection the woman may contract before or during pregnancy. Common colds, flu, stomach and intestinal viruses, strep throat, sinusitis, and even pneumonia will not harm the fetus. There are, however, important exceptions to this general rule, and these are presented here.

AIDS.   (See the discussion of AIDS test, pp. 21–23.)

Chlamydia.   Chlamydia is a bacterium that causes more infections (conjunctivitis and pneumonia) in newborns than any other germ. Like gonorrhea, chlamydia resides primarily in the cervix; it may or may not cause symptoms. The baby is exposed during birth. Depending on the population of women surveyed, between 2 and 40 percent harbor chlamydia and between 18 and 50 percent of the babies of these women pick up chlamydia during birth. Not all will become ill. Even without preventive treatment only about one-third of infected babies will develop conjunctivitis. Conjunctivitis is prevented (and treated) with erythromycin eye ointment, routinely instilled in the eyes soon after birth.

Chlamydia can also cause pneumonia in infants less than three months of age (with peak occurrence between four and twelve weeks). Erythromycin taken by mouth is the usual treatment.

The current recommendation for preventing infections in newborns is to treat infected women whether or not they have symptoms. Women considered at high risk for infection are tested in prenatal visits. In some settings all women are tested. Again, erythromycin is the preferred antibiotic for treatment. (Chlamydia infection in adults is discussed on p. 134.)

Chicken Pox (varicella).   The chicken-pox (varicella) virus can pass from an infected woman during pregnancy to her fetus, causing *congenital varicella syndrome*. This illness consists of withering (atrophy) and scarring of the skin of the arms and legs; the eyes and central nervous system can also be affected. The rate of transmission to the fetus during the first trimester is between 1 and 2 percent. If a woman develops chicken pox from five days before to seven days after giving birth, severe infection of the fetus or baby can result, with death rates as high as 30 percent.

Fortunately, most women enter pregnancy having had chicken pox as children and are, with occasional exceptions, immune. Universal immunization of children with the recently developed varicella vaccine will not only result in near 100 percent immunity in pregnant women, but will also largely eliminate the nuisance and complications of this usually mild childhood illness. Shingles will also become a thing of the past. This disease is a painful result of reactivated varicella virus, which remains dormant in the body for life, but can flare at any time, usually later in life.

Cytomegalovirus.   *Cytomegalovirus* (CMV) is the leading congenital infection in humans, infecting 1 percent of all babies. Of the approximately 3 million babies born each year in the United States, 30,000 are infected. About 3,000 of these infants are obviously sick at birth, and about 600 die. The 2,400 who recover are likely to sustain nerve damage, deafness, vision impairment, mental retardation, and stunted growth. Of the 27,000 infected infants who appear well at birth, between 2,700 and 7,600 will develop, in various combinations, hearing impairment, inflammation of the eyes, impaired vision, tooth infections that lead to loss of baby teeth, and intellectual defects.

Infection with CMV stimulates an immune response and antibody formation. Like the herpes and chicken-pox viruses, CMV goes into hiding and stays in the body for life. In common with these other viruses, CMV may reactivate, and does so in about 2 percent of pregnancies. During reactivation the virus multiplies, disengages from its hiding place, and travels throughout the body. During this period of dispersal, the virus can pass across the placenta to infect the fetus and can settle in the woman's cervix, where the baby can be exposed during birth. Fetuses are at greatest risk for becoming infected and for being more severely infected in women who become infected with the virus for the first time during pregnancy, about 2 percent of all women. Women with reactivated infection are less likely to transmit the virus, presumably because their antibodies provide a degree of immunity. CMV can also pass into breast milk. Women known to be actively infected should avoid breast-feeding.

If a rise in antibody levels shows that a woman has a primary infection or is infected through reactivation, prenatal testing of the fetus should be offered. Testing in this case includes checking the amniotic fluid for the virus and using ultrasound to determine whether fetal structures have been affected.

Infected newborns can harbor and excrete CMV for months, even years. They are thus a major reservoir for the virus, and day-care centers are prime sites for its spread. Since most infected babies do not usually appear ill, pregnant women, women who could become pregnant, and women who work in day-care centers are at particular risk.

Several measures may help prevent the infection of nonimmune, pregnant day-care workers. First, women can be offered blood testing for antibodies to the virus. Those who are not immune and continue to work should wash their hands frequently; use gloves, especially when handling diapers or respiratory secretions; and avoid mouth-to-mouth contact or excessive kissing. At home, another common setting for infection of nonimmune pregnant women, it is best to minimize contact with the urine of toddlers known to be infected as well as with their saliva by limiting kissing and the sharing of drinking glasses and zutensils.

In older children or adults with healthy immune systems, CMV infection is mainly subclinical, causing no symptoms at all, or it may cause symptoms similar to those of infectious mononucleosis—sore throat, fever, swollen glands, and an enlarged liver. CMV infection is a major problem for individuals with AIDS and for those undergoing dialysis for kidney failure. Drugs that are effective in these settings in controlling (but not eliminating) the virus are unsafe for use during pregnancy.

Fifth Disease. Infection of a pregnant woman with the virus (parovirus B19) that causes *fifth disease*—so named because it once was the fifth most common infectious rash in children—can be damaging or lethal to the fetus, but the risk of viral transmission to the fetus is very low. The virus does not cause congenital defects. Rather, it destroys red blood cells, which can result in heart failure. Most women (and men) are immune to fifth disease (also known as *erythema infectiosum*) because of previous exposure to the virus, usually in childhood. An antibody test is available to determine previous infection and immunity. Women who are exposed to individuals with fifth disease (usually children) should talk with their midwife or doctor about the desirability of being tested for immunity. If infection of the woman is proved through antibody testing, it is recommended that weekly fetal ultrasounds be done for about twelve weeks after exposure to check for signs of heart failure. If signs are present, transfusion of red blood cells to the fetus through the cord must be considered.

Fifth disease in children and adults typically causes fever and a distinctive rash—an intensely red facial rash with markings as though someone had slapped the cheeks. The redness characteristically does not affect the skin around the lips. Commonly, a lacey red rash appears first on the arms, then spreads to involve the trunk, face, buttocks, and thighs. The rash can recur for weeks and sometimes months. Infection in adults can cause arthritis and a mild respiratory illness. Many infected individuals have no symptoms but are nonetheless contagious, primarily through airborne spread of the virus. The disease is most contagious before the rash appears, when it is least suspected. No treatment for this viral infection is available, and permanent control awaits the development of a vaccine.

Gonorrhea.   The newborn can pick up the bacterium that causes gonorrhea during passage through the birth canal of an infected woman whether or not she displays symptoms of the infection. Gonorrhea infects the baby's eyes, causing a virulent conjunctivitis that can sear the corneas and even cause blindness if untreated. Gonorrheal conjunctivitis is prevented by routine treatment of the eyes of the newborn with erythromycin ointment very soon after birth (see p. 268). Testing of pregnant women for gonorrhea and the topic of gonorrhea in adults are discussed on page 137.

Group B Streptococcal Infection.   Until control measures were put in place in the 1990s, group B streptococcus (different from the bacterium that causes strep throat) was responsible for between 12,000 and 15,000 infections in newborns per year in the United States, affecting two to three babies per thousand. This deadly germ is still the most common cause of bloodstream infection (sepsis) and meningitis in newborns. Without prompt recognition and treatment of the disease, about half of infected newborns will die; and half of those who become ill and develop meningitis will show long-term neurological effects.

The group B streptococcus is carried in the intestines of about 10 percent of women and spreads from the anus to the vagina. Usually, it causes no symptoms in the woman. The baby picks up the bacterium during passage through the birth canal and can also acquire the infection after birth. About 40 percent of infected mothers transmit the bacterium to their babies.

The signs of illness in the newborn are nonspecific and include irritability, fever, vomiting, lethargy, and labored breathing. Even mild symptoms may indicate a potentially lethal spread of bacteria throughout the body. Prompt diagnosis and treatment are essential.

To prevent infection of the baby antibiotics are provided to women in labor who have tested positive for infection or are at high risk for having group B streptococcus in the cervix or vagina. Risk factors include premature (less than thirty-seven weeks) labor (see p. 309), maternal temperature during labor of 100.4 degrees Fahrenheit (38.0 degrees Celsius) or higher, membranes having been ruptured more than eighteen hours (see p. 314) at any gestational age, and previous birth of an infant with group B strep disease. This preventative approach has proved very successful. An immunization against this infection is greatly needed.

Hepatitis. As discussed on page 23, hepatitis B, transmitted from an infected woman to the fetus or to the baby at birth, is an important health risk to the baby. Current policy is to immunize all infants at birth with hepatitis B vaccine and to give gamma globulin as well to infants whose mothers test positive for hepatitis B. Fortunately, the hepatitis C virus, an even more common infection in pregnant women, is infrequently passed from mother to baby. As yet, there is no vaccine to protect against this virus.

Herpes. There are two types of herpesvirus, *type 1* and *type 2*. Type 2 produces the familiar cold sores of the mouth and lips. Type 1, which causes blisters on the genitals of men and women, is a very common sexually transmitted disease. After the first episode of infection, herpesvirus remains in the human host indefinitely, erupting periodically as visible, painful lesions (usually on the lips or genitals), although often it is so mild as to go unnoticed. During a flare-up or an initial attack the virus can be transmitted to others. Thus, herpesvirus in a woman's birth canal can be picked up by her infant during labor and delivery. A first-time infection of a woman around the time of delivery is especially contagious. Infections acquired earlier in pregnancy and associated with the development by the woman of antibodies against the virus are generally of less consequence.

Herpes infection of the newborn can be fatal or disabling, even when the baby is treated with the partially effective drug therapy now available. At present, the best way to keep a baby from getting herpes is to prevent his or her exposure to the virus. There are three primary means of doing so: cesarean section; safe-sex practices; and drug therapy given to the woman, her partner, or both.

When herpesvirus is known to be present in the vagina, a cesarean section is performed to keep the baby is away from the infected environment. For this approach to work, the amniotic membranes must either be intact or have been broken no more than four to six hours before the operation. Electronic fetal monitoring is avoided because this technique requires breaking the amniotic sac and attaching electrodes to the fetal scalp, thereby providing a route of entry for the virus.

Women considered most at risk for shedding virus that can be transmitted at birth are those with visible herpes sores, so performing C-sections on these women will prevent most infections. However, this practice will not prevent all infections because herpesvirus may be present in the birth canal in the absence of visible sores; women may be shedding virus in the vagina who show no symptoms or signs of infection.

Another preventive approach begins with testing both partners for antibodies to the herpesvirus. When the woman has no antibodies and her male partner does have them, indicating past infection and the potential for future flare-ups, safe-sex practices should be initiated to prevent viral transfer. Treating the man with daily suppressive doses of the antiviral drug acyclovir can further decrease the chances of transmission. If the man has an episode of herpes infection (with visible sores), it is recommended that the couple avoid genital contact altogether in the last several months of pregnancy. If the man has cold sores of the mouth (caused by type 2 herpesvirus), oral-genital contact should be avoided, since herpes type 2 can also infect the woman's genitalia, from where it can be passed to the infant. Finally, a woman with a history of recurrent infection can take acyclovir from thirty-six weeks until birth to reduce the chances of flare-ups during labor.

After the birth, people with cold sores of the mouth or lips should avoid kissing or nuzzling the infant, cover any exposed lesions, and wash their hands before handling the baby.

Listeriosis.   *Listeria monocytogenes* is a bacterium that can infect the pregnant woman and the newborn. The woman (and nonpregnant adults) can develop an influenza-like illness, known as listeriosis, with fever, malaise, headache, back pain, and GI symptoms. Infection of the woman in pregnancy can result in spontaneous abortion and stillbirth. In the infant, infection can cause life-threatening illnesses, including pneumonia, meningitis, and septicemia (bloodstream infection). Fortunately, Listeria infection is not common in humans.

Listeria is widespread in streams, sewage, silage, and soil and infects primarily farm animals. It is passed in their stools, from which it can contaminate vegetables grown with infected manure. It is commonly present in chicken, particularly commercially prepared chicken, and in unpasteurized cows' and goats' milk and soft cheeses made from these milks. Thorough washing or cooking of vegetables is preventive, and pasteurization of milk and thorough cooking of chicken usually destroys the organism. Pregnant women are advised to avoid store-bought chicken salad.

Monilia.   *Monilia,* a yeast *(Candida albicans)* commonly present in the vagina, can cause vaginal infection in the woman and *thrush* in the newborn (see p. 80). Although many women with monilial infections have an itchy vaginal discharge, which leads to early diagnosis and treatment, the infections may also be silent (with no obvious symptoms) or go unnoticed.

Rubella.   Rubella, or German measles, a mild viral infection of childhood, which was nearly universal before the introduction of the rubella vaccine, can severely damage the growing fetus. The capacity of some viruses to damage the fetus was first established in connection with rubella, as investigators noted that epidemics of rubella preceded the birth of a significant number of babies with a group of birth defects known as *congenital rubella syndrome*. These include deafness, a small brain, and mental retardation.

The development of an effective vaccine (see p. 140) against this virus was given impetus by the serious problem of infection of the fetus. Now girls and women are routinely immunized against rubella, and the occurrence of rubella-induced birth defects has been virtually eliminated (see also p. 19 on testing for rubella immunity and Before You're Pregnant Dos and Don'ts, p. 12).

Syphilis.   *Syphilis* is an infection caused by a corkscrew-shaped bacterium (*Treponema pallidum*) that can reach the fetus of an infected woman by crossing the placenta from her blood to that of the fetus. Infection can cause widespread and progressive damage to any part of the body of the fetus, including the brain, eyes, and bones. Although treatment with antibiotics can arrest infection of the fetus, damage already done cannot be reversed. Because of the danger of syphilis, women are checked for the presence of the disease with a blood test at their first prenatal visit and, if indicated, at later visits as well. If syphilis is diagnosed during pregnancy, antibiotic treatment is given to the woman (see p. 154).

Toxoplasmosis.   Toxoplasmosis is an infectious disease caused by a one-celled, amoeba-like microorganism called *Toxoplasma gondii*. Commonly found in the feces of cats, it is also encountered encysted (in dormant form) in the raw meat of several animals, especially pigs, and in contaminated fruits and vegetables. One-fourth to one-third of all people have contracted this infection at some time in their lives, usually without being aware of it, as reflected by the presence of measurable antibodies to toxoplasma in their blood. These individuals are subsequently immune. Infected humans harbor the cyst form of this organism in their tissues, apparently without ill effect.

If a nonimmune woman becomes infected during pregnancy, the fetus can become infected in turn, suffering possible widespread damage, especially to the brain and eyes. The baby may have mental retardation, epilepsy, and blindness. The infected woman may have no symptoms at all or may show symptoms that resemble those of infectious mononucleosis: sore throat, fever, and enlarged lymph glands in the neck. The rate of transmission to the fetus is about 30 percent.

A pregnant woman can avoid exposure to toxoplasma by not eating raw meat, especially pork; washing hands carefully after handling raw meat; and avoiding contact with stray cats. If the pregnant woman has a pet cat, she should wear disposable gloves and a face mask (against dust) while changing the litter or delegate this task to someone else. Litter should be changed daily to prevent toxoplasma larvae from maturing to the stage of infectivity. The cat should be confined to an area where it cannot hunt birds and rodents, kept away from the stool of other cats, and fed canned or cooked food rather than raw meat.

To determine the risk of fetal infection, maternal antibodies are first measured; if their level has risen, the amniotic fluid is examined for toxoplasma genes. Infection of the amniotic fluid suggests, but does not prove, fetal infection.

For the woman who has become infected but whose fetus has not, antibiotics can prevent spread to the fetus. Even when there is evidence of possible fetal infection, antibiotic treatment can limit the damage. However, most women will elect an abortion under these circumstances. It appears to make sense to test pregnant women for toxoplasma antibodies in populations in which the risk of infection is high. Whether it would be beneficial to test all pregnant women is not clear.

Tobacco

Women who smoke or who are exposed to smoke during pregnancy place themselves and their fetuses at risk. The components of smoke in a woman's blood, including thiocyanate, carbon monoxide, and nicotine, pass freely across the placenta into the fetus's blood and can be detected in umbilical-cord blood at birth.

Exposure to smoke also increases the likelihood of complications in the pregnancy, including spontaneous abortion (see pp. 298–303); placenta previa and abruptio placenta (pp. 303–305); premature rupture of the membranes (p. 313); intrauterine growth retardation (see p. 296); and premature labor and delivery (pp. 309).

Babies of women who smoked during or after pregnancy are more likely to die of sudden infant death syndrome (SIDS; see p. 273), as children to be more susceptible to respiratory infections (colds, bronchitis, ear infections), and as adults to be more likely to develop lung cancer even if they themselves do not smoke. The damage to their lungs occurs before these children are born and is often exacerbated by postnatal exposure to smoke. As teenagers, these children are more likely to become smokers themselves. There is even some evidence that a taste for nicotine develops both from prenatal exposure and breast milk.

Alcohol

Despite widespread publicity surrounding the risks of alcohol to the fetus, the use of alcohol by pregnant women is on the rise. The most recent statistics, from 1995, are that 15 percent of pregnant women drink (up from 9.5 percent in 1992) and 3.5 percent drink heavily. Over 50,000 babies are harmed each year by this behavior.

The babies of women who drink heavily during pregnancy are at risk for a cluster of defects that are apparent at birth and may impair functioning for life. These defects are known as *fetal alcohol syndrome* (FAS) and are grouped into four categories.

1. Prenatal growth retardation
2. Central nervous system abnormalities, including a small head and brain (microcephaly), a delayed development, attention deficit disorder, hyperactivity, learning disabilities, and seizures
3. Multiple abnormalities of the face, including small eyes, an underdeveloped groove in the skin between the upper lip and the bottom of the nose, an upturned nose, a thin upper lip, and small, flat cheeks
4. Malformations of the heart and other organs

Only in recent years have babies with FAS been followed up in adolescence. Researchers from the University of Washington Medical School (where in 1973 FAS was first described in the United States) and the University of Vancouver (Canada) reported in 1991 in the *Journal of the American Medical Association* that the characteristic facial abnormalities of affected children become less pronounced with time, but that these children tend to remain short and have small heads. The average IQ was low, 68, but there was considerable variation. Average school performance was at a second- to fourth-grade level, with striking deficits in arithmetical skills. Common maladaptive behaviors included having poor judgment, being easily distracted, having a conduct disorder, and having difficulty perceiving social cues.

FAS is a leading cause of mental retardation in the United States, affecting between 0.2 and 1 percent of all children. In 1993 the rate of FAS in the United States was 6.7 per 10,000. The lifetime-care costs for one affected child are estimated to be $1.7 million. The consequences of chronic high-dose alcohol exposure in utero are devastating.

The mothers of babies with FAS have been alcoholics, drinking over four shots of hard liquor (or the equivalent in beer or wine) per day during pregnancy. Some experienced delirium tremens (D.T.'s) or alcoholic stupor during labor. Fetuses exposed to lower amounts of alcohol, two to four shots per day, have demonstrated lesser degrees of the physical and mental effects of FAS. These are referred to as FAE (fetal alcohol effects). The severity of FAE or FAS appears to be related to the extent of exposure to alcohol, but the precise dose-response relationship (how much alcohol over what period of time in what stage of fetal development to produce what abnormalities) is not well understood.

It is not known and probably never will be known for certain whether it is safe to drink any amount of alcohol during pregnancy. The safest policy is simply to abstain, as indicated in the familiar warnings on the labels of alcoholic beverages and on signs posted in restaurants and stores that sell alcoholic beverages. Some authorities believe that this campaign overstates the problem and at the same time fails to reach the alcoholic women who most need the advice. Several studies have suggested that social drinking may not be very risky. One such study, reported in the *British Medical Journal* in 1991, involved 592 women. During early pregnancy, 43 percent of the women consumed no alcohol, 48 percent consumed one to five drinks weekly, 6 percent had five to ten drinks weekly, and 3 percent had more than ten drinks weekly. A follow-up of the children of these women at eighteen months of age found that the children of drinkers had the same motor and mental development scores on a standardized assessment as the children of nondrinkers. However, eighteen months is a short follow-up time in rapidly developing children, and such studies need to be extended into later childhood. Findings of another study, done at about the same time at

the National Fetal Alcohol Research Center in Detroit, suggest that fetal alcohol effects begin to show up only in women who regularly drink
more than three shots of whiskey per day (or its equivalent in beer or
wine). I do not believe that either of these studies justifies the use of alcohol during pregnancy. I would say only that they are somewhat reassuring to the woman who consumed a small amount of alcohol before
she knew she was pregnant.

For questions about alcohol exposure during pregnancy (which tend
to arise when a woman consumed alcohol before knowing she was pregnant), genetic counselors are good resources.

Caffeine

The risks of caffeine for the fetus are not well understood. However,
there is some reasonably good evidence that large doses, over 300 milligrams per day (one cup of coffee, tea, or cola drink contains about 100
milligrams), are associated with spontaneous abortion (see p. 298) and
intrauterine growth retardation (see p. 296). Thus the safest policy is to
avoid or to limit caffeine consumption to no more than one to two cups
daily during pregnancy and when pregnancy is planned.

Marijuana

The impact of marijuana smoking on the fetus has been difficult to assess, partly because marijuana smokers also commonly drink alcoholic
beverages and smoke tobacco (see previous sections) and tend to have
inadequate diets. Any defects noted in the babies of marijuana smokers
may be the result of the interaction of several factors, making it difficult
to isolate the specific contribution of marijuana.

With these reservations, the best available evidence is that marijuana
use is likely to result in smaller babies and in babies who have features
similar to those found in fetal alcohol syndrome (see p. 143). The best
recommendation, of course, is to avoid marijuana during pregnancy.

Cocaine

The impact of cocaine exposure on the fetus is not yet well understood.
The evidence to date, based on retrospective studies, is that chronic co-

caine exposure is associated with low birth weight, intrauterine growth retardation (see pp. 296–298), small head size, brain injury in utero from strokes, abruptio placenta (see p. 304), premature rupture of the membranes (see pp. 313–314), and premature labor (see pp. 309–313). At birth, many exposed babies temporarily demonstrate significant impairment not only of orientation, but also of motor and state regulation, as measured by the Neonatal Behavioral Assessment Scale (see p. 233). They often also experience tremors, eat poorly, are irritable, and, occasionally, have seizures. Later, cocaine-exposed babies are more likely to die from sudden infant death syndrome.

The precise role of cocaine (or crack) in these varied adverse outcomes is not clear, because many of the mothers of these babies also have engaged in other behavior that can harm the fetus, such as cigarette smoking and poor nutrition. Although long-term effects on the growth and development of these infants and children have not yet been completely defined, there is cause for great concern, particularly in view of the widespread use of cocaine within certain segments of society.

X Rays and MRI

The possibility of harm to the fetus from x-radiation has aroused great concern, much of it originating in the aftermath of the atomic bombing of Japan at the end of World War II when, after the population was exposed to extraordinary levels of radiation, an increase in spontaneous abortion and birth defects was observed. The risk of radiation exposure to the fetus from diagnostic X rays, including CT (computerized tomography) scans, is very, very low, however, certainly not high enough to contraindicate medically needed studies. Nevertheless, unnecessary exposure is best avoided, especially in the first trimester when organs are being formed. If a study can be delayed, or fewer views taken, so much the better. The following guidelines are suggested:

1. A sexually active woman in her reproductive years should assume that she is pregnant unless proved otherwise by onset of menses in the previous ten days; use of oral or long-acting hormonal contraceptives; use of an IUD; having had no sexual intercourse since the last menstrual period; having had her tubes tied; or a negative result on a pregnancy test (see p. 53). A

woman should avoid nonemergency X rays if there is any question of pregnancy.

2. If an X ray is needed during the first trimester of pregnancy, the pelvis should be excluded from the X-ray field if at all possible.

3. Women should always wear a shield over the pelvis and abdomen when having X-ray studies (including dental X rays), whether or not they are pregnant. Such shields offer some, but not complete, protection.

4. If there is a medical indication for a diagnostic X-ray study during pregnancy, the importance of the information needed almost always outweighs the remote risk of harm to the fetus. However, each situation must be evaluated on its individual merits. Radiologists can be consulted on this question.

5. In the highly unlikely event that a woman receives a relatively large amount of radiation to her pelvic area (more than five rads and far more than that of any diagnostic study) in the first trimester of pregnancy (possibly before she knew she was pregnant), her fetus may be at increased risk for birth defects; the exact risk is not known, perhaps 1 to 3 percent. For some couples, even a risk of this magnitude (which is less than the overall pregnancy risk for a major fetal defect) may be enough to justify a therapeutic abortion after careful review with a physician or genetics counselor.

This discussion does not apply to the therapeutic use of X rays administered in much larger doses, usually to treat cancer. These doses can be sufficient to damage the fetus.

Magnetic resonance imaging (MRI) is not known to cause harm to the fetus. This technique, which uses magnetic waves, not X rays, is being studied as a tool for assessing the dimensions of the birth canal when the fit of the baby is in question (see Disproportion, p. 289).

Environmental Toxins

There is a still limited but increasing body of knowledge about the effects of toxins from the polluted environment on babies and children exposed after and before birth. According to studies done at Wayne State University in Detroit and at the University of Maryland, children who were exposed in utero to concentrations of PCBs (polychlorinated biphenyls) just slightly above normal concentrations were more likely to demonstrate poorer short- and long-term memory during infancy and early childhood as well as deficits in IQ when tested at age eleven. The long-term effects of exposure to PCBs, if any, are unknown. Used as insulating materials in electric transformers and capacitors, PCBs are among the most widespread and stubbornly persistent of environmental contaminants. Although these chemicals are now banned in the United States, they are still being produced and used in other countries and can spread far and wide. Residues from earlier production in the United States persist and can be detected in body tissues. Eating fatty fish from contaminated lakes and rivers has been a major source of exposure.

Information about the accumulation of toxic chemicals in another species of mammal, the polar bear, is sobering. Since 1968, researchers have detected increasing concentrations of toxic contaminants in the tissues and milk of these bears, including PCBs and dioxins (notorious as an ingredient of Agent Orange, the defoliant used by the U.S. military in the Vietnam War) and DDT (the pesticide whose devastating impact on animal life was described by Rachel Carson in her landmark book, *Silent Spring*). Produced in the factories of North America, Asia, and Europe, dioxins are taken up by small marine organisms, such as amphipods, that are eaten by fish that are eaten by seals that are eaten by polar bears. The same pattern of exposure affects humans, who are also at the end of the food chain. For example, the breast milk of women tested in the Canadian Arctic has been reported to contain about six times the quantity of PCBs found in women in the nearby province of Quebec.

Lead is another environmental toxin for which there are some research data. Lead mobilized from the bones of a previously exposed woman can be transferred to the fetus or through breast milk to the baby after birth, with negative consequences for neurological and intellectual development. Lead added to gasoline and then discharged in exhaust fumes is a major source of exposure. Lead has been banned from gasoline in the United States, but is still used elsewhere.

The effects on humans of long-term exposure to pesticides used in agriculture is unknown, but is of considerable concern. Methyl bromide, a commonly used pesticide, indirectly affects humans after it is chemically transformed, as it depletes the atmospheric ozone layer that protects us from harmful ultraviolet radiation. Methyl bromide may also affect humans directly when it enters the body. Scientists are searching for safe substitutes for methyl bromide (peach oil is receiving particular attention) which will be phased out according to an international environmental treaty. Further addressing exposure to agricultural pesticides, the U.S. Congress passed the landmark Food Quality Protection Act in 1996, which requires the government to reassess its standards for food.

Daily exposure to industrial solvents during the first trimester of pregnancy has been identified as a cause of birth defects, particularly in the case of female workers who themselves develop toxic symptoms while using these chemicals. These solvents are used in printing, graphic design, laboratory work, and cleaning (including dry cleaning). If exposure to solvents cannot be avoided, the best advice is to wear a protective mask.

Because of concerns about pesticides, an increasingly popular option is to eat organically grown foods, which are pesticide-free fruits and vegetables, often used in a plant-based diet (see p. 94). Commercially sold organic baby foods are also now available (pioneered by the Well Fed Baby company in California). Organic produce has the added advantage of being grown without synthetic nitrogen fertilizers. These fertilizers, combined with pesticides, in the short run result in higher crop yields. In the long run, however, they contribute to soil erosion and water pollution, resulting in destruction of fish and marine plant habitats. These issues are being addressed in various ways by the U.S. Department of Agriculture. Organic farming contributes to soil preservation because it stabilizes soil with organic matter, including manure and cover crops grown off-season and plowed under during planting time, which forms compost. This soil retains water and is less vulnerable to being blown away as dust during dry seasons.

Another option for curtailing pesticide use and exposure that is rapidly coming into use despite some controversy is genetic engineering. Generally, consumers don't know when a particular food is genetically engineered (potatoes, soybeans, corn, and cotton are the most common plants so altered). In this process, a gene that controls the production of a protein that is toxic to a pest insect or mold is introduced into the genetic makeup of the plant, rendering it resistant to attack. Plants are also being engineered to tolerate higher levels of pesticides, which could result in increased pesticide use. The pros and cons of organic farming versus agriculture that relies on certain kinds of genetic engineering are many and complex.

There is little doubt about the importance of gaining a better understanding of the effects on humans and on the environment of the chemicals we produce. Under the direction of Congress, the Environmental Protection Agency (EPA) has launched an ambitious and highly sophisticated program to test such chemicals (including those in cleansers, solvents, food additives, cosmetics, nutritional supplements, plastics, and petroleum by-products), starting with the 15,000 chemicals that are produced in amounts of 10,000 pounds or more per year, plus all pesticides. The United States has taken important steps to address the problem of environmental toxins. Because pollution knows no national boundaries, international efforts are critical as well. An organization called Mothers and Others for a Livable Planet is working to address these issues (see Appendix).

Hot Tub and Sauna Use

There is now reasonably good evidence that women should avoid the warming effects of hot tubs and saunas early in pregnancy. As reported in the August 19, 1992, issue of the *Journal of the American Medical Association*, researchers at Boston University found that the fetuses of women exposed to heat sources during the first trimester were at increased risk for neural tube defects (see p. 24). Use of a hot tub increased the risk 2.8 times; sauna, 1.8; fever, 1.8; and electric blanket, 1.2. There is little information yet about the risks of such heat exposure during the last two trimesters.

Video-Display Terminals

Concern has been expressed about the effects on the fetus of radiation from computer screens, an issue for many women. Research to date has so far revealed no demonstrable risk.

Automobile Safety

Without preventive measures a woman of childbearing age is more likely to be killed or crippled by an automobile accident than by disease or other threat. Seat belts, air bags, and better car design have significantly reduced these risks. Both lap belts and shoulder harnesses can be used safely in pregnancy. The shoulder harness can be used in the usual way, and the lap belt should be fastened over the hips beneath the uterus. For maximum protection of the pregnant woman, all other passengers need to be restrained, too, since a crash can send unrestrained riders flying with unbelievable force (over one ton at a car speed of twenty-five miles per hour) that can seriously harm them and others.

Expectant parents should plan ahead for their baby's car safety by obtaining a crash-tested infant restraint before the baby's birth, so that even the first ride will be a safe one. This can be a seat designed for infants only or a seat that can be converted as the baby grows. Infant-only seats are rear facing, have a three-point or five-point harness, and can be used for babies up to a year old and up to twenty pounds (some models fit heavier babies). Some have a detachable base that remains in the car; some can be locked onto a shopping cart. Convertible car seats are bulkier and can become forward-facing seats for toddlers. It is important to follow the instructions carefully when converting the seat and readjusting the harness. Both types of restraints are held in place by the car's own safety belts. It is not safe to carry an infant or child on one's lap, even when sitting in the backseat. It is also unsafe for a child who weighs less than forty pounds to use the car's safety belts without a restraining seat. (However, the standard belt is better than no restraint at all once a child can sit up alone.) The American Academy of Pediatrics has a listing of the various types of car seats in pamphlet form and on its web page (see Appendix).

Other sources of information on car safety for children are also listed in the Appendix.

Exposure to Noise

A mounting but still limited body of evidence about the sensitivity of the fetus and newborn to excessive noise with an associated risk of hearing loss and emotional distress has led the American Academy of Pediatrics to call for more research on this topic. As a precaution, the Academy recommends that pregnant women be exposed to less noise in the workplace (e.g., airport jet traffic) and in entertainment settings (boom boxes in cars, rock concerts, and loud disco music—risky to the hearing of adults as well).

The Academy has also identified the neonatal intensive care unit, where premature babies are cared for with a variety of noise-emitting equipment, as a setting with risks for hearing loss. Recommendations for staff include monitoring the noise levels in incubators, eliminating tapping or writing on the tops of incubators and hoods, gently closing incubator doors, and wearing soft-soled, quiet shoes. For more information, contact the Committee on Environmental Health of the Academy (see Appendix).

Obesity

The effects of obesity on pregnancy are mainly negative. Consequences include a greater likelihood of needing a C-section along with an increased risk of complications; larger babies who are more difficult to deliver vaginally; and increased incidence of preeclampsia (p. 307), shoulder dystocia (the shoulder of the baby gets stuck during birth; see p. 315), late fetal death, and congenital abnormalities among babies born prematurely. Finally, obese pregnant women are more likely to remain obese and to become more obese after giving birth. On the positive side, obesity appears to protect against a baby's being small for his or her gestational age (see p. 296 on intrauterine growth retardation).

Obesity has become a major and growing public-health problem in the United States, as is evident in most public places—malls, beaches, markets, and so on. In my own state of California, where so much food is produced, the highest-ranking health official has attributed obesity in part to the trends toward decreased consumption of fruits and vegetables (only 3.8 servings of fruits and vegetables consumed per person per day in 1997) and eating out, especially in fast-food restaurants. More than one in five American women in the peak childbearing years, between the ages of twenty and twenty-nine, is obese. When an obese woman becomes pregnant, the best she can do for the welfare of her baby is to hold her obesity in check. Pregnancy is not the time to lose weight. For the obese nonpregnant woman, the best advice is to achieve a normal weight before becoming pregnant. (Also see Before You're Pregnant Dos and Don'ts, p. 12.) Rather than going on a diet, I recommend simply eating healthfully, with an emphasis on plant-based foods and reduced fat, a diet that will satisfy hunger without adding pounds (see p. 87).

There is another benefit in using pregnancy as an opportunity to evaluate eating and exercise practices. By adopting healthy family eating habits, parents can help prevent obesity in their children. Children fed on what has become the three American food groups of salt, fat, and sugar are growing ever fatter. The percentage of obese children has nearly doubled since 1980, and studies show that childhood obesity may be a risk factor for heart and circulatory problems in adults. Poor eating habits are even fostered in schools. Cash-strapped schools gain revenues through contracts with soft-drink corporations and fast-food chains for exclusive marketing rights in school facilities. Thus caffeine consumption and dependence are fostered, as well as nutritionally valueless eating habits.

Compounding these dietary deficiencies are reductions in physical activity, as children turn to television watching, playing video games, and surfing the Net. Lack of sidewalks and bike paths in the suburbs is associated with a steep decline in biking to school, and there is a heavy reliance on cars even for children who live within walking distance of school. There are growing trends to snack frequently—in front of the TV, at the movies, in the car, and usually on fast foods, and to eat on the run (only 24 percent of us eat breakfast, lunch, and dinner regularly; more and more we eat while we work rather than take the time from our hectic, multitasked lives simply to eat a meal. For further discussion, see page 87, on nutrition, and page 95, on exercise.

TREATING THE FETUS

Of all recent developments in prenatal care, one of the most exciting is the ability to treat an ill fetus. The field of *fetal medicine* has come into its own as our ability to evaluate fetal health and to take action or not based on that evaluation has improved. In the following discussion I will touch on the highlights of this developing field, focusing on the active treatment of the unborn.

One of the oldest treatments involves the fetus whose survival is threatened by anemia with heart failure, most commonly caused by incompatibility of the Rh D blood types of the woman and the fetus (see Blood Type, p. 16). In this case, the fetus can be saved by a blood transfusion performed in utero. Blood cells are injected into the fetus's abdominal cavity or into an umbilical blood vessel through a needle that has been passed, under ultrasonic guidance, through the woman's skin, abdomen, uterus, and amniotic fluid. Several such transfusions may be needed to ensure the survival of the fetus.

The fetus can be treated with drugs, which are transferred across the placenta. Antibiotics are used in this way to treat syphilis (see p. 141). (In this example, the woman is treated at the same time.) Similarly, fetuses with heart failure caused by rapid beating of the heart (*tachycardia*) as a result of an abnormality in impulse generation have been treated with digitalis.

Fetuses with underfunctioning thyroid glands (*hypothyroidism*) and goiter (enlargement of the thyroid) have been treated by injection of thyroid hormone directly into the amniotic fluid. In swallowing the amniotic fluid, the fetus also swallows the hormone. Similarly, overfunctioning of the fetal thyroid gland (*hyperthyroidism*) has been treated by having the woman take a drug to decrease thyroid activity. A malfunctioning or overfunctioning fetal adrenal gland can be selectively suppressed by having the woman take adrenal hormones.

If a premature birth is necessary for the health of the mother, the baby, or both, the lungs of the fetus can be matured to a more functional level by giving the woman cortisone-like hormones (see p. 163 on L/S ratio).

The fetus in severe distress during labor (determined by fetal monitoring and scalp-pH sampling) can be resuscitated prior to an emergency cesarean section with oxygen given to the woman (and hence to the fetus), or the woman can be given drugs (see p. 312) to stop uterine contractions. Also, the woman can be positioned to roll the uterus off her major abdominal blood vessels, thereby increasing blood flow and oxygen supply to the placenta and fetus.

Prenatal surgical treatment for problems that would damage the fetus if uncorrected is in its infancy. A pioneer in fetal surgery is Michael Harrison of the University of California Medical Center in San Francisco, where an international registry of fetal surgery is maintained. One example of prenatal surgery is surgery to correct or ameliorate blockages of the urinary tract. Ultrasound can detect obstructions of the male urinary tract, which can lead to stretching and progressive destruction of the kidneys. Obstructions of this type are located at the juncture of the bladder and urethra, so-called posterior urethral valves. At several medical centers, operations have been performed to relieve such obstructions by passing a plastic catheter (a small, thin tube) through the fetus's abdomen into the bladder to drain off excess urine into the amniotic fluid. An alternative approach, with some advantage for younger fetuses in whom the tubes tend to block off with time, is to open the uterus under anesthesia and operate directly on the fetus. In the case of bladder obstruction, an incision is made into the fetal bladder that allows the urine to drain through a valve into the amniotic fluid. After birth, another operation is performed to remove the valves and close the incision. More recently, valves have been removed before birth using a cystoscope to enter the fetal bladder.

Operations have also been performed on fetuses to relieve a diaphragmatic hernia. In this condition, one of the diaphragms (the muscles that separate the lungs from the abdomen and that play an important role in breathing) is missing. The result is that the abdominal contents, for example, stomach and intestines, move (herniate) into the chest space that is normally occupied by the lungs, and the lung collapses. A technically difficult operation can correct the hernia after birth, but the lungs nonetheless may not expand and function. Also, although technically achievable, full surgical correction in utero has not resulted in the birth of babies who survive. The current approach is to perform open fetal surgery to expose and then tie off the fetus's trachea (windpipe). In so doing, the fetus's lungs become distended with fluid, forcing the abdominal contents out of the chest and into the abdominal cavity. After birth, the tie around the trachea is released and the definitive correction of the diaphragm is performed.

Fetal surgery has been successfully performed to remove tumors of the lung and spine that could seriously compromise the fetus's chance of survival. After initial disappointment with the results of operations to relieve hydrocephalus (and thereby prevent brain thinning and damage), surgeons are now revisiting this complex topic with some promising results. Joseph Bruner and Noel Tulipan at Vanderbilt University Medical Center have pioneered a procedure that places catheters into the dilated fluid chambers of the brain (ventricles) to drain the excess fluid into the amniotic fluid. Definitive surgery is then performed after birth.

Surgical intervention may be required to protect and even save the life of a twin fetus in a state of heart failure because its circulatory system is joined with that of a nonviable mate lacking a heart (the one heart has to do the work of two and gives out). Charles Rodeck and his associates at University College Medical School in London have developed a procedure to interrupt the flow of blood to the abnormal twin by coagulating a communicating blood vessel with a heat probe passed into the uterus and blood vessel under ultrasonic guidance.

Fetal surgery has led to several exciting discoveries that are possibly even more significant than correction of anatomical malformations. One discovery is that an incision into the skin of a fetus early in gestation heals without scarring—a phenomenon with far-reaching implications for clinical practice. Another major finding is that early in gestation a fetus, unlike a child or an adult, will not reject certain cells injected into its body. The injected cells will survive and reproduce, coexisting with the fetus's own cells. If the DNA in a fetus's own genes is defective, resulting in disease, the transplanted normal cells can make up for the deficit. Thus some inherited diseases could potentially be cured by cell transplant. Additionally, after birth the baby is more likely to accept an organ donation from the donor of the cells transplanted before birth. Cell transplantation in utero thus may pave the way for easier and more successful organ transplantation. The kinds of cells currently being transfused and studied are called bloodstem cells; these are the undifferentiated parent cells that give rise to the various circulating blood cells (white and red cells and platelets).

New Contributions of the Fetus and Baby to Medicine in General

The newborn baby and fetus are providing answers for dealing with several vexing medical problems, with the promise of more good things to come. One such problem is finding replacement bone marrow for a patient whose own marrow has been destroyed through a disease process, such as leukemia, or by drugs or therapeutic radiation. Blood stem cells, abundantly present in umbilical-cord blood for about twenty minutes following birth, are providing a solution. These cells are capable of repopulating a patient's depleted or absent marrow without being rejected by the immune system. Right after birth these cells are isolated from the rest of the cord blood, typed, and frozen. This aspect of transplantation research is in its early stages, but so far looks very promising. Several medical centers (New York University is a leader in the United States) are now storing cord blood in blood banks. Some private companies are offering this service to parents for use in their own families; unfortunately, this practice diverts stem cells from the blood banks that respond to calls for cells from anywhere in the world.

Other tissues that have routinely been discarded at birth are now seen as a source of cells that can treat diseases. The amniotic membranes (which line the uterus and are attached to the placenta) have found a new use in surgery (pioneered at Tokyo University) to repair a damaged cornea (the normally transparent center of the surface of the eye), thereby improving a patient's vision. Umbilical-cord tissue is being used in plastic surgery, as it is a relatively inexpensive and abundant source of human collagen.

A major problem faced by surgeons who treat babies with birth defects is obtaining enough skin to cover and close the repair. Unlike adults, babies do not have much skin to donate to themselves, and some repairs require a lot of skin. Researchers at Harvard Medical School have found a way to take snippets of skin from the fetus, using minimally invasive surgical techniques, and grow the skin tissue in the laboratory for use by the baby after birth. The same approach has been used with bladder tissue, and it seems likely that it will work for other tissues as well. This process allows definitive repairs to be made earlier and with fewer (even one) operations.

Arguably the most stunning development in the field of prenatal medicine is the ability to grow in the laboratory the earliest, prefetal (embryonic or *pluripotent*) cells, before differentiation into various tissues (heart, blood stem cells, pancreas, and so on) has occurred. James A. Thompson at the University of Wisconsin and John Gearhart at Johns Hopkins University, along with their colleagues, have been able to maintain cells derived from the blastocysts (see Growth of the Fetus, p. 59) of in vitro fertilized eggs (from women being treated for infertility) and from germ cells from five- to seven-week-old aborted fetuses (germ cells are the cells that are not committed to forming specific tissues but become the next generation of sperm and eggs) in culture media. These cells, now known as *human embryonic stem cells*, must be made acceptable to a future patient (to avoid immune-system-mediated rejection). One planned approach is to introduce the self-recognition gene from the patient into the stem cells. The stem cells would then be directed to differentiate into the type of tissue the patient needed, for example, normal heart tissue to replace damaged heart tissue. In this way, a universal spare-parts system could be developed. In addition, having these body tissues would facilitate the testing of drugs for effectiveness and safety. How quickly this technique will become available to treat human disease will depend on the resources committed to develop it. The federal government, constrained by laws prohibiting research on embryos, has recognized a distinction between pluripotent stem cells, which are incapable of developing into human beings, and embryos, which are, thereby allowing the funding of further research and development. Laws regarding such research are currently being reevaluated.

We don't know very much yet about how pluripotent cells are directed to form various tissues. Research into this question is moving rapidly. Once we understand this process, we will be in a better position to understand how development goes astray with resulting malformations and chromosomal aberrations (such as in Down syndrome), as many birth defects result from errors in early stages of tissue differentiation.

TESTS OF FETAL WELL-BEING LATE IN PREGNANCY AND DURING LABOR

What a Woman Can Tell

There has been some interest in seeing whether women can assist in identifying fetuses in difficulty by counting the number of fetal movements that occur over a set period of time. This is called the *kick count*. A good time to do a kick count is after dinner, when the fetus is commonly most active. Before starting, the woman should empty her bladder. In a spot from which a clock or watch is visible, the woman lies on her side or relaxes in a comfortable chair. She writes down the start time and begins to count fetal movement. After counting ten movements—any she can feel—she writes down the number of minutes that have passed. She should immediately report to her doctor or birth attendant if the kick time is two hours or more.

It is not clear whether information gleaned from kick counts effectively changes perinatal outcomes. I suggest, however, that a woman who notices a *significant decrease in fetal activity*, even if she cannot precisely describe it, report this promptly to her doctor or birth attendant. An increase in activity, on the other hand, has not been shown to predict fetal problems and is probably a good sign.

Principles of Fetal Heart Rate Monitoring

1. The fetal heart rate reflects fetal oxygen supply, which depends on the delivery of oxygen to the placenta from the woman's circulation, the health of the placenta, and the flow of blood through the umbilical cord from and to the fetus.

2. Contraction of the uterus temporarily cuts off the blood supply to the placenta, enabling the fetus to draw only on oxygen already present in the placenta at the time of onset of the contraction.

3. The fetus whose oxygen supply is already borderline when the uterus is not contracting will be tipped into a state of oxygen deprivation during a contraction. This lack of oxygen will be reflected in a prolonged slowing of the fetal heart rate, with slow recovery.

4. During a uterine contraction the fetal heart rate normally slows in response to pressure on the fetal head and returns to its baseline as the contraction ends. In fetal-monitoring terms, this is called an *early deceleration*. However, if the placenta is functioning inadequately and oxygen supply to the fetus is marginal to begin with, a contraction will tip the fetus into a state of oxygen deprivation and the heart rate will drop. The rate will not recover until well after the contraction is over. In the language of monitoring, this is called a *late deceleration*. A third kind of deceleration, called *variable deceleration*, bears no consistent relationship to uterine contractions. It is believed that this pattern is caused by compression of the umbilical cord by pressure from the fetus or by twisting.

5. Normally, the fetal heart beats at a baseline rate of between 110 and 150 to 160 beats per minute. A rate of 100 to 110 is termed *mild bradycardia* (literally, "slow heart"), and a rate less than 100 is called *marked bradycardia*. *Tachycardia* (literally, "fast heart") is mild if the heart rate ranges from 160 to 180 and marked if it is greater than 180. Tachycardia alone is not an indication of fetal distress, since it may be due to maternal fever, drugs given to the woman, or intrinsic abnormalities in the rhythm of the fetus's heart. Similarly, mild bradycardia without other changes is not necessarily a sign of fetal distress. Severe bradycardia has several

causes, among them congenital heart defects in the fetus, sudden lowering of the blood pressure in a pregnant woman with hypertension, or decreased oxygen supply to the fetus.

6. Another term used in connection with electronic fetal monitoring is *variability*, which refers to the variation in heart rate from beat to beat. When a fetus is awake and healthy, its heart rate accelerates and decelerates from second to second. Although these changes are probably too subtle to detect by listening to the heart with a stethoscope, the internal electronic fetal monitor, which senses the fetal heart as an electrocardiogram, produces a continuous printout of the heart rate, which presents variability visually. Decreased variability is observed when the fetus is asleep, when the woman has been medicated with a drug such as Demerol, morphine, or Nisentil, when the fetus is experiencing distress or when labor is premature.

The Nonstress Test

The basic principle of nonstress testing (NST) is that a healthy fetus's heart rate will increase in response to movements of its body that occur when it is awake. In the standard method of performing the test, an external ultrasound monitor is used to detect the fetus's heart rate, which is recorded on a moving strip of paper for twenty minutes. When the woman feels a kick, she depresses a switch, which identifies the movement on the paper with a mark that can be related to the heart rate at the time. If necessary, fetal movement can be stimulated by making a loud noise near the uterus. The most widely accepted standard of normality is two increases (accelerations) of fifteen beats per minute over baseline, lasting fifteen seconds, per ten minutes. A normal test is called negative, or reactive. An abnormal test is called positive, or nonreactive. This terminology is somewhat confusing in that negative means normal and positive means abnormal.

Another version of the nonstress test simply clocks the fetal heart rate with a stethoscope over five minutes. The fetus is considered reactive when a single acceleration of fifteen beats per minute lasting ten seconds is observed. This form of the nonstress test is less expensive than ultrasound monitoring and more readily available. It may also have advantages over the use of ultrasound in women with obesity or hydramnios (p. 295), in whom the ultrasound waves are dampened by the intervening fat or fluid.

The Fetal Biophysical Profile

The nonstress test is a good screening test for fetuses at high risk for distress. Its results are often combined with ultrasound assessment of amniotic fluid volume, fetal body tone, and limb and breathing movements into the fetal biophysical profile (BPP). The BPP is thought to predict fetal well-being as accurately as the contraction stress test (discussed in the next section) and is much easier to administer. With a normal BPP the chance of a fetal death in the following seven days is less than 1 in 1,000. Basing decisions about whether to intervene in a high-risk pregnancy based on the BPP alone has resulted in a fetal death rate lower than that achieved in low-risk pregnancies.

Contraction Stress Testing

Contraction stress testing involves monitoring the fetal heart rate with an external monitor while the uterus contracts. The relationship between contractions and fetal heart rate is interpreted according to the standards used in electronic fetal monitoring (see p. 164). The contraction stress test is done in the labor and delivery section of the hospital and is usually performed on women and fetuses who have failed the nonstress test. It takes from one to two hours. For fifteen to thirty minutes, baseline uterine activity and the fetal heart rate are recorded along with fetal movements. If spontaneous uterine contractions lasting forty to sixty seconds occur approximately three times in ten minutes, the test can be done without oxytocin stimulation. In the absence of demonstrable uterine activity, oxytocin is used to produce such contractions (see Drugs That Contract the Uterus, p. 195) or nipple stimulation is tried to cause the woman to release her own oxytocin.

The correlation between a negative (normal) contraction stress test and a favorable outcome for the baby is very good. Only 1 in 1,000 fetuses die within one week of a negative test result. Positive (abnormal) contraction stress tests are divided into nonreactive and reactive groups, not discussed here. A positive test is associated with a significant increase in the incidence of intrauterine growth retardation, low five-minute Apgar scores (see p. 231), and increased occurrence of fetal distress during labor.

In the case of a positive (abnormal) test, 25 to 75 percent of fetuses will be normal. To help distinguish normal fetuses from fetuses that would benefit from prompt delivery, other tests are used, including the biophysical profile, cord wave analysis (see p. 162), and cord-blood sampling (discussed next).

Umbilical Cord Blood Sampling

Blood for diagnostic purposes can be obtained from the fetus by passing a needle (attached to a syringe), under ultrasound guidance, through the woman's abdominal wall and the wall of the uterus into the fetus's umbilical vessels. The fetal blood can be analyzed for oxygen concentration; diseases of the blood cells, such as sickle-cell anemia (see p. 38), thalassemia (see p. 40), and low platelets; abnormalities of blood-clotting proteins, found in hemophilia (see p. 42); and antibodies to microorganisms such as toxoplasma (see p. 141) and cytomegalovirus (see p. 135).

Using the information obtained from the fetus's blood, physicians can make decisions regarding therapy. In some instances treatment may be administered using the ultrasound-and-needle technique, for example, in transfusing blood cells into the umbilical cord of an extremely anemic fetus. As techniques of gene analysis have improved, the indications for obtaining fetal blood have changed; the same information can now be obtained with less risk by studying the genes of fetal cells shed into the amniotic fluid or by detecting the DNA of infectious agents, such as toxoplasma.

Doppler Velocimetry of the Umbilical Artery

Measuring blood flow with ultrasound in an alternately contracting and relaxing artery is known as *Doppler velocimetry*. (*Doppler* is the last name of the inventor of this technique.) This test can be applied to the umbilical artery, which pulsates synchronously with the fetus's heart. The role of this test in assessing fetal health is still experimental.

How Effective Are Tests of Fetal Well-Being Before Labor?

The effectiveness of the tests of fetal well-being used before labor is unknown, despite the widespread use of these tests, particularly the nonstress test, the contraction stress test, and the fetal biophysical profile. When they are normal, they seem to be good predictors of the viability of the fetus and baby; when they are abnormal, however, their predictive value is unclear.

The L/S Ratio as a Test of Lung Maturity

Late in normal pregnancy certain cells in the fetal lungs produce fat-rich chemicals that coat the inner walls of the air sacs, which are collapsed before birth. This coating prevents the sacs from sticking together after respiration begins and the sacs fill with air. A major problem for premature babies, particularly those younger than thirty-two weeks' gestational age, is that these surface chemicals have not yet been produced. These babies are at risk for developing *respiratory distress syndrome* (see p. 309).

Some of the surface chemicals produced by the fetal lungs are washed up through the airways to the mouth and out into the amniotic fluid. Two of the chemicals secreted are lecithin (L) and sphingomyelin (S). The ratio between these two (the L/S ratio) is a good predictor of maturity of the lungs. Amniotic fluid for L/S measurement is obtained by amniocentesis.

An L/S ratio of greater than 2.0 indicates that the risk of respiratory distress is slight, unless the woman is diabetic; the fetus has an illness caused by incompatibility between its blood type and that of the woman, usually involving Rh D (see p. 16 on blood type, Rh D status, etc.); or the fetus is very sick, for any reason, at the time of testing. In newborns, if the L/S ratio is 1.5 to 2.0, respiratory distress will occur 40 percent of the time; if the L/S ratio is below 1.5, distress will occur 73 percent of the time.

Thus the L/S ratio is a useful, although imperfect, measure of fetal lung maturity. Whenever preterm delivery is considered, as, for example, in suspected intrauterine growth disturbance (see p. 296) or preeclampsia (see p. 307), the risk of continued intrauterine life must be weighed against the dangers of prematurity, particularly of respiratory distress syndrome. The L/S ratio helps in this decision. Babies who are candidates for premature birth and have an abnormal L/S ratio are treated with corticosteroids.

Monitoring the Fetal Heart During Labor

Please read pages 159–160, Principles of Fetal Heart Rate Monitoring in Labor, in preparation for the discussion that follows.

Intermittent Fetal Heart Monitoring in Labor. The traditional way to monitor the fetal heart rate is to listen with a stethoscope; more recently, a handheld ultrasound device, called a Doppler, has become available. Skilled attendants can use a stethoscope or a Doppler much as an electronic monitor is used; they can follow heart-rate patterns through a contraction and identify the normality or abnormality of the pattern. A stethoscope or Doppler can also be used to monitor the fetal heart rate during a nonstress test (see pp. 160–161). Intermittent monitoring has the advantage of allowing the woman to move around freely.

Continuous Electronic Fetal Heart Rate Monitoring During Labor. Continuous electronic fetal monitoring (EFM) records uterine contractions and the fetal heart rate over time. The uterine contractions are measured by a pressure gauge strapped to the woman's abdomen. The changing shape of the uterus during a contraction is sensed and transmitted as electrical signals, activating a needle that imprints a lumpy line (blip) on a rolling strip of graph paper. The fetal heart rate can be detected with an external ultrasound monitor, placed on the abdomen over the uterus, or internally, by a wire leading through the vagina and attached to the fetal scalp that detects the electrical impulses from the fetus's heart. For detecting the variability of the heart rate, the internal monitor has a decided advantage over the external monitor.

The electrode commonly used for internal monitoring is attached to the fetus by twisting the corkscrew-shaped wires at its tip into the skin of the scalp or by attaching them with a clip. It is likely that the fetus feels the jab of attachment, although observations made on newborns receiving injections or having blood drawn lead us to believe that the pain is probably experienced for only a short time.

Complications of internal fetal monitoring are rare, but not insignificant. They include infection of the scalp of the fetus at the site of attachment of the electrode; damage to fetal blood vessels, with resulting hemorrhage in the case of a low-lying placenta (see pp. 303–305 on placenta previa); and an increased risk of infection within the amniotic cavity. Internal fetal monitoring is contraindicated when the woman has AIDS (see p. 21) or active genital herpes (see p. 138) because these viruses can gain entrance to the fetus through the break in the skin of the scalp at the point of wire attachment.

An important practical issue of internal fetal monitoring is that the woman must lie in bed for as long as the wires are attached. Telemetry systems, in which the fetal heart rate is broadcast to the monitor without maintaining connections by wire, have been developed, but such systems are not widely available.

How Effective Is Fetal Heart Rate Monitoring? Although the fetal heart rate is now monitored in all labors, we do not actually know that this practice makes a difference in the health or survival of babies, even though it appears obvious that it should. No studies have compared monitoring with no monitoring The time to conduct such a study was many decades ago, when monitoring was first introduced. Today, a new practice such as this would not be allowed without a controlled trial. Now that monitoring is so deeply embedded in practice, however, it is unlikely that such a study will ever be conducted. Even when fetal distress is identified by monitoring, there is no evidence that birth by C-section (in other words, as fast as possible) is better than vaginal birth, even though common sense would say it is.

Comparison of Intermittent and Continuous Electronic Fetal Heart Rate Monitoring. There is general agreement among obstetricians that continuous electronic monitoring has an advantage in labors classified as high risk (for example, because of preeclampsia), when instant information about the fetus is a necessity. With respect to labors that start out as low risk, there have been nine randomized control studies involving over 17,000 labors (including labors at term and preterm). The studies compared women whose fetuses were intermittently monitored (listened to every fifteen minutes during the first stage and every five minutes during the second stage of labor) with women whose fetuses were continuously electronically monitored. Fetal scalp-blood sampling for pH (see p. 167) was available in all labors as needed.

These studies did not demonstrate any differences between the groups in the initial newborn assessment at the time of birth, in the number of deaths of babies during labor or birth, or in the number of infants requiring care in the intensive-care units of the hospitals. The studies did show a higher incidence of cesarean births in the electronically monitored labors. In the largest study reported, one difference, the significance of which is unclear, was that for reasons unknown, more, but a still very low number, of intermittently monitored babies, especially those whose mothers received oxytocin (see p. 195) to stimulate their labors, had a convulsion during the newborn period. However, there was no difference between the groups in the proportion of babies with seizures who survived, nor was there any difference between the groups in the frequency of cerebral palsy or in the mental or neurological development of the babies as of their fourth birthdays. In summary, either method of fetal monitoring appears acceptable in labors considered low risk; intermittent monitoring appears to have an edge in preventing cesarean delivery. In high-risk labors, when instant information about the fetus is deemed essential, electronic monitoring may have an advantage. In actual practice, however, many obstetricians use electronic monitoring in *all* labors partly (and justifiably) because they are afraid of lawsuits alleging that brain injury to an infant would have been prevented if electronic monitoring had been used.

None of the studies to date have included women who have had a previous cesarean section and were attempting a vaginal birth. However, there is no obvious reason to believe that the outcomes would be different. The American College of Obstetrics and Gynecology approves of both ways of monitoring and has even more liberal guidelines for frequency of intermittent listening during the first stage—every thirty minutes.

There are no studies that have compared the amount of time required of professional staff to monitor by the two approaches. A common view is that continuous electronic monitoring requires less staff time—one nurse (in this era of shortages of nurses) can watch several patients. However, it is worth noting that the best outcome statistics among babies and mothers have been achieved in settings where there is one-on-one continuous attention by a birth attendant who monitors intermittently.

Fetal Scalp-Blood Testing During Labor

The critical measure of the well-being of the fetus during labor is the amount of oxygen in its blood. Since the fetal heart rate reflects oxygen supply to the heart, it is a good, although indirect, measure of blood oxygen. More precise monitoring would measure the oxygen level itself. The technology to do so on a continuous basis, using a noninvasive sensor attached to the fetus and red and infrared light, has just become available. At present the closest indicator of fetal oxygen in wide use is blood acidity, measured by what is called the *pH*.

To perform this test, an endoscope (illuminated tube) is inserted through the cervix and pressed against the fetus's head. The skin is then wiped clean with a cotton swab, sprayed with ethyl chloride to stimulate increased blood flow, and coated with a silicon gel to cause the blood to coalesce as easily collected globules. Immediately after a uterine contraction, one or two tiny cuts are made through the skin to a predetermined depth. The blood is collected in a long, pointed glass tube and analyzed.

A pH reading of 7.25 or greater (more alkaline, as opposed to acidic) is considered normal; 7.20 to 7.24, borderline; and less than 7.20, abnormal and indicative of too little oxygen in the blood. Generally, in the latter case, the baby should be delivered promptly. However, the test is not always reliable. Rarely, pH results with high readings can be associated with hypoxia (lack of oxygen), and some low readings can be associated with normal oxygen values. A deceptively low reading, which indicates danger when there is none, can occur when the fetus's scalp is swollen and the blood is not circulating well, when the blood of the woman is too acid, or when the blood sample is inadvertently taken from the woman rather than from the fetus.

The pH can be deceptively normal under the influence of pain medications and anesthetics given to the woman, as well as when infection is present, when the blood of the woman is alkaline, when the fetus has certain congenital anomalies, and when the blood sample was obtained other than immediately after a contraction.

Overall, if a fetus's scalp-blood pH is normal, there is an 80 percent chance of a favorable Apgar score after delivery and a 20 percent chance of an unfavorable one. (See p. 231 regarding the Apgar assessment of the need of a baby for resuscitation.) If the pH is low, there is a 60 percent chance that the Apgar score will be low. Thus, although the scalp-blood pH test is very useful, it is a far from perfect means of identifying fetuses in trouble.

Fetal-scalp sampling should not be done when a fetus is suspected to have hemophilia or when the woman has an infection that could be transmitted to the fetus at the sampling site: herpes (see p. 138), HIV (see p. 21), hepatitis (see p. 138), gonorrhea (see p. 137), or cytomegalovirus (see p. 135).

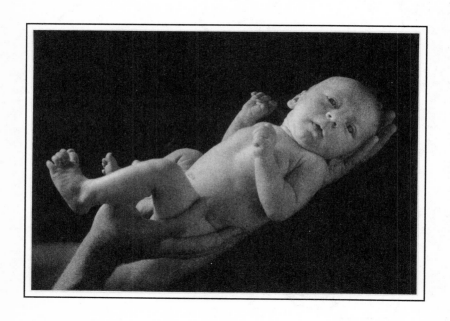

CHAPTER 4

Choices in Childbirth

STAGES OF LABOR

By convention, labor is divided into three stages. The *first stage* begins when regular contractions are occurring and the cervix is dilating (opening up). The passage of a mucous plug (bloody show) or spontaneous rupture of the membranes (breaking of the bag of waters) also counts as evidence that labor is starting. In a first labor the complete absorption (incorporation) of the soft, thick, tubelike cervical canal into the body of the uterus (a taking up of the cervix, also known as effacement) is also evidence of the onset of labor. (In subsequent pregnancies the cervix usually thins out before contractions begin.) The first stage of labor lasts until the cervix is completely dilated, marking the onset of the *second stage* (see Figure 4.1). The first stage is further divided into latent and active phases. I discuss these later on. The second stage, which begins with full cervical dilatation, ends with the birth of the baby, when the *third stage*, the delivery of the placenta, begins.

The progress of the first stage of labor is judged according to the diameter (width) of the cervix. The size of the opening ranges from zero (completely closed) to fully dilated, at an average of ten centimeters (just under four inches) with a full-term baby. The smallest discernible dilatation is noted as a fingertip; that is, it allows for the introduction of the tip only of the examiner's finger. The cervix may be dilated one to two centimeters before labor begins, especially in first pregnancies.

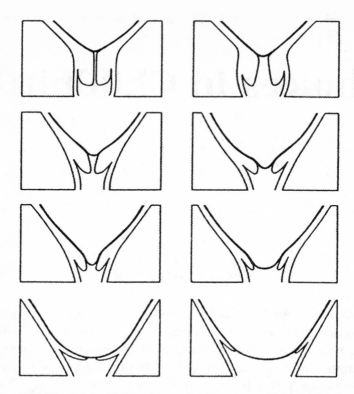

FIGURE 4.1   Dilatation and effacement (thinning) of cervix. Left-hand column shows cervix in a first birth; right-hand column shows the cervix after two or more births.

Painful uterine contractions without evidence of cervical activity (effacement; dilatation; or the indirect evidence of cervical activity, occurrence of a bloody show, or rupture of membranes) do not constitute labor. These are common late in pregnancy and are referred to as Braxton Hicks contractions (after the name of the physician who described them; see p. 66). Braxton Hicks contractions are characteristically irregular in their timing. They change unpredictably in length, strength, or frequency and often stop with a change in activity. Shifting from standing to lying down (or vice versa) or taking a warm bath will often make them stop. In contrast, labor contractions increase in regularity, duration, strength, and frequency. They grow stronger with activity.

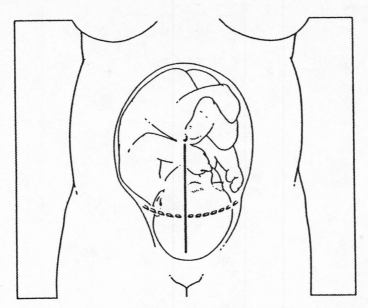

FIGURE 4.2   Axis of birth canal (bold line) and midpelvis
(dotted line)

Another important consideration in assessing the progress of labor is
the location of the fetus in relation to the birth canal (see Figure 4.2),
that is, how far into the birth canal the fetus has descended. The level of
descent is known as the *station*. The midpelvis is called station zero.
When the head reaches station zero, it is said to be engaged (see Figures 4.3 and 4.4). Above the level of the midpelvis the station is called
negative; below the midpelvis, positive. Plus one, then, means one centimeter below or beyond the midpelvis; minus two means two centimeters above the midpelvis. Descent of the fetus is recorded in sequence as
minus three, minus two, minus one, zero (at the midpelvis), plus one,
plus two, and plus three (when the baby's head is visible).

In addition to determining the location of the fetus, it is important to
determine which part of the fetus is entering the birth canal—head,
face, hands, or buttocks (see Breech Presentation, p. 277)—and how it
is oriented to the birth canal. The presenting body part, say, the point
of the head (known as the *occiput*), can usually be identified during a
vaginal examination. Determining the way the head, or other present-

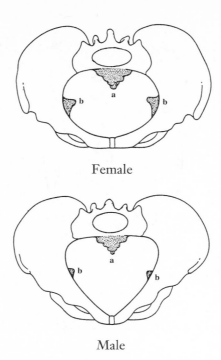

Female

Male

FIGURE 4.3   Pelvis seen from above, showing sacrum (a), ischial spines (b), and symphysis pubis (c).

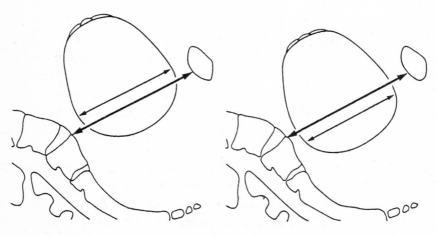

FIGURE 4.4   Descent of fetus's head into the birth canal, known as engagement. Bold line shows distance between sacrum and pubic bone.

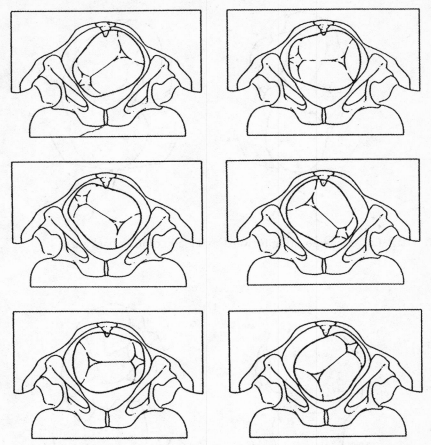

FIGURE 4.5   Positions of head during labor as seen from below, showing fontanels

ing part, is rotated in the 360 possible degrees requires identification of
its landmarks, or topical characteristics, with reference to an imaginary
line or axis that follows the course of the birth canal. In the case of the
head, *sutures*, or *fontanels*, distinguish the front from the back of the
skull. These sutures are the seams between the still-unknit bones of the
skull. The fontanels are the triangular spaces at the junctions of the sutures, a large one in front (anterior) and a smaller one in back (posterior) (see Figure 4.5). Using these landmarks, it is possible to determine
whether the head is facing forward, backward, or crossways. In medical
terms, the location of the occiput is described as being to the left or

FIGURE 4.6   Head pointing forward   Head pointing backward

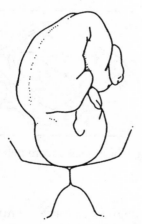

FIGURE 4.7   Head pointing right   Head pointing left

right of center, pointing forward (anterior), backward (posterior), or crossways (transverse), ninety degrees to the right or left of the midline. Thus, LOA (left occiput anterior, the most common position), means that the occiput (the *O*) is directed left and forward. For a summary of the various positions, see Figures 4.6 and 4.7.

Touching the head of the fetus reveals whether the scalp is swollen. Swelling is called *caput succedaneum*; a caput signifies that the ring of

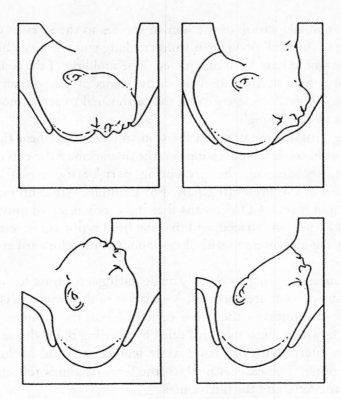

FIGURE 4.8   Caput—swelling of fetus's scalp as a
result of pressure from the cervix or vagina

pressure exerted by the cervix on the scalp has interfered with the return of blood from the skin in the center of the ring. The presence of a
caput (see Figure 4.8) indicates that the cervix is not yielding to pressure from the head and may mean some degree of obstruction to the
descent of the fetus. At times a caput can be several centimeters thick,
suggesting a greater degree of descent (a lower station) than is the case.

Another effect of pressure on the fetus's head is known as *molding*, the
shaping of the head by the architecture of the birth canal. At birth a
baby's head, unlike that of the adult or child, can be squeezed and elon-
gated because the separate bones of the skull have not yet fused (see
Figure 4.5). The seams are open and the bones can overlap. This over-
lapping of the bones can often be detected in a vaginal examination.
Molding is seen at birth in the form of elongation of the head and usually reverses spontaneously within a few days. The capacity of the head

to mold is an adaptation of the human species to the stresses of labor. The give of the skull prevents it from cracking and permits a birth that otherwise would have been obstructed. The molding of the fetus's head is complemented by the looseness of the joints of the woman's pelvis, which also allows for some give of the birth canal to accommodate the fetus as it passes through.

During a vaginal examination the woman will usually hear the examiner report his or her observations on the dilatation of the cervix, its effacement, the station, the presenting part of the fetus, and the orientation of the presenting part. For example, "six centimeters, 80 percent, minus one, LOA" means that the cervix is six centimeters dilated and 80 percent effaced, and that the head is one centimeter inside the midpelvis and oriented with the occiput pointing forward and to the left.

These measurements are usually made during a contraction, when dilatation and descent are maximal. A variation of this principle is used to assess the roominess of the pelvis early in labor; the examiner pushes the fetus down and into the birth canal by pressing the abdomen on the top of the uterus with one hand while feeling the head in the vagina with the other. The ease with which the fetus descends reflects the fit between the fetus and the birth canal.

As previously mentioned, the first stage of labor includes two phases of cervical dilatation, the *latent phase* and the *active phase*. The active phase is further divided into the *acceleration phase* and the *deceleration phase*. The latter part of the acceleration phase and the early part of the deceleration phase are referred to as the *transition*, in which the cervix opens rapidly, from about seven centimeters to full dilatation. Transition is often the hardest part of labor, and its pain may be intense. It is often accompanied by nausea and vomiting.

Each stage and phase of labor has its own characteristics. A sensitive attendant, or the laboring woman herself, particularly if she has given birth before, can often tell the status of labor by the frequency, duration, and intensity of contractions, the presence or absence of pressure sensations in the birth canal, and the presence of associated symptoms, such as nausea or vomiting.

Early in the latent phase of the first stage, contractions are five to thirty minutes apart and last from fifteen to forty seconds. They are often described as mild cramps, gas, back pain, or pressure. During the active phase, the contractions come two to five minutes apart, are forty-five to sixty seconds in duration, and are stronger and more intense. In transition the contractions occur one and one-half to three minutes apart, last for forty-five to ninety seconds, and are the strongest they will be during the whole labor. Often, one contraction follows another so rapidly that resting between them may be impossible. Once full dilatation is achieved (the beginning of the second stage of labor and the end of the first), the contractions may space out to three to five or more minutes apart, so that some women are even able to doze off between them. As the fetus descends to the perineum, many women report a burning sensation. The contractions are now less intense, and discomfort shifts from the uterus to the rectum and vagina and includes a sense of pressure and an urge to push. This urge should be followed to the extent that it feels comfortable to do so. (See discussion later in this chapter on pushing during birth.)

The configuration of the birth canal varies along its course. It is not like a curved tube or tunnel with a constant diameter throughout. At the entry to the birth canal the widest measurements are the oblique distances running from the right back to the left front and from the left back to the right front. At the outlet of the canal, the widest dimension is from front to back, from the tip of the spine (coccyx) to the juncture of the pubic bone in the front (see Figures 4.3 and 4.4). As the fetus descends in the birth canal, it turns and twists to accommodate to these shifts in dimension. The fetus apparently plays an active role in moving along. In the LOA position, the head approaches the perineum at an angle and then moves to a direct front-to-back orientation just as the baby is being born, while the shoulders and back, following behind higher in the canal, are still at an angle. When the head fully emerges, it immediately turns back into alignment with the rest of the body. As the shoulders are born, they move into a direct front-to-back position with one shoulder under the pubic bone as the other emerges over the coccyx. As the shoulders turn, the head turns with them, and the baby's face looks directly to the side. (See Figures 4.9 and 4.10.)

Although the posterior position (occiput pointing to the back) is a normal, but minority, presentation from which babies are safely born, it is often associated with the prolongation of labor and the experience of back pain. If a fetus is posterior and progress in labor is slow, efforts are usually made to help the head (and the fetus) to rotate forward, either

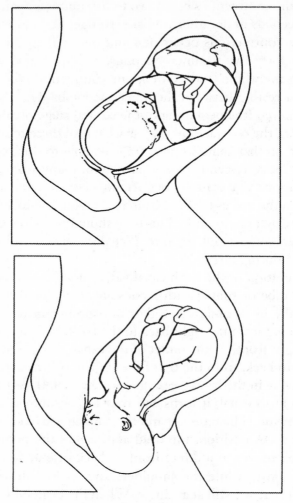

FIGURE 4.9   Descent and rotation of fetus
in birth canal

by having the woman change position or by having the attendant turn
the head manually in the vagina.

TIMING YOUR CONTRACTIONS

Place your hands on your uterus and feel for its tightening and then relaxing. You will usually experience some pain at the same time. In early
labor, contractions last between twenty and sixty seconds and the tight-

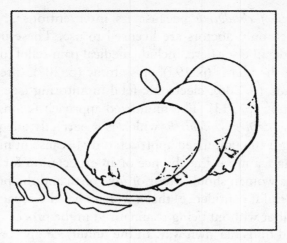

FIGURE 4.10   Rotation of head during birth

ness should be felt over the entire uterus. Time the contractions from the start of one contraction to the beginning of the next.

When to Call the Hospital, Birthing Center, or Birth Attendant

For a first labor, call if you can no longer talk through contractions or when your contractions come regularly every three to five minutes over one hour, last at least forty-five to sixty seconds, and are much stronger when you walk.

For second or subsequent labors, call when contractions occur every five to seven minutes, last forty-five to sixty seconds, and become stronger when walking.

Also call if your bag of waters breaks or if you have bright red vaginal bleeding, not to be confused with the bloody show, which is the dark, blood-tinged mucus passed from the cervix as it dilates.

The Active and the Unhurried Approaches to Labor and Birth

There are two major approaches to labor and birth, which I call the *active* and the *unhurried*. Each approach has its own solutions to the central problem of pain in labor. The active approach is often called the *medical model of childbirth* because its interventions are drugs and surgery, which only doctors are licensed to use. These interventions, discussed in detail elsewhere, include medical pain relief (p. 197), drugs that contract the uterus (p. 195), episiotomy (p. 208), forceps and vacuum extraction (p. 206), electronic fetal monitoring (see p. 164), and cesarean section (p. 213). The unhurried approach is most commonly referred to as *natural childbirth*, which is a perfectly adequate term. I prefer calling it the unhurried approach only because in my analysis its distinguishing feature is the absence of an expectation for how long or in what way a woman should labor or give birth and the presence of an expectation (call it confidence) that a woman has the capacity to handle the pain of labor without being traumatized in the process. She sets her own pace and finds her own way. In the unhurried approach interventions include patience; lots of hands-on, one-on-one care; psychological support and encouragement; relaxation; changes in position; a soothing environment; body contact with attendants and close ones; and, more recently, immersion in a warm tub for labor and delivery. Labor pain is managed rather than eliminated. An essential part of managing this pain is the mind-set that in the right environment and with the right support, it *can* be done. Although critics of the active approach describe the unhurried approach as noninterventive, I do not agree; it is just that the interventions used are different.

Although the two approaches are very different, they are both safe and they both work. Both are being refined and improved. For example, the active approach now offers the dual spinal-epidural anesthetic, a major advance in pain relief (see p. 203), and the unhurried approach now includes water birth, also a major advance (see p. 193). Which approach is best for you depends on individual preferences, availability (of birth attendant and facility), and cost. In general, the active approach is practiced by physicians and the unhurried approach by midwives. Some physicians are also skilled practitioners of the unhurried approach. You will need to select a birth attendant based on your preference, assuming that you have a choice. (See Birth Attendants and Birth Settings, p. 6.) If a medical complication develops in a labor using the unhurried approach, as occurs in a minority of circumstances, a physician (and often an anesthesiologist and pediatrician) will be needed.

The goals of the active approach are that no woman should suffer from pain in labor and that labor should be handled with whatever tools are needed to accomplish delivery within a defined number of hours, usually twelve. Enter the hospital at a certain time and leave at a predictable later time, baby in arms. The active approach is usually applied to first labors because they normally last longer than subsequent labors, but it can be used with subsequent labors as well. (For many women, second and later labors seem to take care of themselves.) A quick delivery and shortened hospital stay are perceived as using scarce hospital resources efficiently and as fitting in with the widely accepted goal of containing health-care costs, although the active approach is probably more expensive than the unhurried one. The active approach can also be viewed as fitting better into the busy parents' schedule.

The unhurried approach is based on the observation that women normally vary in the durations of their labors, just as they do in their heights and blood pressures, and that there is no exact figure for how long a labor should be. As long as there is no expectation about how long a labor *should* last, the fetus and the woman are doing well, and the woman and her birth attendant both believe things are going well, there is no need to do anything other than provide support, in all of its many forms, to the woman throughout the process. In these conditions well over 90 percent of women will give birth without most of the interventions that are a part of the active approach.

There is evidence that the unhurried approach is less costly. Statistics compiled in 1995 on charges in birthing centers, which offered only the unhurried approach, show that the average birth cost $3,241, whereas a hospital birth in the same community at the same time averaged $6,378. The estimate of annual savings for just 100,000 births in birthing centers (a small fraction of all births in the United States each year), including savings resulting from performing fewer cesarean sections, was a sizable $1.4 billion. However, this estimate is probably high because the costs of hospital care for uncomplicated births include paying, in part, for the standby resources needed for complicated births—operating rooms, specialized equipment, highly trained personnel, and so on. Because of these unavoidable built-in costs, which birthing centers do not have, exact financial comparisons are difficult, if not impossible. Nonetheless, it does appear that the unhurried approach has economic benefits.

The differences experientially between the two approaches can be startling. They certainly were for me as an observer. Having been educated only in the medical model, my first exposure to the unhurried approach, with care provided by midwives at the Booth Maternity Center in Philadelphia in the mid-1970s, was a real eye-opener, nothing short of astonishing. Women of all backgrounds and ages simply had their babies, without any of the high-tech devices to which I was accustomed, and did perfectly well in all respects. I had to question the need to do anything different for any women at low risk for labor problems.

Between the pure examples of the active and unhurried approaches as I have presented them, there are gradations that combine elements of each. Because the active approach is in a sense easier and less demanding, the woman who wants the unhurried approach needs to consider the setting in which she will labor very carefully and the extent to which the institution (or home) and her attendants will be supportive of her preferences. For example, repeatedly asking a woman in the second stage of labor whether she would like an epidural anesthetic, as is sometimes done in hospitals, instead of simply providing, matter-of-factly, nonmedical methods of pain relief implies that the pain will sooner or later become unbearable.

My concern is that of access and choice. Support for the active approach can easily be found anywhere in the United States, whereas support for the unhurried approach is limited or nonexistent in many communities. Although the percentage of births attended by midwives, the primary practitioners of the unhurried approach, increased from 1.7 percent in 1980 to 9 percent in 1998, midwives still attend only slightly less than one in ten births in the United States. The active approach remains dominant. Consider recent statistics showing that labor inductions are up 14.0 percent, as many as 30 percent of women may receive oxytocin to stimulate their labor contractions, more than 80 percent of labors are monitored electronically, epidural anesthesia use has increased, and about 10 to 15 percent of women need assistance from forceps or a vacuum extractor in delivering (or, more to the point, being delivered of) their babies.

Many women do not even know that there is a way to labor and deliver other than by the active approach. It is the only choice available in their communities, which means, in essence, they have no choice. Judith Rooks, in her book *Midwifery and Childbirth in America* (which is also an excellent history of how we have come to have the maternity-care system we have), expresses this concern very well when she links (correctly, in my opinion) the availability of the unhurried approach (she uses a different term) to the supply and distribution of midwives: "Given the examples of other countries; given the safety, effectiveness, and benefits of midwifery care; and given the importance of the qualitative aspects of the childbearing experience to many women and families, it is wrong to deny any American woman the option of choosing to have a midwife as her primary-care provider if her pregnancy is normal."

In the same vein, doctors Murray Enkin, Marc Keirse, James Neilson, and midwife Mary Renfrew, authors of the second edition of the highly respected and influential book, *A Guide to Effective Care in Pregnancy and Childbirth* (see Appendix), which is derived from the Oxford database of clinical trials, include in the category of "Forms of Care That Are Unlikely to Be Beneficial" the following: "Involving *obstetricians* in the care of *all* (my emphasis added) women during pregnancy and childbirth" and "Not involving obstetricians in the care of women with serious risk factors." Under the category of "Forms of Care That Are Likely to Be Beneficial" they list "Midwifery care for women with no serious risk factors." Pointedly absent in this category is care by physicians of such women. Clearly these editors recognize that the great majority of women will do very well if offered the unhurried approach with midwives as their attendants.

There is some evidence that more women would like to have the *option* of the unhurried approach. For example, a 1995 survey of the largest HMO in the state of Washington (Group Health of Puget Sound) found, according to Rooks, "that 8% of reproductive-age women were interested in the idea of a midwife-attended home birth and might choose that option if the cooperative would provide the same benefits for a home birth that it provides for a birth in one of the H.M.O. hospitals."

Elements of the Active Approach

Although elements of the active approach are practiced in many hospitals, the packaging of them as the active management of labor has been achieved and popularized by the Royal Maternity Hospital of Dublin. In that institution active management involves (1) a strict definition of labor onset that includes regular and painful uterine contractions at least once every five minutes in association with, in first labors, complete effacement (taking up; see p. 172) of the cervix, bloody show, or spontaneous rupture of membranes or, in all labors, progressive dilatation of the cervix (in many second and subsequent pregnancies the cervix is dilated before labor onset); (2) purposeful rupture of the membranes (see p. 187) of all women in labor in whom such rupture has not occurred spontaneously (this intervention alone has been proved to shorten labor); (3) use of oxytocin (see pp. 195–197) in first labors (only) when the cervix dilates at less than one centimeter per hour; and (4) cesarean section if delivery does not occur within twelve hours. The primary birth attendant in the Dublin program is a midwife who gives one-on-one care to the laboring woman.

Elements of the Unhurried Approach

The following list summarizes the major elements of the unhurried approach.

1. Choose a midwife as your birth attendant or a physician who is skilled in midwifery (hard to find). Unhurried births are the stock-in-trade of midwives. Also consider having a doula with you (see p. 10). Don't look to your significant other to play the role of doula. Your partner, who inevitably is too emotionally involved with you to provide the *professional* input you need, does have an important contribution to make, however.

2. Don't start the labor clock ticking by going to the hospital or birthing center too early and then staying there if you're not in active labor even though you're experiencing contractions. Otherwise, expectations of how long you should be in labor will come into play, and if you don't meet these expectations you are more likely to become disappointed and lose your nerve and the odds that medical interventions will be proposed and accepted will increase. If you're not in active labor, go home. (The criteria used in Dublin are good ones to use in determining whether you should stay or leave.) Then, stay at home until you are in active labor. Stay in phone contact. Make it a point to be on the phone with your attendant *during a contraction*. As

obstetrician Alan Schapker (Medical Director of the Bethany Birth Center in Phoenix) pointed out in a talk at the 1995 annual meeting of the National Association of Childbearing Centers, if you can talk through a contraction, it's not time to head out. If possible, have the doctor, midwife, or nurse check you in the office, as the hospital, for many people, raises anxiety levels because of its association with illness. The less anxiety the better in labor.

3. Avoid having your membranes deliberately ruptured (amniotomy; see 186). Because of concerns about infection, the clock really starts ticking loud and clear after this procedure is performed and puts pressure on all to achieve delivery within a certain time. Spontaneous rupture of the membranes at term has almost the same implications for duration of labor as does amniotomy.

4. If possible, do not use an electronic fetal monitor strip, often standard procedure on arrival in the labor and delivery unit. Use of a fetal monitor can increase anxiety, symbolizes the medical model, and has no evidence-based rationale. It puts you in the mind-set for an active-management approach.

5. Don't ask for predictions on the duration of your labor. Expectations will then be set, which, if not met, will increase your concern that something may be wrong and that something has to be done about it.

6. Labor is one situation that you can't control, so don't even try. Go with the flow. Surrender.

7. As midwives Susan Melinkow (of Sharpthe Birth Place, San Diego) and Holly Schochat (of Northwest Hospital, Tucson) suggest, when labor stalls, consider psychological as well as physical factors. For example, when encouraged to talk, a woman whose labor is going nowhere might identify and express a fear that she won't love this baby as much as her first, that her husband won't love the baby, or that she feels guilty about having this baby because she had an abortion with her last pregnancy. The mere communication of such concerns, no matter how silly or embarrassing they may seem, has unblocked many a labor. The woman lets go of her resistance and the baby is born.

8. Keep your environment simple and relaxed. Labor is not the time to host a party for your friends and relatives, particularly during the first stage. Wait until the second stage of labor if you want a few close friends and family members with you.

9. Find the positions that work best for you (see Positions During Labor and Delivery, p. 204). In general, avoid giving birth while lying flat on your back; avoid the use of stirrups; and keep control of your legs.

10. Take advantage of the benefits of being massaged and stroked, of being held and hugged, of having your hair combed. Counterpressure against a sore back can be a blessing. A cup of tea, dim lights, and music all have their place. Also consider nontraditional methods of pain relief, such as foot massage, acupuncture, and guided imagery and visualization (for example, of waves on the ocean). Labor is the time of times to be soothed, praised, babied, accepted, heard, and not criticized.

11. Consider a water birth (see p. 193).

Research on the Active Approach

In Dublin, active management has resulted in excellent outcomes, including a cesarean delivery rate of less than 6 percent, which is remarkably low by U.S. standards even when allowance is made for possible differences in the populations of women served. Further, 30 percent of the women seen in the Royal Maternity Hospital require oxytocin and about 20 percent have epidural anesthesia, both of which are used only in first labors.

The Dublin experience has attracted much attention in the United States as a possible approach to reducing the high C-section rates. Two well-conducted studies have tested the results. In both studies the control group received many of the interventions received by the active-management group, but did not receive them as consistently or under the same guidelines with respect to the time elapsed from the onset of labor. As reported in 1992, José Lopez-Zeno and colleagues at Northwestern University conducted a controlled trial of active management during first labors and achieved a cesarean-section rate of 10.5 percent, compared with 14.1 percent in the control (usual-care) group. In this study, not using midwives, the average length of labor was shortened by 1.66 hours, and significantly fewer infections occurred among the women who were actively managed. Almost three-fourths of the women at Northwestern in both the active management and the control groups received epidural anesthesia.

Another controlled trial of active management was conducted under the direction of Fred Frigoletto at Brigham and Woman's Hospital in Boston in 1995. This study used one-on-one nursing, with the nurses changing only at shifts. The average duration of labor was shortened by 2.7 hours, and there was no difference in the C-section rate of 19 percent in each group. Fifty-four percent of the women in the active management group and 64 percent in the usual-care group requested epidural anesthesia.

With the active-management approach using epidoral anesthesia the woman may well be able to watch television during labor and delivery will usually involve the use of stirrups, washing of the perineum, and the covering of the woman's legs and lower abdomen with sterile drapes. Unlike unhurried labors, which are often noisy and spontaneous, actively managed labors tend to be neat and orderly.

Why the differences in results between the Dublin and the U.S. versions of active management? A major element in the care provided in Dublin was the one-on-one attention by a midwife using the midwifery approach to labor and delivery. This is very likely a crucial element. This notion is echoed by the authors of *Active Management of Labor, The Dublin Experience* (see Appendix and p. 185), who conclude that "No form of management of labor can be really effective unless it can be practiced by nurses independently, almost, of doctors. This requires a level of mutual confidence between nurses and doctors which is not too often found."

Research on the Unhurried Approach

Research data on the unhurried approach are limited. The best sources of data are birthing centers, which emphasize the unhurried approach. Another source of data on the unhurried approach is home births. Although less common in the United States than in other countries, home births are still popular among a small segment of the U.S. population (about 1 percent) and holding steady. (Until the twentieth century the home was the *only* place to give birth; Richard Nixon was the last U.S. president to be born at home.)

Freestanding birthing centers were pioneered during the 1970s. The Maternity Center Association of New York, under the leadership of nurse midwife Ruth Lubic, opened a center in a converted brownstone house on the upper east side of Manhattan. The Booth Maternity Center of the Salvation Army (which also included a hospital component), under the leadership of nurse midwives Kitty Ernst and Ruth Wilf and obstetrician John Franklin (and over the sometimes very strong opposition of obstetricians, especially in New York), was opened in Philadelphia. In the United States freestanding birthing centers now number 145, with 85 more under development. Most centers are certified by the National Association of Childbearing Centers (see Appendix), an organization that maintains very high practice standards and collects statistics on every birth at its centers. Nurse midwife and researcher Judith Rooks reported the association's statistics in the December 28, 1989, issue of the *New England Journal of Medicine*. The data came from the 84 centers certified at the time and involved 11,814 women admitted for labor and delivery. Overall, the outcomes were excellent and comparable to or better than the best achieved in a hospital setting among similar women. The intrapartum and neonatal mortality rate was (a low) 1.3 per 1,000 births—0.7 per 1,000 when infants with lethal malformations are excluded from the statistics. Using very conservative indications, slightly over 16 percent of the women were transferred during labor to a hospital, and 2.4 percent were transferred as emergencies. Women with first pregnancies were more likely to be transferred than those with later pregnancies (29 versus 7 percent). The rate of cesarean sections (all performed in hospitals) was (a low) 4.4 percent (see pp. 213–220 on cesarean birth), and no women died. Seventeen percent of the women had episiotomies. Of the rest, 34.0 percent had no vaginal tears, 45.7 percent had minor tears, and slightly over 2.0 percent had deeper tears. Internal continuous electronic fetal monitoring (see pp. 164–166) was used in 1.1 percent of the labors (the rest were monitored by intermittent listening to the fetal heartbeat), and 95 percent of the women drank liquids or ate while in labor (see pp. 194–195). Forty-three percent of the women took showers, baths, or both. Twenty-four percent of women in their first labor and 6 percent of women in a later labor received analgesics for pain relief (see p. 197). (Other forms of anesthesia, such as epidurals, were not available in the birthing centers.)

Freestanding birthing centers emphasize continuity of care by nurse midwives and, more recently, lay midwives (physicians usually participate as consultants to the midwives or, in some cases, as birth attendants); secure transport services and backup arrangements with hospitals and obstetricians; strong prenatal education; and treating pregnancy, labor, and delivery as normal, happy experiences. They do not administer oxytocin to augment labor, nor do they (with few exceptions) use electronic fetal monitors or epidural or spinal anesthetics. They place great emphasis on helping women find *what works best for them* in labor, drawing on each woman's own strengths. They encourage laboring and delivering in an upright position (see p. 204 on position in labor and delivery). Their excellent outcomes probably reflect the combined effects of these policies and practices, which differ from the standard hospital-based approach and offer a revealing comparison. As a model of care, the birthing center that meets the standards of the Commission for the Accreditation of Birth Centers (based on the nationally recognized Standards for Birth Centers published by the National Association of Childbearing Centers) has much to recommend it, including reaching women in need of services who have fewer financial resources and reducing the costs of care by as much as 30 to 50 percent. More and more hospitals are adopting a birthing-center approach within their own walls or grounds (side by side with the active approach as an option) and achieving similar results, with an added advantage of easier access to facilities and personnel in case of complications.

I find it intriguing that the results of midwife-attended birth in birthing centers are not that different from midwife-attended birth using the active-management rules followed in Dublin (I do not have access to data on duration of labor in the birthing centers). What this seems to say is that if you want these kinds of results, use midwives, doulas, or nurses who provide one-on-one care.

The classic setting for the unhurried approach is the home. The best natural laboratory for research on outcomes of home births has been the Netherlands, where national health policy, a nonactive intervention philosophy of birth, and an excellent support system, including maternity aides who stay during labor and the baby's first week, have enabled midwives and general practitioners to continue to attend many births at home. A study that analyzed data compiled by the Central Bureau of Statistics found no significant differences in outcomes between cities with an almost 100 percent rate of hospital births and cities of similar demography with a 50 percent rate of hospital births.

Following international trends, in the Netherlands between 1960 and 1990 the proportion of deliveries occurring in the home declined from 70 to 35 percent and is continuing to drop. However, birth at home continues to be very safe. In a 1990 report of almost 9,000 births, the perinatal death rate was 0.14 percent, and only 3.1 percent of infants were admitted to the hospital in their first week. (Data on mothers transferred to hospitals are not available.) The overall cesarean-section rate in the Netherlands, including births for which labor began at home, is less than 5 percent. Studies from the United Kingdom, Switzerland, and the Netherlands reported in 1996 showed similar excellent results. In these countries, home birth is a recognized and supported option with a defined transport and transfer system in place if hospitalization is required. These elements are crucial.

Home birth in the Netherlands has benefited that nation's entire system of maternity care. Through the repeated experience and highly visible model of successful normal births in the home, as well as through the prominent role of midwives in hospitals as well as at home, a philosophy of nonintervention in maternity care (relative to other countries) is maintained even for hospital births. The rate of cesarean sections in the Netherlands was 2.0 percent in 1969, 3.0 percent in 1975, 5.0 percent in 1980, and 6.0 percent in 1987. In the United States the rate was 5.3 percent in 1969, 10.2 percent in 1975, 15.2 percent in 1978, and 24.0 percent in 1988. (See p. 7 regarding controversy over just how high a C-section rate should be.)

In the United Kingdom, the National Birthday Trust Fund's survey of 6,044 planned births in 1994 and the 1996 study of the Northern Region Perinatal Mortality Survey Coordinating Group found no evidence to support the claim that the safest policy is for all women to give birth in the hospital.

In the United States, midwives and, to a lesser degree, physicians who have attended women at home, often facing hostile opposition from the organized medical community, along with the women who have had home births, have played a critical role in establishing a beachhead for the unhurried approach to labor and delivery. For a long time, the home was the only place where unhurried births could occur.

Research Comparing the Active and the Unhurried Approaches

There are no comparison studies of the two approaches beyond the data already presented. There are no randomized control trials comparing births in hospitals in birthing centers, and at home. It is unlikely that there will ever be such trials, as it is highly unlikely that women would accept the randomization required. Because women who choose a particular setting for labor and birth are self-selected and may differ in important characteristics, such as motivation and attitudes toward pain, it is difficult to know whether the different outcomes observed result from care in labor peculiar to the site of birth, from characteristics of the women themselves, or, as is more likely, from a combination of the two.

WATER BIRTH

Water birth (warm-water immersion for labor and delivery) is the latest and, perhaps, one of the most interesting developments in support of the unhurried approach to birth. It is gaining in popularity in the United States and has had a major impact in other countries, such as the United Kingdom, where a majority of hospitals under the National Health Service are now equipped with tubs. It is estimated that well over 50,000 water births have occurred worldwide, with no reports of life-threatening complications for either the mother or the baby. A 1999 study in the United Kingdom of 4,032 water births (217 of 219 maternity centers responded to the survey) that occurred between 1994 and 1996 showed that deaths of babies and admission to the special-care nursery were no different for babies born in water than for babies born vaginally but not in water, all in low-risk pregnancies. The small numbers in this study somewhat limit the strength of its conclusions. Although these data are impressive and the enthusiasm for water birth is undeniable, no controlled trials of its effectiveness have been done to date. I hope that such studies will be carried out.

The use of water as part of labor started in Europe as a comfort measure during labor (see discussion of the birthing center at Pithiviers, France, in Exercise and Relaxation, p. 95). Women liked it so much that they refused to get out to deliver their babies. To everyone's surprise, the babies did just fine being born in the water, with no risk of drowning. (They don't begin breathing until they're brought up from the water.) I can just imagine the early scenes of French doctors tearing their hair out when faced down by a woman who defiantly wouldn't budge when told it was time to leave the tub and go to the delivery room— "But, but . . . Madame Ladieux, please be reasonable!"

Water appears to provide enough external support to the woman to elevate (float) her to a new level of coping. A favored birthing position is on hands and knees. By avoiding bearing down with her contractions and by gently pushing between them (a practice encouraged by midwives in most deliveries), the woman eases the fetus through the birth canal while gradually stretching it. (Episiotomy rates with water birth in the United Kingdom have reportedly dropped from 60 to 10 percent.) Finally, the mother reaches down to cradle the baby and pull him or her into the water and, shortly thereafter, into the air. The mother delivers her baby; the midwife is an ever-alert bystander.

A major resource for water birth in the United States is Global Maternal/Child Health Association, under the leadership of nurse Barbara Harper (see Appendix). As part of its educational and support services, this organization has produced a powerful and moving videotape of a woman laboring and giving birth in water. Particularly memorable are the woman's haunting sounds and twisting dance as, eyes shut and fully in control, she retreats deep into herself (defying all the rules about the importance of breathing in a certain way and maintaining eye contact), where she must be accessing all the enormous innate (and often untapped) strength that a woman brings to childbirth. What an extraordinary sense of fulfillment this woman must have experienced, one that will last a lifetime. My prediction is that just as birthing centers, rooming-in, and support for breast-feeding in hospitals developed in response to public demand (women voting with their feet), so, too, water birth will become an increasingly available option.

FLUIDS AND FOOD

The rationale for the traditional hospital rule that women in labor should avoid eating and drinking and rely on intravenous fluids (IVs) exclusively is that if a general (gas) anesthetic (see p. 203) is required as part of an emergency delivery (usually by cesarean section), there is a risk that during the induction of anesthesia, the woman will vomit and breathe the stomach contents into her lungs. This is indeed a serious problem; chemical pneumonia and even death can result.

However, this traditional policy has been modified in light of new evidence and considerations. First and foremost, proper anesthetic technique (compression of the upper airway by pressing on the neck) can prevent aspiration of vomited stomach contents during anesthesia induction until a tube is secured in the airway. Second, general anesthesia is little used today, certainly compared with fifty or more years ago when the policy of no food or fluid by mouth was developed. Third, it has not been proved that a stomach empty of fluids and food will prevent the aspiration problem. Even in the absence of food, the acid in the stomach is highly irritating to the lungs if aspirated. Given this evidence, the policy of no food or drink has been substantially liberalized in many hospitals. In birthing centers and for home births it has never been an issue. For example, in the study of outcomes in birthing centers cited on p. 190, 40 percent of the women who eventually required a C-section had drunk clear fluids or eaten solid foods during labor and none aspirated when anesthesia was administered.

Early in labor it makes sense to eat easily digested carbohydrates, such as bread, fruit, rice, and pasta, and light proteins, such as cheese and yogurt. As labor progresses, the emphasis should shift to high-calorie liquids. In general, water, sports drinks, iced tea, and noncitrus fruit juices are well tolerated. Added honey or sugar can provide calories for women who want to drink plain water. Optimally, women should consume eight ounces of fluid and 200 calories an hour (a tablespoon of honey contains 64 calories; one cup of grape juice, 167 calories).

Some home-birth attendants have observed that citrus and apple juices and dairy products can cause vomiting in heavy labor. They advise women to freeze cranberry or grape juice in ice-cube trays to use in the event of nausea. Crushed ice from these juices, plain ice chips, or small sips of cool water tend to be kept down if taken in small amounts between each contraction. Dry toast or crackers also often help reduce nausea.

DRUGS THAT CONTRACT THE UTERUS

The drugs *oxytocin* (trade names Pitocin and Syntocinon), *ergonovine maleate* (Ergotrate), and *methylergonovine maleate* (Methergine) stimulate contraction of the uterus. Oxytocin is the synthetic form of a hormone normally secreted by the pituitary gland to contract the muscles of the uterus and the glands of the breasts, leading to the ejection of milk. In the postpartum period, the secretion of this natural hormone accounts for the afterpains of uterine contractions familiar to nursing mothers, particularly with their second and subsequent babies. The secretion of natural oxytocin is stimulated by nerve impulses that reach the brain and pituitary gland from the breasts during nipple stimulation. Thus, stimulation can initiate and augment labor as well as initiate both the letdown of milk and the uterine contractions that help prevent postpartum hemorrhage. Because synthetic oxytocin is metabolized readily and lasts but a short time in the blood, it is ideal for augmenting uterine contractions in labor. It is less effective in initiating labor, but is used for that purpose.

When used intravenously to enhance labor, oxytocin is delivered through a constant-infusion pump set to regulate the amount of hormone entering the woman to produce the right intensity and frequency of contractions. Intrauterine-pressure monitors inserted via a tube through the vagina are sometimes used to measure the intensity of uterine contractions during oxytocin stimulation.

Oxytocin is also used to initiate (induce) labor if deemed necessary to the woman's or baby's health, for example, in cases of preeclampsia (see p. 307) or prolonged pregnancy (see p. 306). Finally, oxytocin is used to help contract the uterus after the baby is born, which decreases postpartum bleeding (hemorrhage). For this purpose oxytocin can be given by injection or added to an intravenous infusion already in place.

Multigravidas (women who have had more than one full-term pregnancy) are more sensitive to oxytocin than are women who are pregnant for the first or second time. They experience more cramping and pain from administered oxytocin or from the natural hormone they produce themselves. (As mentioned, their afterpains are characteristically more intense.)

Ergonovine is a chemical derived from the ergot fungus found in rye and other grains or produced synthetically in the laboratory. Ergonovine causes uterine contraction. Unlike oxytocin, the effects of ergonovine last for hours, making it unsuitable during labor but useful for maintaining a contracted uterus after delivery of the placenta.

Ergonovine and methylergonovine are administered by injection after the placenta has been delivered and should be given along with oxytocin, not alone. They can also be given by mouth to maintain the uterus in a contracted state. Both can be used to contract the uterus and prevent bleeding after a D & C (pp. 302–303). Because of the undesirable side effects of ergonovine preparations, including nausea and elevated blood pressure, they are less frequently administered today.

Prostaglandins are another widely used group of naturally occurring chemicals that cause uterine-muscle contraction and can be used to initiate labor. They are placed in a gel base and inserted into the vagina or into the cervical canal. They ripen the cervix for labor and stimulate contractions of the uterus. (Once labor is under way, oxytocin can be administered as needed.) Prostaglandins, given intravenously, are also used to contract a baggy (hypotonic) uterus after delivery of the placenta. (See also the discussion of use of prostaglandins in therapeutic abortion on p. 316.)

MEDICAL PAIN RELIEF

In my discussion of the two major approaches to labor and birth, the active and the unhurried, I stated that the central focus of each was pain relief. The elements of the unhurried approach, which I described in some detail, are mainly directed toward this goal. Here I will discuss the role of drugs and of various ways of administering them.

Analgesics

Analgesics and anesthetics are medications used for pain relief. Analgesics reduce pain to make it tolerable, whereas anesthetics are intended to eliminate it completely. Analgesics in everyday use include aspirin, ibuprofen (Advil, Motrin), and acetaminophen (Tylenol). Moderately strong analgesics include codeine and oxycodone-aspirin (Percodan). The strongest analgesics include morphine, meperidine (Demerol), alphaprodine (Nisentil), nalbuphine (Nubain), and fentanyl.

The analgesics most commonly used in labor are meperidine, fentanyl, nalbuphine, and butorphanol. To counteract the nausea associated with them, these drugs are sometimes combined with the antihistamine promethazine. These analgesics are given by injection or intravenously; if given intravenously, the dose is controlled by the woman, within certain safety limits. In addition to relieving pain, analgesics produce some drowsiness and euphoria. Many women find that these drugs help them regain their strength during a long, difficult early labor.

Analgesics pass through the placenta to the fetus, where they can depress the centers in the brain that drive respiration, an effect of clinical importance only when, after birth, the baby must breathe on his or her own, not in utero when the work of respiration is being done by the woman. Analgesics can also sedate the fetus, resulting in drowsiness that can interfere with the baby's responsiveness and feeding during the first few hours after birth or even longer. Because of their depressant and sedative effects, these drugs are used mainly in the first stage of labor. Barring an unexpectedly rapid birth, as in an emergency cesarean section, their effect on an infant's respiration should be over long before delivery. If the effect is not over, and if the baby's respiration is depressed, assistance can be provided as needed with a breathing bag and oxygen. The drug naloxone hydrochloride (Narcan) can also be administered to the baby to reverse the respiratory-depressant effects of analgesics.

Anesthetics

Anesthetics are drugs designed to eliminate rather than simply relieve pain. Two broad classes are used: blocking drugs, which disrupt impulse transmission in nerves, and inhaled gases, which shut down pain transmission and perception in the entire nervous system, including the brain, and put the patient to sleep. Lidocaine (Xylocaine) is an example of the former, and nitrous oxide, the latter. Improvements in anesthetics over the past fifty years have been substantial and offer women almost complete pain control that is also safe.

Nerve Blocks

Nerve-block drugs are used in pregnancy to achieve local, peripheral-nerve, spinal, and epidural anesthesia. The names designate the site of action of the anesthetic: the peripheral nerves of the skin or vaginal surface (local anesthesia); the pudendal nerves, which supply the vagina and perineum (pudendal nerve block); the nerve roots within the spinal fluid (spinal anesthesia); or the nerve roots outside the spinal cord (epidural anesthesia). Each type will be discussed in turn, along with the recent practice of combining spinal and epidural anesthesias.

Local Anesthesia.   *Local anesthesia* is accomplished by injecting the blocking drug directly into the site to be numbed, blocking the end branches of the nerves within that site. In pregnancy, local anesthesia is used just before an episiotomy is done (see p. 208), before the repair of an episiotomy, or tear, and in numbing the skin through which the needle used in spinal or epidural anesthesia will be introduced.

Pudendal Nerve Block.   The two pudendal nerves are situated in the lower back corners of the vagina and are identified within the vagina by feeling (palpating), on the right and left sides, a specific prominence in one of the pelvic bones adjacent to which the nerves run. A successful *pudendal nerve block* will anesthetize much of the perineum and vagina and reduce the pain associated with vaginal stretching and tearing, whether spontaneous or by episiotomy, during birth. A very long needle is needed to reach these nerves, which are very deep in the vagina. To guide the needle to the sites, one at a time, the physician positions a fingertip on the bony landmark and slides the needle along the same finger to its destination. Pudendal block is infrequently used because epidural block accomplishes the same goals better and also eliminates labor pain.

Spinal Anesthesia.   In *spinal anesthesia,* the blocking agent is injected into the spinal canal through a needle that is inserted between the vertebrae of the lower back. The drug bathes the spinal nerves within the canal before they exit the cord. Both sensory and motor nerves are temporarily blocked, so that the woman's lower abdomen, pelvic area, and legs are numbed and cannot be voluntarily moved. The level of anesthesia (that is, how high on the abdomen the anesthesia reaches) is largely determined by how much drug is given and by the position the woman assumes immediately following the injection. For a vaginal delivery, the goal is to anesthetize only the perineum and legs. For a cesarean section, anesthesia should reach the lowest ribs. Spinal anesthesia is given only after full cervical dilatation. Thus it is of no help with pain during the first stage of labor.

Spinal anesthetic is administered while the woman is sitting or lying on her side. First, the skin is cleaned with an antiseptic solution. Then a sterile drape with a central hole is placed over the lower back. The anesthesiologist numbs the skin with a local anesthetic, infiltrating the solution down to the spinal column so that the channel between skin and spinal column is anesthetized. The woman is then asked to curl forward to open the spaces between the vertebrae. A thin, hollow needle containing a removable stylet is pushed through the numbed channel until it passes through the meninges into the spinal fluid just below the end of the spinal cord and nerve roots. The stylet is removed, and the location of the needle in the spinal canal is verified by the return of clear spinal fluid. A syringe containing the anesthetic solution is then attached to the needle, and the medication is introduced between uterine contractions. For a vaginal delivery, the woman is asked to sit up for forty-five seconds to allow the medication to settle to the bottom of the spinal canal. For a cesarean section, the woman lies first on one side, then on the other, to allow the anesthetic to travel upward in the canal to block the nerves that supply the entire abdomen. The level of anesthesia is controlled to some extent by tilting the operating table up or down as indicated. The anesthesiologist checks the level by checking the woman's response to the prick of a needle moved up or down the abdomen.

In vaginal delivery, spinal anesthesia interferes with the woman's ability to push. The higher the level of anesthetic, the more her capacity to push is impaired. In addition, spinal anesthesia requires that the woman lie on her back with her legs in stirrups during delivery, further interfering with pushing. As a result, forceps or vacuum extraction (p. 206) is more likely to be needed, as well as episiotomy (p. 208).

Spinal anesthesia carries several risks. The most common is a drop in the woman's blood pressure brought on by blockage of the sympathetic nerves that control the tone of the muscles within the walls of arteries. When the arteries dilate, the same volume of blood is contained in a larger volume of vessel, and thus the pressure of the blood falls. This drop in blood pressure is made worse if a woman lies flat on her back to deliver; in this position, the uterus rests on the large vein in the back of the abdomen (inferior vena cava), interfering with the return of blood to the heart and the pumping of blood from the heart. For this reason, the delivery table is tilted to the side. (See pp. 204–206 on position in labor.) The expected fall in blood pressure is also minimized by boosting blood volume with fluids given intravenously before beginning the procedure. If a drop in blood pressure occurs despite these measures, medication is given to contract the dilated muscles in the arteries. Because of the risk of low blood pressure, spinal anesthesia is not used when a woman's blood volume is already compromised, for example, when blood loss has occurred or when preeclampsia is present (see pp. 307–309).

An undesirable consequence of spinal anesthesia, much less common today than in the past, is headache. A spinal headache is caused by the leakage of spinal fluid through the puncture site into the space surrounding the spinal cord, the epidural space. The reduced volume of spinal fluid leads to shifting of the brain, with added stress on its pain-sensitive attachments to the inside of the skull. Spinal headache is minimized by using a very thin needle, which produces a very small hole and a very slow and small leak. When it occurs, bed rest and analgesics are helpful. If these measures fail, injection of a small amount of the woman's blood into the epidural space near the puncture site has proved effective in sealing it. The effects of spinal anesthesia on bladder function may necessitate the use of a catheter during the first twenty-four hours following delivery.

A dreaded but rare complication, which results from the inadvertent introduction of an excessive dose of anesthetic into the spinal canal, is blockade of all nerves below the neck, thereby producing paralysis of respiration and a precipitous fall in blood pressure. In this emergency, hypotension (low blood pressure) is treated by using the measures previously discussed and by elevating the legs to maximize the volume of blood returning to the heart. Respiration is assisted by measures ranging from bag breathing by the anesthesiologist to intubation of the airway and mechanical ventilation.

Spinal anesthesia is avoided in women who have had allergic reactions to local anesthetics, whose skin at the injection site is infected, or who have chronic low back pain, which could be aggravated by the spinal needle.

While spinal anesthesia is used primarily in emergency situations, the same technique using a narcotic drug as well as an anesthetic along with an epidural anesthetic is gaining in popularity and will be discussed below.

Epidural Anesthesia.   *Epidural anesthesia* eliminates pain in both labor and delivery. It is by far the most popular approach to medical pain relief, whether used alone or in combination with spinal anesthesia. In epidural anesthesia the nerve roots are numbed after their exit from the spinal fluid into the space in the spinal canal just below the lower pole of the meninges (which surround and contain the spinal fluid). This compartment is called the epidural space. Within it are the nerve roots that serve the parts of a woman's body involved in labor and delivery, including the uterus, cervix, vagina, and perineum. In the epidural space the sensory nerves that transmit external stimuli are less well insulated and more susceptible to blockade than are the nerves that stimulate muscle contraction. Thus, when nerve roots in the epidural space are blocked, pain and other sensations are eliminated. Some voluntary movement is preserved, but not enough to permit walking. An epidural is given only after labor is well established, during the active phase of the first stage. If given too early it can dampen or even stop uterine contractions. Even when given in the active phase, an epidural may temporarily slow labor. Epidurals definitely lengthen the second stage of labor because of reduced uterine forces pushing the fetus into the birth canal. Recent studies suggest that the fatigue of the laboring woman after receiving an epidural can be reduced if she waits for an hour before beginning to push in the second stage (unless the urge is there) without affecting the duration of labor or the well-being of the baby. This delay in pushing is sometimes referred to as laboring down or passive second stage.

The procedure for performing an epidural is similar to that used for a spinal. Once the needle enters the epidural space, a thin plastic catheter is passed into it. Often the woman will experience a twinge of pain in her back or leg as the catheter touches a nerve root. When the needle is withdrawn, the catheter is left in place and the anesthetic solution is injected into the space. The catheter external to the skin is taped to the back. A major advantage of epidural block, in contrast to spinal block, which is a one-shot deal, is that additional anesthetic solution can be given as needed. The anesthetic solution can be given as a continuous infusion or, more often in practice, as a top-off every ninety or so minutes. The advantage of the intermittent-dosing approach is that less total drug is used and fewer drug-related effects occur. Studies have shown that women can successfully self-administer the anesthetic solution as they need it by controlling the infusion pump.

Epidural anesthesia is not always completely effective even when administered by an experienced physician. In one study, 85 percent of women were free of pain, 12 percent had partial relief, and 3 percent experienced no relief at all. An epidural given to relieve labor pain, with the catheter pointing upward (toward the head) to direct the solution to the nerves supplying the uterus, may not effectively numb the perineum during the second stage. As with spinals, epidurals can also cause a decrease in blood pressure, which responds to the same measures used for hypotension in spinals.

A serious complication can result if the anesthetic solution is inadvertently injected through a vein into the woman's bloodstream. This risk is markedly reduced by gently pulling back the plunger of the syringe before injecting solution to check for blood and by using a small test dose to see if the woman experiences any systemic reactions.

A disadvantage of epidurals is that both mothers and babies are more likely to develop a fever. For the baby, fever raises the question of infection, which must then be evaluated with blood, urine, and sometimes spinal-fluid tests. There is no evidence that use of epidurals results in greater use of forceps or vacuum extraction. Whether the rate of cesarean sections is increased cannot be answered with the data available at this time.

Dual Spinal-Epidural Anesthesia.   A more recent and increasingly popular use of spinal and epidural anesthesia is to use them in combination in what is called a *dual spinal-epidural*, or *walking epidural*. In this approach a narcotic drug as well as an anesthetic is used for the spinal and a lower dose of anesthetic, sometimes also with a narcotic, is used for the epidural. The great advantage is that there is no loss of muscle control and the woman can be up and about and push effectively. It is a major advance in anesthesia for labor. Undesirable side effects of the narcotic are itching, retention of urine in the bladder, and nausea and vomiting. These effects can be reversed with the narcotic antagonist *naloxone*.

General Anesthesia

Although less commonly used in obstetrics today than blocking agents, general anesthesia with inhaled gas, the oldest of the anesthetic methods used in childbirth, still occupies an important place in labor and delivery. General anesthesia with chloroform was introduced by the

Scottish physician Sir James Simpson in 1847 and was popularized by Queen Victoria during the birth of her eighth child in 1853. The great advantage of general anesthesia is ease of administration and rapid on-set of action. Thus, in emergencies in which time is critical, usually when an urgent C-section is needed, it is the anesthesia of choice. Nitrous oxide, self-administered by the woman during a contraction, is a general anesthetic used in labor.

The disadvantage of general anesthesia used for birth, even with the improved gases available today (chloroform is no longer used), is that they pass directly to the fetus, anesthetizing it as well. This is usually not a problem during cesarean birth unless the fetus is already having problems with the oxygenation of its blood (see fetal distress, p. 154). Use of nitrous oxide during labor has no demonstrable effect on the fetus or baby. Of course, with general anesthesia for delivery the woman is not awake during birth. A more serious concern with general anesthesia for delivery is that the woman may vomit and aspirate stomach contents into her lungs, producing a chemical pneumonia. This problem is preventable with proper anesthetic technique. (See discussion of fluids and food on p. 194.)

Learning About Anesthesia

In some hospitals anesthesiologists meet with pregnant women and their partners to answer their questions about anesthesia and the role of the anesthesiologist. Some obstetricians routinely refer patients for these consultations, which may be regarded as part of childbirth education as they are equally informative to those who have definitely decided they want anesthesia and those who would use it only if needed. The topic of anesthesia is also covered in most childbirth-education classes. Couples should inform themselves about anesthesia prior to, rather than during, labor, when decisionmaking is more pressured.

POSITION DURING LABOR AND DELIVERY

In a traditional hospital birth, a woman lies on her back with her legs in stirrups. This supine, or *lithotomy*, position is often associated with episiotomy and the use of anesthesia and forceps. It was designed primarily to allow the physician easier access to the birth canal and perineum for the manipulations that often characterize this type of delivery. In fact, the supine position makes these interventions more likely, and it has come under criticism for several reasons.

First, when a woman lies flat on her back, the uterus rests on the large vein that runs adjacent to the spine. Compression of this vein results in a diminished return of blood to the heart and outflow from the heart to various organs, including the uterus and placenta. Thus, the fetus's access to oxygen is reduced and the margin of safety during contractions, when oxygen access is normally reduced, is narrowed. Fetal distress may result (see p. 154), particularly for fetuses already compromised. Moreover, the uterus, deprived of its normal circulation, is less able to contract effectively, potentially interfering with labor. Another problem is that bearing down during the second stage is more difficult for the woman and less effective when the woman is lying on her back than when she is vertical. Finally, Michel Odent, obstetrician at the famous birthing center at Pithiviers in France, claims that tearing of the perineum is reduced to a very low level when the woman gives birth in the upright position, and episiotomies are rarely needed.

The position for birth in preindustrial societies is almost always either standing (by holding or being held up) or squatting, in both cases taking full advantage of the force of gravity to push the baby out. X rays of the pelvis show that the outlet of the birth canal is increased by as much as 28 percent (almost a third) when a woman squats! An increase of this magnitude can make the difference between a vaginal and an operative delivery.

The upright position (standing, sitting, or squatting), is also an excellent one in which to labor, especially if it relieves pain. There has also been an impression among some birth attendants that walking can shorten labor. Research findings on this question have been conflicting. A small controlled study from the University of Southern California showed that walking was as effective as oxytocin in stimulating labor. A larger randomized control study done by Steven Bloom and colleagues at the University of Texas in Dallas, reported in 1998, showed no effect of walking on the duration of labor.

The upright position also appears to be as advantageous in delivering the placenta as it is in delivering the baby. Although there have been no controlled studies, clinical observations suggest an advantage in expelling the placenta while squatting.

The results of a randomized control study of birth in the squatting position were reported in the July 8, 1989, issue of the *Lancet*. With squatting there were fewer forceps deliveries (9 percent versus 16 percent) and shorter second stages of labor (thirty-one versus forty-five minutes); there were fewer perineal tears, but more labial tears. In addition, 82 percent of the women who squatted in birth also maintained the upright position for most of the second stage. The women reported great satisfaction with being vertical during the latter part of labor and during delivery. Squatting also appears to offer advantages when the baby's head is posterior and when a small rim of cervix (anterior lip) remains as an obstacle to further progress.

Another position that is more effective than lying on the back is sitting up, at least at a forty-five-degree angle, drawing the legs up if desired to provide more effective pushing and to enlarge the dimensions of the birth canal. (The newer birthing chairs, returning to designs used for centuries and then abandoned, help women achieve this position.) If the woman is seated in bed, she either brings her buttocks to the edge of the bed or elevates her buttocks with a firm object (such as an inverted bedpan covered with a soft pad) in order to provide room for the emerging baby.

Another effective position for labor and delivery, but one that has not yet been subjected to critical evaluation, is lying on the side with the upper leg held up by an assistant and the back and buttocks near the edge of the bed. The attendant stands behind the buttocks with one hand supporting the perineum and the other arched over the uplifted leg to control the baby's head. This position also helps the woman to see her baby emerging. A closely related position is kneeling on one knee with the other leg bent at the knee and the foot flat on the bed or mat.

FORCEPS AND VACUUM EXTRACTOR

Forceps and the vacuum extractor are tools used to assist in vaginal births by pulling the baby through the birth canal. Forceps are metal instruments, which look like tongs, with blades at one end that fit around the baby's head and handles at the other that lock together. The vacuum extractor is a suction cup (usually plastic) attached to a hollow handle and air pump. The cup is applied to the baby's head during a contraction of the uterus, and a vacuum is created within the cup by the air pump to seal it to the head. The suction is released when the contraction is over.

In the United States, vacuum extraction has become the favored of these two techniques among most birth attendants. Both methods are used when progress through the birth canal has stopped or when birth must be accomplished quickly because the baby is in difficulty. One or the other technique is used in 10 to 15 percent of vaginal deliveries.

Several complications for the baby can result. A 1999 study from the University of California at Davis looked at all births in the state that occurred between 1993 and 1994 among women having their first baby. The study considered only babies who weighed between 2,500 and 4,000 grams at birth. Bleeding between the scalp and skull (*cephalohematoma*, see p. 241) was increased from 2 percent for spontaneous vaginal births to 6 percent when forceps or a vacuum extractor was used. Five percent of babies with cephalohematoma also had thin (hairline) fractures of the underlying skull. In fewer than 1 in 800 vacuum-extractor- and 1 in 600 forceps-assisted births, bleeding of some type occurred within the skull (intracranial bleeding). In contrast, such bleeding was found in fewer than 1 in 900 babies born by cesarean section performed after labor had begun and in fewer than 1 in 2,500 babies born by unassisted vaginal delivery or cesarean section performed before the onset of labor. The highest rates of intracranial bleeding were found when cesarean section was performed after a failed attempt at assisted vaginal birth, 1 in 333, and when both forceps and a vacuum extractor were used, 1 in 277. Although we do not know the long-range significance of intracranial bleeding, it seems prudent to avoid it. What we can conclude from these statistics is that when the likelihood of a successful assisted vaginal delivery appears low (for which we need better predictors), it should probably not be attempted, nor should forceps or a vacuum extractor be used in sequence after one of them has failed.

Regarding long-term outcomes, a 1991 report from Israel of 52,282 infants born in Jerusalem between 1964 and 1972 is reassuring about the safety of both forceps and vacuum extraction. In this study, reported in the journal *Lancet*, there was no evidence of medical or mental impairment at age seventeen years among those who had been delivered by either of these methods. How to relate the two studies cited here is not clear, but certainly the data presented do not argue against the appropriate use of either forceps or a vacuum extractor.

A rare complication of vaginal birth assisted by forceps or a vacuum extractor is damage to the nerves that control the muscles of the arm, which can result in a permanent palsy. A complication from forceps is a temporary weakness of the face, usually in one side only, caused by pressure of the blade just below the ear on the nerve that controls the facial muscles.

For the woman, forceps use in contrast with use of a vacuum extractor, according to a study reported in 1998 by Abdul H. Sultan and his colleagues in London, is more likely to increase the hidden tears and functional injury to the rectal sphincter muscle (affecting bowel control) that commonly occur with vaginal birth.

EPISIOTOMY

An episiotomy is an incision or surgical cut made with (sterile) scissors or a scalpel in the perineum, the area between the lower junction of the labia and the anus. The incision may be made in the midline (median) (the more common practice in the United States) or angled to the side (mediolateral) (see Figure 4.11). Its purpose is to widen the opening of the vagina to ease passage of the baby's head. An episiotomy typically is repaired (sewn up) following delivery of the placenta, using absorbable sutures that dissolve and so do not require later removal. Polyglycolate sutures (Dexon or Vicryl) have been shown to be associated with less pain. If a spinal or epidural anesthetic has not been administered, a local anesthetic is injected to ease the pain of an episiotomy and its repair.

The traditional medical view of episiotomy, which once informed its nearly routine use, was expressed in a past edition of the well-known textbook *Williams Obstetrics* as follows:

> It substitutes a straight, neat surgical incision for the ragged laceration that otherwise frequently results. It is easier to repair and heals better than a tear. It spares the fetal head the necessity of serving as a battering ram against perineal obstruction. If prolonged, the pounding of the fetal head against the perineum may cause intracranial injury. Episiotomy shortens the second stage of labor.

This view has to be understood in the context of the labor and delivery practices of the times. During delivery, most women lay flat on their

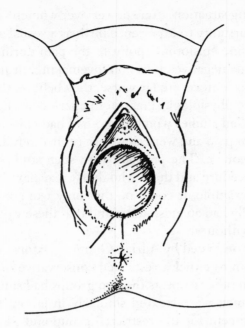

FIGURE 4.11   Episiotomy: midline or angled to the side

backs with their legs in stirrups. In this position it is difficult to push the
baby out. Anesthesia further compromised women's capacity to bear
down. Babies often needed assistance in navigating the birth canal and
often had to be pulled out with forceps. At the very least, it seemed, the
barrier to birth presented by the perineum had to be removed; hence
the policy of routine episiotomy.

Episiotomy is alleged to prevent vaginal and pelvic relaxation following birth and to prevent urinary (stress) incontinence, but there is no
evidence to support these claims. Episiotomy is valuable in removing a
barrier to progress of labor when the perineum is the barrier, especially
when the baby is in distress and must be delivered quickly.

The topic of episiotomy has aroused strong feelings. In the past especially, the policy of many obstetricians was *always* to do an episiotomy.
At the opposite extreme, Sheila Kitzinger, a well-known English midwife and childbirth educator, once called the procedure "ritual genital
mutilation," in which males (as most physicians at the time were men—

a rapidly changing situation) exert power over women's bodies and deny women the opportunity to experience birth as a sexual act.

Critics of routine episiotomy point to the pain during healing of the episiotomy and its negative effects on lovemaking, urination, and defecation. These discomforts are far worse, they believe, than the pain of a natural and more physiological tear in the perineum. Indeed, in several early noncontrolled studies women who had had episiotomies reported more postpartum pain and were slower to return to full activity, including sexual intercourse. The problem with such studies is that women who had the procedure and those who didn't may have been different to start with. For example, it could be that only women who were most likely to tear badly had an episiotomy and that these women would have been worse off without it.

In one study, conducted by Adrian Grant at Oxford, women were allocated at random to either a restricted conservative or a liberal use of the procedure; in other respects the two groups had similar characteristics and the women were treated similarly in labor. The episiotomy rates were 10 percent for the restricted group and 51 percent for the liberal group. Interestingly, there were no differences between the groups with respect to the amount of pain reported after birth, the time it took for the perineum to become pain free, or problems controlling urination. The only other difference in outcomes was that women in the restricted group were more likely to have resumed sexual intercourse within a month after delivery (presumably because it was less uncomfortable for them). Despite the differences in episiotomy rates, there was little difference in the frequency with which suturing of the perineum was required. The women who did not receive an episiotomy were more likely to tear on their own, so that not having an episiotomy did not spare women from tearing and being sutured.

In 1992, a randomized control study from Canada under the direction of Michael Klein, professor of Family Medicine at McGill University, persuasively showed that women who had episiotomies had worse outcomes in all respects than did those who did not have episiotomies: more pain, poorer perineal tone, and a slower return to sexual function. Vaginal tears sustained during delivery healed better than did episiotomies. This study provided convincing evidence that there is no justification for routinely doing episiotomies. The only valid reasons for doing an episiotomy are distress in the fetus that necessitates a quick delivery or an inability of the woman to overcome the resistance of the perineum to delivery, which is an unusual circumstance.

More recently, a report in 2000 from the Brigham and Women's Hospital in Boston compared women who had a midline episiotomy, women whose perineum spontaneously tore during delivery, and women who had neither tearing nor episiotomy. In this study, the presence of flatus incontinence (inability to control the expulsion of intestinal gas) and stool incontinence was determined at three and six months after delivery. The women who had had episiotomies fared worse than did the women in the other two groups, whose outcomes were similar, except at six months, when there was not significant difference in fecal incontinence among the groups. The findings in all these studies should allow us to take a more relaxed view of perineal tearing during delivery.

A number of measures taken during delivery appear to minimize perineal tearing. (Few of these have been subjected to controlled clinical studies.) What follows is based on the experience of many practitioners.

1. As long as the woman and the fetus are doing well, birth should be gradual and unhurried, allowing the perineum to stretch slowly. Women should push only if pushing increases their comfort.
2. To prevent undue stretching, the woman can respond selectively to her urge to push, according to the status of her perineum. Attendants can give verbal feedback and show her the effects of her pushing with a mirror. If pushing causes excessive stretching, the woman can stop pushing and allow her uterus to do the work alone. A gentle push between contractions can then ease the baby's head out. (For more on pushing, see p. 95 on exercise during pregnancy.)
3. Maintenance of flexion of the baby's head (chin to chest) results in the smallest part of the head pushing through the vulva. Flexion is supported by downward pressure on the top (vertex) of the head by the attendant's hand during contractions.
4. Supporting the perineum by maintaining constant counter-pressure with the hand applied to the perineum as it gradually stretches is thought to minimize tearing.
5. Position during delivery may also be important. There is accumulating evidence that the upright position—standing or

squatting—minimizes tearing, another good argument for avoiding lying flat on the back during delivery.

6. Water birth (see p. 193) may contribute to less tearing of the perineum and to decreasing the need for an episiotomy.

7. Preparation of the perineum through Kegel exercises, which have a toning effect on the muscles and fascia, is believed to make these muscles more stretchable and less likely to tear. This notion is analogous to the idea of preventing muscle strain in joggers and other athletes by stretching the muscles before running or playing a sport. (See pp. 95–112 on prenatal exercise and pp. 53–59 on the physical examination.)

A recent and important insight pertaining to episiotomies and vaginal births in general has been provided by Abdul H. Sultan and his colleagues in London. These researchers reported in 1997 that *visible* vaginal damage (tearing) to the anal sphincter, the set of muscles that controls the bowels, occurred in 3 percent of first deliveries and in no subsequent deliveries. Yet testing revealed that in 35 percent of first deliveries and 44 percent of subsequent deliveries women sustained measurable sphincter damage. According to this study, an episiotomy, as well as the use of forceps, added to hidden sphincter damage, above that caused by vaginal birth alone. Although problems (symptoms) from such injury may not show up until much later in life (along with problems with bladder control), findings such as these enliven the debate on the virtues of elective cesarean birth (see p. 220) as well as the details of the process of vaginal delivery and the rehabilitation of the perineal muscles after birth.

DELIVERY OF THE PLACENTA

The third stage of labor begins with the birth of the baby and ends with the birth of the placenta. To facilitate separation and delivery of the placenta and minimize bleeding (*the* major concern following birth of the baby), an effective active-management approach has been developed. This approach includes giving oxytocin to contract the uterus (see p. 195), cutting the umbilical cord just after the birth of the baby, and gently pulling on the cord to help the placenta separate. (The effectiveness of cord traction has not been critically studied.) Sometimes oxytocin is given on the appearance (birth) of the baby's shoulder. There is some evidence that the squatting position can aid in the expulsion of the placenta. After birth of the placenta, keeping the uterus contracted to prevent bleeding is important. If oxytocin and gently massaging the uterus are insufficient, ergot drugs (see 195) can be given by injection and prostaglandins (see 197) can be given intravenously. If even these measures fail, the uterus can be compressed between the hands of the attendant, one in the vagina pushing up, and the other on the abdomen pulling down.

If the placenta is not delivered within a half hour of birth, or if there is brisk bleeding (more than the normal sixteen ounces of blood lost at delivery), it must be removed by hand to prevent significant blood loss. (In the past, postpartum hemorrhage was a major cause of the death of mothers.) Manual removal is uncomfortable to the mother and may require anesthesia. Once removed, the placenta is carefully inspected. In the unlikely event that a large piece is missing, the uterus must be explored manually under anesthesia to identify and permit removal of the fragment left behind. In one of several thousand births (the exact incidence is not known) the placenta or a section of it grows into the wall of the uterus, making separation either difficult or impossible, depending on the depth of penetration. This situation is called *placenta accreta*. Unless the placenta can be removed manually, the only treatment is removal of the uterus (hysterectomy).

CESAREAN BIRTH

Cesarean section (C-section) is the surgical procedure used to deliver a baby through an abdominal and uterine incision. Legend has it that the operation is named after the first Roman emperor, Julius Caesar, who supposedly was born this way, although his mother did not survive. Documentation reveals that C-sections were attempted as early as the seventeenth century, but the procedure was not performed in large numbers until the end of the nineteenth century, and even then the maternal death rate was high. Consistent success, that is, with both baby and mother surviving, did not occur until well into the twentieth century. By the time of World War II, cesarean section had proved to offer dramatic benefits in dealing with such life-threatening problems as placenta previa, placental abruption, eclampsia, and severe disproportion (all discussed in Chapter 7). During the 1960s and 1970s doctors increasingly recognized that cesarean section could benefit maternal and infant health even when a life was not immediately at stake. For example, babies delivered by cesarean section were found to do much better in terms of neurological problems (that is, there were fewer cases of cerebral palsy, learning problems, and so on) than babies delivered by forceps while still high in the birth canal (so-called *midforceps* delivery). With certain kinds of breech presentations babies delivered by C-section were also found to do better than babies delivered vaginally.

Although there is no question that cesarean section has been enormously beneficial, some doctors, midwives, and childbirth educators believe that too many of these operations are being performed. Figures for C-sections hover at one-fifth of all births and close to 1 million deliveries per year, making C-sections the most frequently performed major surgical operations. A critical reappraisal of the reasons for cesarean delivery has already led to some leveling off in the percentage of deliveries by surgery. However, we are still far from achieving the goal, set by many involved professional organizations but not agreed to by all, of a U.S. national C-section rate of 15 percent by the year 2000.

The childbirth-education movement has responded to the increased frequency of cesarean sections with a constructive critique. For example, educators have urged that the term *cesarean birth*, rather than *cesarean section*, be used to emphasize that a birth, not merely an operation, is occurring. Fathers are welcomed in the operating room, and early parent-infant interaction is encouraged despite the surrounding distractions. Discussion of cesarean birth is now included in prenatal classes, and organizations have been formed to meet the needs of women who have undergone or will undergo cesarean sections and of those who contemplate vaginal birth after a cesarean (VBAC). (See Appendix for these resources.)

A Typical Cesarean Birth

In most hospitals, cesarean section is performed under spinal, epidural, or dual spinal-epidural anesthesia (see pp. 198–203). General anesthesia (see p. 203) is reserved for emergencies, when there is no time for starting spinals or epidurals, or when they have not worked. Before beginning the operation, the lower abdomen is shaved from just below the navel to the pubic bone. A catheter is inserted in the bladder and left in place until after the operation. The skin is vigorously scrubbed with surgical soap, and sterile drapes or an adherent plastic covering is placed over the abdomen to leave only the lower belly uncovered. The operating table is tilted about fifteen degrees to the side to roll the uterus off the great vein in the abdomen, the inferior vena cava, so that the return of blood to the woman's heart and the flow of blood to the placenta will not be compromised. The obstetricians and surgical nurse wear gowns, caps, masks, and gloves; all other people present, including the husband or partner, labor coach, or doula, wear surgical scrub suits, masks, and caps in the operating room. Obstetricians reserve the right to ask nonprofessional participants to leave the room during an emergency. Policies on participation by husbands or partners may vary from one hospital to another. Women are advised to clarify this issue ahead of time.

A vertical screen is usually placed above the woman's upper chest so that she cannot see the surgeons. However, she is able to hear them and can carry on a conversation with those around her. Ideally, she should feel no pain, but if she does, she should report it so that measures to stop it can be taken. She may feel some tugging and pressure, especially during the delivery of the baby. Once the amniotic sac is opened, she will hear the noise of the suction machine drawing the amniotic fluid from the uterus into a collecting bottle. Following the removal of the amniotic fluid, the obstetrician reaches into the uterus to take hold of the baby's head, which is then worked through the incision. The assistant presses the top of the uterus to help push the head out. In a breech delivery the legs are delivered first.

After the head is born, the obstetrician clears the amniotic fluid from the baby's nose and mouth with a bulb syringe. If meconium (the baby's stools) has been passed into the amniotic fluid, this suctioning is more intense and is done with a plastic catheter. As the rest of the baby is delivered, the obstetrician will usually ask the anesthesiologist to inject a dose of oxytocin (see p. 195) into the mother's intravenous infusion to cause the uterus to contract. It is also common practice to give the mother a single dose of intravenous antibiotics to prevent uterine infection; so that the antibiotics do not pass to the baby, they are given to the mother after the umbilical cord is clamped. The cord is cut, and the baby is handed to the nurse or pediatrician, who carries the newborn to a nearby warming table. The baby may be further suctioned and examined. When clearly doing well on his or her own, the baby is wrapped, capped, and handed to the father or other designated person.

Meanwhile, the surgeons remove the placenta and sew up the incisions in the uterus and the abdominal wall. From beginning to end the surgery usually takes between thirty and forty-five minutes. Afterward, the mother is wheeled to the recovery room. The baby can usually remain with the parents, though there may be a brief period during which he or she is taken to the nursery for weighing, measuring, and eye treatment. Breast-feeding can begin right away.

During the postoperative period medications are administered to the mother to deal with the pain of the incision. Blood pressure, pulse, urine flow, amount of bleeding, and the tone of the uterus are checked regularly.

By the day after surgery, many women can drink fluids, and the intravenous infusion can be slowed and pulled out after forty-eight hours. The bladder catheter is removed after twelve hours. On the second and third days, gas pains from ineffective bowel action are common, and a rectal suppository or enema can be helpful. Women can walk with assistance on the day after surgery. Early walking promotes quick recovery and prevents the formation of blood clots (thrombi) in the veins of the legs (see Venous Thromboembolism and Phlebitis, p. 321). By the fourth day skin sutures or clips can be removed. On the fifth, or even the fourth, day, mother and baby can go home.

Risks of Cesarean Section

Even though the C-section has become a remarkably safe operation and death of the mother exceedingly rare, it is, nonetheless, major surgery and has risks. These risks include phlebitis, uterine infection, urinary tract infection, and the complications of anesthesia. A C-section carries all the economic costs of major surgery and also causes a delay of at least one week before a woman can return to her normal activities.

Improvements in the operation continue to be made. Some of the now-standard techniques mentioned are of recent origin, including tilting of the operating table to the side; use of intravenous antibiotics at the end of the surgery; early walking to prevent phlebitis; and the favored use of epidural anesthesia, alone or in combination with spinal anesthesia.

When Are Cesareans Necessary?

The cesarean birthrate in the United States increased from 5.5 percent of all births in 1970 to 15.2 percent in 1980. The rate was up to 24.7 percent in 1988, dropped to 23.5 percent in 1990, and dropped to 21 percent in 1998. The rates vary considerably from one hospital to another for reasons not well understood. Certain hospitals clearly have a higher rate in part because the women they serve are at higher risk for complications of labor and delivery. However, even when dealing with similar populations of women without risk factors for complications and using a similar, but not identical, approach to care in labor and delivery, the rate can vary, from 5 to 6 percent in the Royal Maternity Hospital in Dublin to 19 percent in a U.S. teaching hospital (see Research on the Active Approach, p. 188).

A 1980 National Institutes of Health (NIH) report that looked at ways to reduce the rate of cesarean sections concluded that the diagnostic categories that had the largest effect on the increase in the rate between 1970 and 1978 were repeat cesarean, breech presentation, dystocia, and fetal distress. A category not considered at that time, still small in numbers but of growing interest, is *elective cesarean birth*.

Repeat cesarean section has been identified as the category most amenable to correction. One obvious way to reduce this category is to reduce the others; without an initial section there can be no repeat. Until twenty years ago, once one section had been done the die was cast for all births that followed. Doctors applied the dictum (first pronounced in 1916), "Once a section, always a section," because they feared that the scarred uterus would rupture during a subsequent labor. This risk is real with the classical vertical (up-and-down) uterine incision, which involves the body, or middle portion, of the uterus rather than its lower segment. The chances of tearing the scar are far less, however, with the transverse (side-to-side), lower-uterine incision now in wide use. This incision cuts through the part of the uterus that is less muscular and contains fewer blood vessels. Thus, in a subsequent labor, if a tear should occur, bleeding, which can threaten the lives of both the woman and the fetus, is less likely. Although obstetricians now make every effort to use only this transverse, lower-uterine incision, it is not always possible to do so.

The current recommendation is to forgo subsequent vaginal birth if a previous vertical incision was made into the body of the uterus or into the lower uterine segment (the risk of rupture is 1 to 3 percent). When there is a vertical, lower-uterine-segment scar, there is a good chance that the incision actually extended into the upper uterine segment, with increased risk for tearing during subsequent labors. If there is a J-shaped incision (as opposed to a curved-line incision) as a result of tearing or deliberate cutting while making the transverse lower-segment incision, repeat cesarean section is also recommended.

Since the 1980s, the "once a section, always a section" rule has been challenged and overturned. Now well over half of women (between 60 and 80 percent) who have had C-sections are successful in delivering vaginally. But just how safe is labor for women who meet the accepted criteria of a previous transverse uterine incision and a fetus weighing less than 4,500 grams (9 pounds, 14 ounces) as determined by ultrasound? Performing research to address this question has been difficult. In the most recent of several well-conducted studies done in the 1990s, Michael McMahon and his associates at the University of North Carolina compared the outcomes in 3,249 women who elected labor with 2,889 who chose a repeat C-section. There were no maternal deaths in either group and no overall difference in complications (morbidity) in the two groups. However, major complications (such as the need for a hysterectomy; rupture of the uterus; or injury from the surgery), although uncommon in both groups, were *twice as common* (1 percent) for the women attempting labor and vaginal birth who eventually required C-sections. (When uterine rupture occurs, the risk of serious complications for mothers and babies is less than 1 percent in hospitals that are equipped to deal with such emergencies.) Another finding of the North Carolina study was that women who were more likely to succeed in delivering vaginally were under age thirty-five, had babies weighing less than 8.8 pounds, and gave birth in a major medical center.

Just as formerly doctors almost automatically recommended repeat C-sections, now they may tend automatically to promote VBAC rather than leave the choice to the woman and her partner after informing them of the advantages and risks of both approaches (see The ABCs of Decisionmaking, p. 1). The sometimes subtle and often not so subtle temptation to push VBACs is increased by managed-care arrangements for health care, because vaginal deliveries are considerably less expensive. Sometimes lost in the debate over whether to encourage VBACs is a more focused consideration of how to *prevent the initial C-section*, the event that creates the need to consider VBACs at all.

In looking at the case of breech presentations, most of which are delivered by C-section, the NIH report recommended vaginal delivery as a safe choice for full-term breech babies under the following circumstances:

The expected weight of the baby is less than eight pounds

The woman has a normal pelvis

The baby is in a frank breech, that is, with legs extended and head flexed

The doctor and his or her assistants are experienced in vaginal breech delivery

As a result of this recommendation, some doctors have been more willing to consider vaginal breech births, but for reasons discussed elsewhere (see Breech Presentation, p. 277), the majority of physicians still favor delivery by cesarean section.

Dystocia, or failure to progress in labor, was also identified by the NIH report as an explanation for much of the increase in the rate of cesarean births in the United States. It seems possible to reduce the number of cesarean sections done for this reason. For example, in 1988, 7.6 percent of all births in the United States were cesarean births because of dystocia, whereas at the National Maternity Hospital in Dublin at about the same time, only 0.7 percent of all births required cesarean sections for this reason. The major distinguishing features of the approach in Dublin were the prompt use of oxytocin if labor failed to progress at a defined rate and one-on-one attendance in labor by a midwife. Aspects of the Dublin approach are now being used in the United States (see Research on the Active Approach [to labor], p. 188).

In considering *fetal distress* as a reason for cesarean birth, the NIH report recommended further studies to improve the accuracy of the diagnosis of fetal distress, the development of new techniques for making the diagnosis, and improved nonsurgical ways of dealing with this problem. In particular, more widespread use of fetal blood testing was recommended. These topics on assessing fetal well-being are further discussed beginning on page 158.

Elective cesarean birth was not considered by the NIH report because it has emerged only recently, and rather unexpectedly, as a consideration. The reasons women give for choosing a C-section over a vaginal delivery include simply not wanting to go through the rigors of labor, given an increasingly safe alternative; not wanting to have their vaginas sore and stretched; and not wanting to deal with what for them and their partners may be less than optimal sexual functioning. Many older women who have problems controlling their bladders and bowels have had repeated vaginal births. Now there is evidence from research studies that in measurable ways, vaginal birth, particularly when tearing or an episiotomy (see p. 208) has occurred or forceps (see p. 206) have been used, is indeed likely to damage the muscles that control the rectal sphincter, both in the short and in the long run. What is not yet known is how these findings relate to such factors as how labor was conducted—for example, using the active or the unhurried approach—the size of the baby, and the use of prenatal and postpartum perineal exercise. Clearly, more attention must be paid to these quality-of-life issues as they relate to pregnancy, childbirth, and women's overall health.

CHAPTER 5

After the Birth:
Care of the Parents

As women now bring their babies home from the hospital or birthing center soon after delivery, and as the number of women having their babies at home remains steady, parents need to depend more on themselves and less on professionals for dealing with common postpartum concerns.

CARING FOR THE BODY

Immediately after giving birth the mother should urinate frequently. An empty bladder will help keep the uterus contracted. To relieve stinging, a woman can dilute her urine by using a squeeze bottle to spray warm water over the perineum during urination, or she can urinate while in the shower with water running over her body. In contrast to stinging localized to the labia, a urinary tract infection is signified by burning on urination in which the discomfort is inside the bladder rather than on the sore perineum and possibly by fever and flank pain. (See Frequency of Urination and Urinary Tract Infection, pp. 72–73.)

The woman may not have a bowel movement for the first several days after giving birth. There is no need to strain, for it is not necessary to defecate immediately, and straining may be harmful. Prune juice, increased fiber, and increased fluid intake can soften or stimulate stools. Hemorrhoids, which may have developed during pregnancy, usually improve on their own after delivery.

The uterus should be checked every fifteen to thirty minutes for the first few hours and hourly for the rest of the day after delivery. If it is not hard, like a softball (or coconut), it needs to be gently massaged until it firms up. If massaging does not work, the midwife or doctor should be informed. Nursing (through the release of oxytocin) also helps, as it results in uterine contractions, sometimes called afterpains. Through human evolution the feeding of the infant has become linked to survival by maintaining contraction of the uterus and thus preventing postpartum bleeding. The uterus should be monitored until it is too low in the abdomen to feel, about the tenth day after delivery. The vaginal flow (lochia) should not be greater than a heavy menstrual period. It should not be green or have a foul smell. By the tenth day the flow has usually become a light pink to brown discharge. Sanitary pads, rather than tampons, should be used for the first two weeks, since tampons may introduce germs into the vagina and the uterus.

The woman may shower when she feels steady on her feet. Tub baths have traditionally been discouraged for two weeks, in the interest of preventing infection from bacteria washed into the uterus. The validity of this precept has not been critically studied. Perineal pain may respond to hot sitz baths (one and one-half inches of water) several times a day. A strong brew of the herb comfrey (available in health-food stores) added to the water is alleged by many midwives to promote healing, but this has not been critically studied.

Ice applied to the perineum during the first twenty-four hours will help reduce labial swelling. If the woman is at home, crushed ice can be packed in a rubber glove tied at the wrist and wrapped in sterile gauze. A sterile cotton ball soaked in refrigerated witch hazel can be placed under a perineal pad over sore regions—rectum, perineum, and labia. Local anesthetics—creams, sprays, or lotions—have been proved to provide pain relief. Foam-rubber rings for sitting are popular. Acetaminophen (Tylenol) and ibuprofen (Motrin, Advil) are safe and effective analgesics. The exercises described in Chapter 2 (pp. 103–106) can be gradually reintroduced (or begun for the first time) as the mother's energy increases and soreness decreases.

CARING FOR THE EMOTIONS

Although every experience is unique, all new parents pass through several developmental stages.

In the first stage, which may be called *taking-in*, mothers think and talk about the delivery a great deal and in considerable detail. As they take stock, they work on resolving any mixed feelings. In this stage a mother can feel focused on herself and inwardly directed and may even welcome being mothered herself.

In the second stage, *taking hold*, a mother becomes energized to take charge of herself and her new baby. She feels less dependent on her family and wants to move quickly into asserting her new role. Pitfalls of this stage of rising expectations and mobilized energy are fatigue and anxiety about one's competence as a mother.

Last, there is a *letting-go*, or settling-in, stage, in which the transition represented by the birth experience is resolved and put away, the baby's separateness is realized and enjoyed, and the parental role is fully incorporated into the parent's identity.

Women often report feelings of grieving after a birth. They discover that the sense of loss they experience is the loss of being pregnant. The unique feeling of fullness within, the self-conscious pride, and the attention of others can all be sorely missed once the baby arrives and steals the show. Mothers sometimes feel like a cross between an anonymous cow that dutifully supplies milk and an underappreciated maid whose job is to clean up messes, while the baby is the focus of everyone's loving attention. To soften this letdown, families can provide a little extra loving and mothering of the mother for a month or so. The result will be a mother who has plenty of love to give because she is receiving much love and who is strong and more confident because she feels valued and special. During this time, when a father is called on to provide a lot of extra attention and do extra work, he, too, deserves extra love.

Mothers often find it hard to imagine a life separate from mothering. One postpartum mother described a feeling of "fluffiness in the head." It is as if they have forgotten how to do anything except care for the baby. Especially troublesome is the inability to find or remember a word or carry on a coherent conversation. This state of mind is probably related to a combination of factors, including hormonal effects, lack of sleep, and intense emotional involvement with the baby. Among the many reactions it can elicit from others in the family are amusement and annoyance. The "fluffiness" soon passes.

The very common swings (lability) in mood, from elation (euphoria) to irritability (dysphoria) that new mothers experience are usually referred to as *postpartum blues* or *maternity blues.* These mood swings are thought to result from a rapid decline in the pregnancy hormones, which have direct and indirect effects on the central nervous system. There is no specific treatment for these temporary mood changes, which must be distinguished from depression (see p. 287).

SEXUALITY

Genital sex usually is temporarily suspended late in pregnancy and early after the birth. As couples well know, however, genital sex is only one expression of intimacy. This is the time for other forms of intimacy—talking, cuddling, holding, caressing, grooming, massage, mutual masturbation, and showering together. Having jointly created a child will forever alter their feelings about each other.

Whether prevention of infection of the uterus should be a concern with intercourse in the weeks after birth isn't clear. Although the American College of Obstetricians and Gynecologists recommends waiting for four weeks, there is no evidence to support this precaution. Simply doing what feels comfortable (what most couples do anyway) appears not to have any dire consequences.

If on the resumption of intercourse the vagina is dry or has tender spots, a water-soluble lubricant, such as K-Y jelly, will help relieve irritation. Adjustments in position will reduce pressure on sore areas. Milk ejection may occur spontaneously with arousal and seem bizarre or humorous to both partners.

Although breast-feeding suppresses a mother's ovulation, it is *not* a foolproof form of contraception. Since ovulation occurs *before* the return of menstrual periods, menstruation is not a reliable guide to resumed fertility. The combination of a condom and foam or jelly is a very effective contraceptive that can be used indefinitely or until other arrangements for birth control are made.

Use of oral contraceptives containing both estrogen and progesterone (combined pills) is generally not recommended during the first several months of nursing. Such contraceptives have been shown to decrease both the volume and the protein content of breast milk in some women. If combined pills are used, nursing should first be well established. In contrast, progestin-only pills (minipills) do not substantially affect breast milk. The minipill and nursing, with its own contraceptive effect, make a very effective *combination* in preventing pregnancy. Minipills can be started right after the baby's birth.

FAMILY CRISES

Interactions of physical and psychological factors can precipitate genuine family crises in the days and weeks following a baby's birth. Examples of tough situations are a sluggish baby who won't nurse, whose mother has sore nipples and painfully engorged breasts and is exhausted; an inconsolable baby, with well-meaning, but intrusive and undermining, grandparents who are interacting with parents who feel frazzled and incompetent; and the superwoman who has older children and, thinking she can do it all, refuses to stop waiting on everyone else long enough to care for herself. In such circumstances, the mother is a prime candidate for exhaustion and for having problems with the baby. (See Depression, p. 287.)

Situations such as these, which in the extreme can be nightmarish, call for active involvement by the doctor, midwife, friends, and others in the family's support network. Phone contact with the doctor or midwife is helpful, for he or she can assess the family's needs, provide support, and offer concrete suggestions. An exhausted mother should be encouraged to get into bed and take her baby with her. She needs to focus on herself and the baby and put everything else on hold. Relatives, friends, and members of a couple's prenatal class (the extended family) can be mobilized to bring cooked food, do laundry and shopping, and care for other children while the parents focus on themselves and the baby.

I vividly remember one mother who became so anxious about adequately feeding her baby that her milk dwindled and her baby became dehydrated, almost to the point of needing hospitalization. A team of nursing mothers, all patients in our practice, was quickly recruited to supplement this woman's depleted milk supply and to allow her to rest and successfully recoup her strength and confidence.

For women whose high-level commitment to neatness is a barrier to relaxation, the postpartum period offers an opportunity to learn that people can take priority over things. A family besieged by well-wishers should consider limited, brief visiting hours and turning off the phone during periods of rest. A voice-mail announcement or personal web site can be used to keep friends and relatives posted. Public-health and Visiting Nurse Association nurses, supervised home-health aides, and commercial homemakers can also provide support. Women can ask the physician or the hospital or birthing center about such resources.

Other support groups for the postpartum period include independent counseling services and childbirth-preparation organizations, such as the local affiliate of ICEA and La Leche League. Some doulas specialize in postpartum care. Chat lines on the Internet are also playing an increasingly important role. Help is usually available if one only asks for it. (See Appendix for a list of resources.)

This chapter is adapted in part by the author from a nonpublished essay, "Postpartum Care," by Peggy Spindel, R.N.

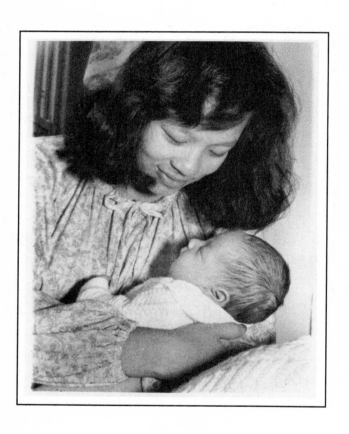

CHAPTER 6

After the Birth: Care of the Baby

The Apgar Score

Immediately after birth the health and well-being of every newborn is judged according to a test named for Virginia Apgar, an American anesthetist who worked at Columbia Presbyterian Hospital in New York. She identified the critical nature of the several minutes immediately following birth and developed a rating scale to help attendants decide whether a baby needs resuscitation.

The Apgar Score rates a newborn baby on each of the following five signs, whose designations begin with the first initials of the name *Apgar* (an unusual correspondence between a name and a rating scale).

Appearance or color
Pulse (heart rate)
Grimace or reflex irritability
Activity
Respiration

Sixty seconds after birth, the baby is rated on these measures using a scale of zero to two. In appearance, the newborn is given a score of two (the maximum) if the skin is pink all over; one if the body is pink but the arms and legs blue; and zero if the entire body is blue. A score of two is given when the pulse is greater than 100 beats per minute, one if it is less than 100, and zero if it is not present at all. An infant who cries vigorously when his or her foot is flicked with a finger is scored two for reflex responsiveness; a grimace or slight cry counts for one; no response is zero. A newborn who makes active motions is scored two for activity or muscle tone; some movement of the arms or legs is rated one; zero is the score if the baby is motionless and limp. Strong efforts to breathe, along with vigorous crying, count for two for respiration; slow, irregular breathing is rated one; no respiration, zero. The five components are totaled to give the one-minute Apgar score (maximum ten, minimum zero).

Most newborns score seven to ten points one minute after birth. Infants with scores of four, five, or six usually require immediate help and oxygen to assist their first attempts at breathing. Mucus in the throat, if present, must be suctioned before they can breathe adequately. A baby with an Apgar score of less than four is unresponsive, pale, limp, usually not breathing, and possibly lacking a heartbeat. Immediate suction is required to clear the airway, and the lungs need to be inflated and deflated rhythmically by external pressure with a bag and a mask that fits snugly over the mouth or attaches to a tube passed into the upper airway (endotracheal tube). Chest compressions to pump blood may also be needed. Several minutes of attention may be necessary before the baby's organs can take over on their own. Premature infants and other infants with breathing difficulties may need continuous respiratory assistance in the intensive care nursery.

Apgar scoring is repeated five minutes after birth, and both scores are recorded. Studies have shown that good scores, especially at the five-minute mark, are strongly predictive of the baby's chances for survival and normal development in early infancy. The one-minute score alerts the attendants to the immediate, sometimes urgent, need for life support, even if brief, to protect the baby from either imminent death or lifelong neurological problems.

AMAZING NEWBORNS

In recent years scientific studies have greatly expanded what we know about newborns' extraordinary capacity to interact with their environment. For example, babies at birth can turn their heads repeatedly toward the source of a human voice, their faces assuming an alert expression as they search out the sound. Babies will choose a female voice over a male voice and prefer humanlike sounds to pure tones in an equivalent pitch range. Babies' responses to sound can be measured by their sucking patterns. Babies pause briefly after a pure auditory tone, then go on sucking steadily. When babies hear a human sound they stop, then continue sucking in a burst-pause pattern, as though expecting something to follow, then pause in sucking to hear more. Babies will notice and follow the picture of a human face, turning a full ninety degrees, but will not follow a scrambled picture of a face, although they will look at it wide-eyed for long periods. Babies prefer the odors of milk to those of water or sugar water, and they can taste the difference between human milk and a cow's milk formula designed to be identical to breast milk. They can even recognize their own mother's milk.

The remarkable complexity and individuality of the newborn are both illustrated and categorized into measurable components by the Neonatal Behavioral Assessment Scale (NBAS) developed by T. Berry Brazelton. This scale recognizes six states of alertness, twenty-six items of behavior, and twenty neurological reflexes. The twenty-six items of behavior are grouped into six types.

1. *Habituation:* the infant's ability to shut out disturbing environmental stimuli
2. *Interactive* (orientation): the newborn's ability to notice and process both simple and complex events in the environment
3. *Motor:* the ability to maintain muscle tone, control motor actions, and perform integrated motor activities
4. *Range of state:* the intensity and variability of the infant's state of consciousness during the assessment
5. *State regulation:* the newborn's ability to control and modulate states while attending to social and inanimate stimuli
6. *Automatic regulation:* the newborn's vulnerability to such automatic behavior as trembling, startling, and changes in skin color

The NBAS is done widely, but not routinely. When it is done, the pediatrician may integrate it (in whole or in part) with the general physical examination while the baby's parents are present. This is a splendid opportunity for them to observe the remarkable capacities of their baby.

By understanding his or her individual temperament or personality, parents are better able to care for the baby, to discriminate between themselves and the baby, and to gain some insight into the responses the baby elicits in them (and vice versa). For example, an intense, easily startled, hard-to-quiet newborn can be expected to be a fussy, even colicky infant. Parents of such a child experience a stressful start, with great potential for self-blame and feelings of inadequacy, desperation, and depression. In addition, they risk playing into the infant's irritability, setting into motion a cycle of mutually stimulating and reinforcing negative behaviors. With the insight derived from watching as the pediatrician examines the baby, however, parents can discover how to help such an excitable infant become calm.

The interactiveness of the newborn grows rapidly in complexity. For example, by the age of three or four weeks, clear differences in the baby's responses to the mother and the father can be seen. As Brazelton wrote in his book *Infants and Mothers*,

> With the mother in sight, it is the baby who is likely to set the pace of their interactions. His face will brighten, his hands and legs will "reach out" gently toward the mother moving smoothly back and forth in a rhythmic fashion. If we watch the baby's face and eyes, we see that they alternately brighten with an intensely interested look as his mother, responding, attempts to engage him, and then become dull as the child retreats into himself and his mother desists.
>
> Father and infant synchronize, too, though their rhythmic pattern is different from that between mother and child and it is the father who is more likely to "set the pace." In our studies we have found that fathers are likelier . . . to "jazz up" the baby. Exaggerated gestures or expressions seem to say, "Come! It's playtime!" At first the baby will watch the father's antics as if trying to take them in and adjust to them. His shoulders will hunch, his eyebrows go up, his face show anticipation. Then the interaction will begin. As the baby gets older he will laugh out loud and bounce up and down in his eagerness to continue the games with his father.

Many of the visible and audible signs and responses of the newborn change over the first few days. After enduring the trying experience of birth and the one to two hours of intense alertness that follow, permitting peak interaction with parents (see p. 244 on parent-infant attachment), many babies withdraw into a state of toned-down activity or disorganization for the next twenty-four to forty-eight hours. The baby may not suck long or hard and appears to have little interest in eating. This normal withdrawal following delivery may confuse parents eager for interaction with their newborn. Nursing picks up once milk comes in, on the third and fourth day, with the baby's increasing hunger timed to coincide with milk production. The nursing that occurs earlier, however, is very important for the baby because the mother's colostrum provides nutrition and immune factors that help ward off infection. This often low-level nursing is also essential for the mother because it stimulates milk production, promotes uterine contraction, and reinforces the closeness between mother and baby that nursing represents.

Reflex Behavior

The newborn is endowed with certain coordinated patterns of behavior known as reflexes, which operate from circuits within the lower centers of the brain and have nothing to do initially with the process of rational thought or purposeful action. Reflexes have essential survival value, which can be clearly seen when noxious stimuli trigger protective responses, such as coughing, gagging, withdrawal, blinking, sneezing, and rubbing of the eyes.

Other reflexes are even more complex. Appropriate stimulation when the baby is in the quiet alert state (awake, making no more noise than a coo, eyes wide open and scanning) will automatically elicit certain reflexes. If the cheek of a sufficiently awake and hungry newborn is stroked, the baby's mouth will turn toward the stroking object, whether it is a finger or, as nature intended, the nipple of the mother's breast. This reflex is known as the *rooting response*. It is completely automatic and orients the baby toward the source of nutrition before the baby can know where food comes from. Sucking occurs by reflex if something touches the lips, the mucous membranes of the mouth, or the soft palate.

If the newborn is startled by a loud noise or sudden change of position, particularly a change involving an element of falling, the arms and legs respond in a characteristic way; they move symmetrically first outward, then upward, and then inward. The hands first open, then clench tightly into a fist, as though the infant were echoing remote primate ancestors in trying to grasp a branch of a tree or the mother's body or hair to prevent a fall or to escape an enemy. The legs go through a similar, although less consistent, sequence of movements. In addition, the baby's head bends down and forward. This reflex, known as the *startle* or *scare response* is named the *Moro reflex*, after the neurologist who first wrote about it.

If pressure is applied by a finger to the palms of the baby's hands or to the balls of the baby's feet, the fingers and toes will curl in to grasp the pressing object. The hand grasp is often so strong that the infant can be lifted partway out of a crib. This automatic response of hands and feet is known as the *grasp reflex*. If the soles of the feet are stroked, the foot will pull up, the toes fan out, and the large toe elevate. This response is known as the *Babinski reflex*, again for the neurologist who first described it.

If the baby is supported under the arms and moved across a tabletop with the feet just touching the surface, the baby's legs will make movements that are very similar to walking. This response to movement and pressure of the feet is reflexive and should not be confused with early walking.

A group of hand-mouth reflexes can be elicited by stroking the baby's cheek or palm. The baby roots toward the stroking finger, flexes the arm, and brings the hand to the mouth. Then the baby opens the mouth, puts in the fist, and begins to suck. Stimulating the baby at either cheek or hand leads to the same complex series of movements.

If a cloth is placed across the baby's nose, the baby will first attempt to mouth it; when this fails, the baby will twist the head and flail with both hands in an effort to remove the cloth. (This reflex makes it all but impossible for a baby to smother in bedding.) If one leg is stroked, the other leg will move over by reflex to push the stroking finger away. Babies withdraw by reflex from painful stimuli such as pinches or pinpricks.

If the baby's head is slowly turned to one side while the baby is lying either prone or supine, the body will predictably assume the attitude of a fencer. The arm on the side toward which the head is turned will be extended, and the other arm will bend at the elbow; the legs will move in exactly the reverse pattern, one bent, the other extended. This response of the extremities to head turning is known as the *tonic neck reflex*. If suspended in air by the feet (a position not harmful or bothersome to the infant but not one I recommend you try), the baby will first assume the fetal position, flexing both arms and legs and curling into an upside-down ball; then the baby will extend the legs and arms outward and arch the back, like a diver in a swan dive.

One of the most remarkable and complex reflex behaviors of a newborn (reported by Swedish physician A. M. Widstrom and colleagues), and one that clearly has survival value, is the ability, if left on the mother's abdomen just after birth, to crawl gradually up to her breast, find the nipple, and start to suckle. At about thirty to forty-five minutes after birth the baby will begin mouthing (sucking the hands and fingers), lip-smacking movements, and drooling, and then inch up to the breast, using the legs to push off. On reaching the level of the nipple, the baby turns the head vigorously from side to side, opening the mouth widely until he or she finds and latches on to the nipple. According to studies by R. H. Vallardi and colleagues, the baby is guided to the nipple by its odor, which is similar to that of amniotic fluid. (See discussion of the importance of prolonged, early mother-infant contact in Bonding and Attachment, p. 244.)

Reflexes are the baby's involuntary behaviors at birth that have critical survival value at this stage of development. In some instances they are the forerunners of voluntary control and demonstrate that the circuits for complex movements are laid down long before the actual movement, for example, walking, begins. Many reflexes persist until voluntary control is developed to the point at which it dominates behavior. Thus, when a baby begins to reach and grasp for objects at the age of about three months or so, the grasp reflex disappears. When the baby becomes more aware of surroundings and visually searches out the bottle or the breast, the rooting reflex vanishes.

For a wonderful presentation, written and pictorial, of newborn behavior, I recommend the book *Your Amazing Newborn* by Marshall and Phyllis Klaus (see Appendix).

APPEARANCE AND PHYSICAL EXAMINATION

During the first day or two babies may have bluish (*cyanotic*) fingers and toes, resulting from a clamping down of circulation to their extremities, perhaps to conserve heat, while the rest of the body is pink. This is quite normal. In a few days the fingers and toes will take on the same coloration as the rest of the body. If a bluish or dusky color remains, the doctor will check for heart or lung disorders.

The breathing rate of newborns is variable. They may breathe as rapidly as sixty or seventy times a minute, then slow down to twenty or thirty times per minute, all within the space of two or three minutes. Breathing may be audible, but it should not be labored or require hard work. Struggling for breath differs from normal rapid breathing and characterizes the breathing of babies with pulmonary difficulties. The vigor and quality of the baby's cry give information about the airway, vocal cords, and general strength. When stirred up, the baby is apt to move all four limbs and thus give an observer an excellent opportunity to detect any impairments of motion. When the baby cries vigorously, the color usually changes from pale pink to beet red.

A newborn's skin is usually dry and flaky, as though the baby were shedding it. The soft, lustrous skin seen in pictures in baby magazines will take weeks to develop. At birth, the skin is covered with a greasy coating known as *vernix*. Even though most vernix comes off with the first sponge bath, traditionally given in hospitals, bits often remain behind the ears and in the folds of the buttocks. It is unnecessary and probably even undesirable to remove vernix; it is better simply to massage it into the skin, as there is mounting evidence that vernix has antibacterial properties and protects against infection. The long hairs on a newborn's body are known as *lanugo*. They characteristically fall out over the first few weeks.

A baby's hands and feet will normally feel cool, and the body will feel warm. Again, the tips of the fingers and toes may be bluish. There is no need to add clothing unless the baby seems uncomfortable.

Forceps used in a delivery may leave indentations on the skin of the baby's face and head, and a vacuum extractor may leave a swollen area of scalp. These marks fade within several days. The small yellow or white spots on the noses, cheeks, or chins of many babies represent trapped collections of sebum, the fatty secretion of the sebaceous glands of the skin. These do not require treatment and fade in a matter of weeks.

Small, faint red spots or blotches are often seen on the upper eyelids, at the nape of the neck, and, less commonly, in a diamond shape over the bridge of the nose and the forehead. Clusters of tiny blood vessels (or capillaries) present in the immediate newborn period and during early infancy account for these markings, which are known as *heman-giomas* (overgrowths of blood vessels). Why they occur is not known. In days long past, hemangiomas at the base of the neck were sometimes called stork bites (since the back of the neck was the part of the anatomy grasped by the beak of the mythical stork who delivered the infant to his or her new home). Stork bites tend to blush and become darker when the baby cries. They disappear gradually over the first year. The diamond-shaped spot on the forehead fades with time, but in some individuals it may persist for life, barely visible except during emotional upsets, when it may flush.

The common *strawberry patch* is a mole *(nevus)* made up of blood vessels. As the name suggests, it looks like a slice of strawberry stuck onto the skin. It typically appears after the immediate newborn period. A small, bright-red spot on the skin is the first sign of the mark, which grows rapidly after the baby leaves the hospital. Such nevi enlarge over the first year and gradually resolve over the next several years. If they are unsightly or interfere with facial-muscle function they can be treated with a laser.

The newborn's skin is highly reactive. When a baby is excited by hunger or stimulated by the poking fingers of a nurse or doctor, large red blotches or mottling may appear transiently over the body, sometimes more prominently in one part than another. Why babies are susceptible to this blotching and mottling is not known for sure, but it is thought to be related to immature regulation of the flow of blood to the skin. These irregularities of coloration have no medical significance, and in several months the exaggerated skin responses disappear.

A common rash seen after the first day or two and for the next several weeks is *erythema toxicum*, which is characterized by a red blotch with a small, white, raised center. It resembles prickly heat (heat rash), which is usually finer. The rash is more prominent on the face, neck, and trunk than on the arms and legs. It comes and goes right before one's eyes. Neither the cause nor the treatment is known, for the condition is so transient and harmless that it has not stimulated the interest of researchers.

Prickly heat, or *heat rash*, is caused by trapped sweat that accumulates deep in the skin and sets up an inflammation. It can afflict people of all ages but is more common in babies. Heat rash manifests itself in small, often pinpoint, red blotches with slightly raised whitish centers. The rash comes and goes rapidly—it may be present in the morning and gone by noon. This condition is best left alone because the application of powders and creams to the skin aggravates the plugging of the sweat ducts and tends, if anything, to make the rash worse. Keeping the baby in a relatively cool environment will reduce heat rash, but may not eliminate it. Fortunately, babies seem to be less troubled than their parents by these rashes.

The head of the newborn can be shaped, or *molded*, as it is squeezed by the birth canal, resulting in a lopsidedness of the head, which corrects on its own within a week. Lopsidedness and flattening of the back of the head are now also seen as a result of babies' being positioned on their backs in sleep, as recommended to prevent SIDS (sudden infant death syndrome; see p. 271). It is important to correct distortions in head shape before the bones of the skull knit together, making the deformity permanent. To correct asymmetry, a towel roll can be placed *under* the mattress to shift the back of the head onto the more prominent (bulged) side. If this repositioning is not successful, the head can be fitted with a plastic band, which is not uncomfortable for the baby, that reshapes the skull over several months into alignment.

The bones of a baby's skull are not knit together as they are in children and adults, allowing them to shift alongside of and override each other to adapt (mold) to the forces in the birth canal without cracking. The normal separations between the bones (*sutures*) can be felt by running the finger over the head. Doing so gives the distinct impression of a small groove separating one bone from the other. Immediately after birth, because the bones may override, the groove feels more like a ridge.

In the middle of the head toward the front is the major (anterior) *fontanel*, or soft spot. There is a smaller, posterior fontanel at the point of the head in back. The coverings of the fontanels are very tough and can be pressed without fear of damage. The boundaries of the fontanels are formed by bones. As the baby grows, the skull bones fuse, closing the fontanels and suture lines. For most infants, the anterior fontanel closes between six months and one and one-half years and the posterior fontanel closes in a few weeks to months. The anterior fontanel in a quiet baby held in a sitting position sinks in and pulsates. When the baby cries, the soft spot tenses. The veins of the baby's head are more visible than are those of adults, largely because they are closer to the surface of the skin and also because there is less hair to conceal them.

Swelling of the scalp from pressure of the cervix during birth, known as *caput succedaneum*, gradually resolves in twenty-four to forty-eight hours and is of no consequence. Trauma to the head during delivery may result in a linear crack (fracture) in the skull and lead to bleeding between the skull and the scalp. The accumulation of blood can be seen as a swelling over the side of the head and is known as *cephalohematoma*. It requires no treatment and gradually resolves over several weeks.

The eyes of the newborn are fully formed. The whites often have small reddish blotches, which are tiny hemorrhages produced by squeezing of the head during delivery. These specks of blood clear in a week or so and have no significance. The color of the eyes varies, from brown in blacks and Asians to blue in whites. Any change of color will occur gradually. The eyes are examined by a nurse or doctor with an ophthalmoscope, an adaptation of a flashlight that has a peephole and magnifying lenses. The lenses of the eyes are checked for cataracts and the retina (the sensing part of the eye) for its normal red color. If this *red reflex* is present, it largely excludes the presence of congenital retinal tumors and other abnormalities. Findings that need prompt further evaluation are absence of the red reflex, rhythmic (usually side-to-side), rapid, jerking movement of the eyes *(nystagmus)*, and drift of one or both eyes out of alignment (lazy eye, or *strabismus*). (During a baby's early attempts to focus the eyes, they may cross for an instant, but this is not strabismus.)

Infants see more than was once thought. They can fix on a red or pale yellow object dangled before their eyes and follow it. Shining a bright light causes the infant's eyelids to shut tightly. If the baby is spun around, the head will turn reflexively in the direction of the spin and the eyes, in a rhythmical series of alternating fast and slow movements (nystagmus), will try to keep up with the spin. When the baby stops short, the eyes continue quick, rhythmical movements in the direction of spin for several seconds. These reactions depend on the complex position-sensing connections in the inner ear and the brain. If pulled up to a sitting position by the hands, the baby's eyes will open much as do the weighted eyes on old china dolls. This response is called the *doll's eye reflex*.

The ears are inspected for proper formation and normal location of the canals. Since vernix in the canal usually blocks the view of the eardrums, they are not routinely checked in the newborn. Fully awake infants usually respond with a startle to any sudden loud noise. Immediate repetition of the noise usually elicits no reaction. The infant seems able to shut out the repeated stimulus as a kind of self-protection.

The lips and mouth, including the gums and palate, are examined for defects. In rare cases, babies are born with teeth, which are usually extras rather than the standard primary or secondary teeth. The tip of the tongue is joined to the floor of the mouth by a little band known as the *frenulum*, which is sometimes quite short. In the past, the concept of being tongue-tied was associated with having a short frenulum and a short frenulum was likely to be clipped. However, babies with short frenula do not typically have problems with sucking or, later, with speaking.

A fuzzy white coating on the tongue, noticed usually after the third or fourth day, signifies thrush, an infection with the yeast *Monilia*. The baby picks up the yeast from the mother's vagina while passing through it during birth.

The newborn's neck is inspected and felt for masses. There are several kinds of congenital cysts, some of which may have sinuses, or small openings, in the skin. Although surgical removal may be required, it is not usually done in the newborn period. The sternocleidomastoid muscles run from the mastoid bone of the skull just behind the ear down to the inner third of each collarbone and are used when the head is bent forward or turned to the side. Bruises of these muscles, which occur during or even before birth, may produce a swelling and later a scarring and tightening, the condition known as *torticollis*, which pulls on one side of the skull more than the other with resulting asymmetry.

Checking the position of the windpipe (*trachea*) is also part of the neck examination. Normally in the midline, it may be tugged to one side with certain abnormalities of the lungs. The thyroid gland at the lower part of the front of the neck is also checked.

The chest should expand and contract symmetrically. Unequal movements of the two sides point to lung problems that require further investigation. Attached to the lowest point of the breastbone just at the top of the abdomen is a distinct bone known as the *xiphoid*. It may be especially prominent and slightly pointed in newborns, but it has no special significance. The doctor listens to the chest with a stethoscope to check on the flow of air in and out of the lungs and to detect any fluid within the lungs.

The rhythm and rate of the heartbeat are also checked with the stethoscope. Heart murmurs are common in newborns, but the majority are normal and not indicative of heart disease. Most disappear promptly. The explanation for these murmurs lies in the radical reorganization of the circulation that occurs at birth. Before birth, blood almost completely bypasses the lungs; with the newborn's first breath, blood begins to circulate through them. This shift in blood flow is accompanied by the opening and closing of various channels within the heart and large blood vessels. The process of reorganization may not be complete for a few days, and blood flowing through partially opened or closed channels generates the swishing noise called a *heart murmur*.

Feeling the pulses in a baby's groin assures the examiner that there is no significant constriction of the aorta, the major artery leading from the heart to the body. Sometimes these pulses are difficult to feel in a newborn, but they can be detected after several days.

The stump of the *umbilical cord* is prominent and firmly attached to the *umbilicus* (belly button). Shiny and moist for the first day or so, the stump gradually dries, shrivels, and falls off in about seven to fourteen days. More than a small rim of redness of the skin of the umbilicus signifies infection and requires medical attention. In newborns, unlike in adults, the size and shape of the abdominal organs—the liver, spleen, and kidneys—can be felt under normal conditions and evaluated. The examiner searches for abnormal masses, such as one caused by a blocked kidney. The bladder normally rises up much higher in the abdomen of the newborn than it does in the abdomen of the adult and can be felt when full of urine. If stools are being passed normally, no additional examination of the anus or rectum is necessary.

The skin of the *scrotum* reflects the maturity of the baby boy. The normal rough appearance develops only in babies whose gestation was close to term. In premature infants the scrotal skin is smooth and shiny. The testicles should be present in the scrotum. Hernias and hydroceles (fluid accumulations) can be detected as swellings in the scrotum, and hernias require repair even in the newborn period. The urethra, the thin tube that runs the length of the inside of the penis, should open at its tip. In a noncircumcised infant, the foreskin may conceal the opening (*meatus*). A forceful stream of urine in boys provides good evidence that there is no obstruction to the lower urinary tract.

The shape of the legs of a newborn has been determined by the forces exerted on them by the uterus and will not change until new forces, particularly weight bearing, come into play. In the case of babies born head first, the legs are bowed and the feet turned inward. In breech babies (born buttocks first), the legs may be rotated outward with the kneecaps close to one another and the feet turned outward. Eventually, all these turns and twists reverse.

The hips are checked for stability of the joints. If the ball of the joint can be disengaged from the socket, the condition known as *developmental dysplasia of the hip* is suggested. Further evaluation with x-ray and ultrasound is then required. If this condition is diagnosed, early treatment is necessary to allow for normal joint development.

BONDING AND ATTACHMENT

In the last twenty-five years research has supplied evidence to support what human experience and evolution did not question until the setting for birth shifted from home to hospital in the twentieth century, namely, that mothers and babies belong together right from the start. From about the 1920s until 1975 babies born in hospitals were kept in nurseries separate from their mothers after brief or no contact at birth. They were brought to their mothers only for feedings, usually by bottle, every four hours by the clock and were otherwise available for viewing only through nursery windows. Fathers were hardly involved. These rigid practices have largely given way to encouragement of as much contact as parents want with their babies, even with today's short hospital stays. Much of the leadership for the demedicalization of hospital practices in newborn care, including the return to favor of breast-feeding, has come from nonprofessional groups representing the concerns of the public. A standout in this activism has been the La Leche League, which was formed in the 1940s in Chicago and overcame considerable opposition from hospitals and doctors to make its point. Today, hospitals that are supportive of unrestricted mother-baby contact and breast-feeding commonly identify themselves as participants in the *Baby-Friendly Hospital Initiative,* as defined by the World Health Organization.

Two distinguished American pediatricians who have studied and reported on the negative effects of separating babies from their mothers are John Kennell, of Rainbow Babies and Children's Hospital, Cleveland, and Marshall Klaus, of the Oakland Children's Hospital. I highly recommend their book, *Bonding: Building the Foundation of Secure Attachment and Independence*. Based on their research and experience as clinicians, these doctors make recommendations, adapted here, for the immediate period after birth.

1. *The first hour.* After the immediate needs of mother and baby have been tended to, parents should have at least one hour alone with their baby so that they can take advantage of the high level of alertness and interactivity exhibited by most babies during this period (see Amazing Newborns, p. 232). Measuring the infant, administering vitamin K and eye ointment, and bathing the infant should be saved for later.

2. *Rooming-in.* Babies should not be separated from their parents unless there are medical reasons for doing so.

3. *Warmth.* After being dried after birth and capped to preserve heat, the baby needs to be kept warm by being placed skin to skin with the mother and covered by a warm, dry towel or a light blanket, or by being placed next to the mother, with a heat panel or warmer over both of them.

4. *Letting the baby find the breast.* If the mother plans to breast-feed, even for a short time, the parents should be asked if they would like to allow the baby to maneuver up to the breast and begin to breast-feed on his or her own (see p. 237).

5. *Early responsibility.* Parents are in charge, taking their cues from the baby, right from the start. The role of the nurse and doctor is that of consultant or, even better, coach.

6. *Incubators and light treatment.* If an incubator is needed for additional heat, it should be brought to the mother's bedside if possible; if light treatment for jaundice is needed (see Jaundice, p. 270), it should be given in the mother's room.

7. *Timing of advice.* Advice by staff should be timed and sequenced according to the mother's needs rather than by the book. If a mother is concerned about her baby's latching on to the breast, staff should stick with that issue rather than discussing other

topics, such as bathing, which the mother is not yet prepared to hear.

8. *New mothers groups and printed instructions.* Information on baby and personal care can be best conveyed in small-group meetings in which mothers have the opportunity to ask questions and share experiences. Important points should be distributed in printed form for later reference.

During the hour or so following birth, the baby is alert to interactions with the parents. This availability can be taken advantage of before the baby becomes sleepy. The richness of the newborn's psychological skills has only recently been described by researchers (see pp. 232–235), even though mothers have always sensed that their babies recognize them from the beginning. For parents and other participants, this responsiveness of the newborn is accompanied by a welling up of intense, at times overwhelming, feelings of warmth and love for the baby and a desire to nurture him or her. Thus it is that babies will make parents of us all.

BREAST-FEEDING

Until the twentieth century all babies were breast-fed and, except in industrialized or industrializing countries, they still are. Human beings evolved with breast milk. Yet, despite the proven considerable advantages of human milk and the major strides made over the past twenty-five years in creating an environment more conducive to breast-feeding, only a minority of American women breast-feed their infants. The percentage of women nursing their infants at birth increased between 1989 and 1995 from 52 to 60 percent; those still breast-feeding their babies at six months rose only from a low 18 percent to a slightly higher 22 percent. Thus, the United States is far short of the goal set by the American Academy of Pediatrics in 1998 that all babies be breast-fed at least until their first birthday. Although these figures underline how far we have to go, they also indicate how far we have come since the 1940s. This was when a group of Chicago mothers, determined to breast-feed despite lack of professional and public support and often in the face of real opposition, formed the La Leche League and spread the word about breast-feeding throughout the industrialized world.

Why is it, then, that more women do not breast-feed or don't do it for very long? Although the situation is changing as more women nurse their babies, many girls and younger women still don't have the opportunity to learn about breast-feeding by being around nursing mothers, as is true for females growing up in traditional breast-feeding societies. Movies and videotapes can make up for this lack of direct experience but only in part. Negative attitudes toward breast-feeding include an (ungrounded) fear that the breasts will sag permanently and lose their attractiveness and that breast-feeding is primitive and animal-like. For some couples, a commitment to an equal sharing of parenting argues for a father's participation in feeding, for which formula is seen as the only solution. (However, a mother can express her milk into a bottle for immediate use or freeze it for later use. A father can then feed it to the baby. The real question may be who will get up in the middle of the night.) This extreme attitude of some couples has always struck me as a rather odd interpretation of the principles of equal rights for women.

Other barriers to breast-feeding are institutional and societal. In the past doctors and nurses actively discouraged nursing because of their own ignorance and their unwillingness to take the extra time required to deal with breast-feeding problems. They genuinely *believed* that commercial formula was better, in part because with formula, it's possible to know how much the baby is getting. Hospital practices of separating babies from mothers, routinely feeding babies water (or formula), and feeding babies according to a fixed schedule (rather than on demand, which is facilitated by rooming-in) all had a chilling effect on breast-feeding. Manufacturers of infant formulas still make it all too easy to use formula by providing free starter supplies for distribution by hospitals. This practice is like saying, "Here is some formula to use in case you don't make enough milk." This message undermines a mother's confidence and is opposite to the expectation of success that is so conducive to getting started with nursing. Further, the cost-saving policy of early discharge of mothers from hospitals or birthing centers without providing for compensatory support services at home deprives mothers of the assistance they often need to sustain nursing at home— tips on positioning, nipple placement, and breaking the baby's suction; encouragement; troubleshooting; relief from other responsibilities when exhausted and sore. Gentle bumps in the road early on often can be navigated easily with timely assistance. Without such assistance, it's

all too easy to give in to the safe and readily available alternative of formula feeding. No mother wants to contend with the fear of her baby's
not getting enough to eat. Perhaps the greatest barrier to continued
nursing relates to the number of women in the workforce; many
women who work outside the home see no alternative to nursing only
until their family leave is over and weaning the baby just before returning to work.

All these factors may make breast-feeding problematic even for the
woman who chooses it. She may have mixed feelings. She may approach nursing to prove that she can do it, or she may sense that the father is going along with her decision to breast-feed but really has
negative feelings about nursing. In such cases, deep down, the woman
may be ready to give nursing up at the first sign of trouble. Such ambivalence doesn't help matters. Nursing works best when women trust
in themselves, feel supported by their families and communities, and
have confidence that they will succeed.

The ingredients of the improving climate for breast-feeding are
many. Today's health-care professionals are far more knowledgeable
and pronursing than were those of the past. Hospital policies have followed suit. Hospitals today generally provide unlimited access to infants for feedings and no longer give supplements. Many hospitals have
banned the practice of routinely distributing packs of formula at the
time of discharge, instead offering educational materials on breast-
feeding and sometimes even supplying a breast pump. Increasingly,
hospitals have professional lactation consultants on staff who are available both during the hospital stay and after the return home. Many
states have passed laws affirming a mother's right to nurse her baby at
job sites and other public places, and national legislation is under consideration. In 1998, Philadelphia became the first city to declare itself a
breast-feeding friendly community.

More and more companies and industries are also doing their part.
The changing climate of the workplace was humorously illustrated on
the cover of the May 11, 1998, *New Yorker* magazine. The drawing
showed a female construction worker, clad in blue jeans, boots, and
hard hat, lunch pail at her side, sitting on a steel girder high above the
street and peacefully nursing her baby, who appeared to be about six
months old. Although the number of companies that sponsor day-care
centers on site, thereby allowing mothers to drop in and nurse their ba-

bies during the workday, is increasing, the practice remains relatively uncommon. An option more likely to grow in availability is company-provided facilities—a lactation support room, as it is called by one prominent corporation—where mothers can pump their breasts in privacy and refrigerate the milk for later use at home. Companies and government organizations that have achieved national recognition for their leadership in providing friendly environments for nursing mothers include Aetna, Eastman Kodak, Cigna, Home Depot, Georgia's Fulton County government, and the Los Angeles Department of Water and Power. In January 1998 the U.S. Secretary of Agriculture issued a policy promising nursing mothers adequate time to pump breast milk while working in the government's fourth largest agency. The Sanvita Corporation now markets its breast-feeding support services to over 300 companies nationally as a benefit that is attractive to nursing mothers and has cut health insurance and absentee costs. For example, since Aetna started its program, it estimates annual savings per nursing employee of $1,435 on medical claims plus the cost of three days of sick leave, for a total savings of $108,737—an almost three-to-one return on investment.

The benefits of breast-feeding are many. From a nutritional point of view it has never been equaled. The more we learn about breast milk, the more we marvel at it. For example, it contains disease-fighting antibodies and white blood cells, which are particularly important for protecting babies against infection in parts of the world where sanitation is poor, but are important to all high-risk newborns, such as those born prematurely or with intrauterine growth retardation. Even in the United States, which generally has high levels of sanitation, human breast milk protects against middle-ear infections (otitis media), colds, and infectious diarrhea; reduces the chances of allergic diseases, such as asthma (particularly if the mother's diet is kept low in such allergens as cow's milk, egg whites, and nuts); and may reduce SIDS (see p. 271). Breast-fed babies are also more likely to score higher on intelligence tests done later in childhood.

Breast-feeding avoids the problems of intolerance seen in babies fed formulas derived from cow's milk; intolerance occurs in 0.3 to 7.5 percent of formula-fed infants, becoming evident in over 80 percent of cases by age four months. It results in vomiting, diarrhea, constipation, nasal allergies, asthma, and eczema. Of course, the wonders of breast milk should really come as no surprise. After all, it has been an essential link in human evolution and survival over many tens of thousands of years.

Breast-feeding is also supremely convenient; it is instantly available without preparation. Nursing from the breast contributes to correct alignment of the baby's erupting teeth. Mothers claim that it promotes a unique physical and emotional closeness. Breast-fed babies smell sweeter, and their stools tend to be softer. (See p. 267 for a discussion of babies' bowel patterns.) Breast-feeding is considerably less expensive than formula feeding, a significant advantage at a time when the cost of living is still a problem for many families. Most breast-fed babies do not require additional foods until at least six months of age, nor do they require vitamin or iron supplements, as vitamins and iron from the mother are secreted in sufficient quantities into her milk. (Fluoride, however, is not passed into the mother's milk and so does need to be added to the baby's diet. See p. 262.) Furthermore, health-care costs (office visits, medicines, hospitalizations, etc.) for breast-fed babies are significantly reduced (to say nothing of inconvenience for parents in lost work, time, etc.). A recent study found that the cost savings averaged between $331 and $475 per baby during the first year of life. Breast-feeding has some contraceptive effect (though it is not at all foolproof), particularly during the first year, and thereby plays an important role in population control in nonindustrialized societies. Breast-feeding also results in some reduction in premenopausal breast cancer and in ovarian cancer and in an improvement in the mother's bone remineralization after giving birth.

All the ingredients for getting nursing off to a successful start are present during the first hour after birth if mother and baby are together in a warm environment with the baby on the mother's abdomen. After the remarkable first hour of high alertness, the baby will show less interest in nursing during the next thirty-six to forty-eight hours, only to have interest return in force about the time the mother's milk comes in.

Both production and ejection of human milk are regulated by hormones produced in the mother's pituitary gland. The primary stimulus for release of these hormones is the suckling of the baby and the emptying of the breasts. In some women the sound or thought of the baby will initiate letting down of the milk from the milk glands into the collecting ducts and possible leaking or squirting of milk from the nipple. (Sometimes this let-down reflex is too active for a particular baby, resulting in some correctable nursing problems, which will be discussed.) During a feeding the cycle of milk production and ejection can occur several times. As babies grow and require more milk, they nurse more and stimulate increased production. The breast is finely tuned to adjust its production according to the baby's needs as expressed by nursing activity. However, the breast can meet a baby's initial demands only if *all* the baby's nursing is directed to the breast. If a baby is also feeding from a bottle, the breast will respond to the lessened total nursing by reducing production. The baby, unsatisfied by the breast, will then need more milk from the bottle, and so on. Eventually, milk production will stop altogether. (This is exactly what happens during weaning.) The basic physiological point is that for nursing to be successful, a baby must have unrestricted access to the breast, without supplementation, from the time of birth. A hungry baby should be breast-fed as often as necessary. Milk production will increase to meet the baby's needs.

Babies nurse best when they are hungry. The mother can learn to identify the earliest signs of hunger rather than wait for the baby to work up to a fit of crying that requires settling down. The mother should follow the baby's lead, not the clock's. During the first few weeks many babies nurse as often as twelve times in twenty-four hours, sometimes with as little as an hour between nursings. Nursings may cluster during one part of the day and be more spaced out at other times. This early feeding pattern can be very tiring for a mother, all the more reason why she needs to be freed up as much as possible from other responsibilities during this crucially important time.

Milk production, letdown, and ejection are remarkably sensitive to a mother's emotions. A sudden emotional shock can stop milk production altogether, and depression (p. 287) can adversely affect nursing. On the other hand, successful nursing is a good sign of maternal contentment and happiness. When a problem in nursing develops, a mother's worry and upset make it even worse; identifying a knowledgeable and supportive expert in breast-feeding, known as a lactation coach, is important for quickly getting back on track.

Although not all crying by a baby is caused by hunger (see Crying, p 263), crying frequently becomes the basis for concluding that nursing isn't working and an excuse for stopping. Often the decision to stop is grounded in mixed feelings about nursing in the first place. As I advise new mothers, be honest with yourself. If you clearly and deeply feel that you want to nurse and your partner supports you fully, you can rest as-

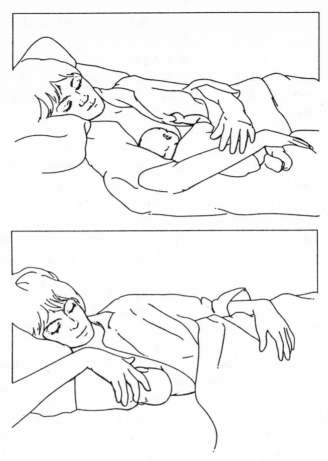

FIGURE 6.1 Nursing positions

sured that you will be able to deal with the baby's crying and continue nursing. You *can* do it! It is also true that an inconsolable baby can trigger so much anxiety in a mother that breast-feeding can be adversely affected, compounding the problem of crying. Consult a lactation coach if you're becoming frazzled.

A baby who is getting enough milk appears content, urinates frequently, and has bowel movements. It is not necessary to weigh babies after a feeding to see whether they have gained weight. Such a practice is bound to make you a nervous wreck and to interfere with milk production. Periodic weighings during well-child checkups will confirm

FIGURE 6.2   Nursing positions, continued

the weight gain that is obviously occurring. Some babies don't cry or even appear hungry and may need special handling to ensure that they are adequately nourished.

A baby nurses by drawing areola, nipple, and the surrounding rim of breast (together forming what is called the teat) into the mouth. The baby is able to latch on by means of the rooting reflex (see p. 235), which leads to turning the mouth in the direction of stroking of the cheek or lips (by breast or finger) and then opening the mouth for the insertion of the teat. The mother needs to cup the breast with four fingers from beneath to support its weight and keep it from pulling away from the baby's mouth and then position the baby to facilitate latching on (see Figures 6.1 and 6.2), all the while supporting the baby comfortably so that he or she need only nurse, not hold up or turn the neck or head. Proper positioning will also minimize trauma to the nipple and maximize the effectiveness of nursing.

Properly positioned, the baby's gums will close over the areola behind the nipple, drawing the teat into the mouth. The nipple elongates under tactile stimulation, and the teat dynamically expands to fill much of the mouth. The teat is held in place by the roof of the mouth (hard palate) from above, the tongue from below, and the lips and gums from behind. When correctly positioned, the baby's lips should be everted (rolled out) on the areola (or on the skin of the breast behind the areola), as opposed to pinched or pursed (as in whistling). The body of the breast should be clear of the baby's nose. The teat is literally milked by a wave of muscle contraction (peristalsis) of the tongue that spreads from front to back, while the length of the tongue maintains contact with the teat throughout. (Sucking milk from a bottle with a nipple involves an entirely different set of coordinated mouth and tongue movements. Many babies, particularly younger ones, are unable to switch back and forth from breast to bottle. Breast-feeding usually suffers in the competition, another reason for avoiding bottles early on.)

There should be no friction or tugging on the nipple itself while the baby is latching on or feeding. The nipple is not designed to withstand such trauma and if subjected to it will become painful and cracked. With correct positioning of the baby there is no reason to limit the duration of nursing, as was often advocated in the past, to protect the nipples. The baby can simply be nursed until he or she shows signs of being full. As one breast feels emptier, the other can be offered. Breast-feeding should not be painful for the mother (with the possible exception during the first few days of nursing of some very brief pain in the teat after the baby latches on). On the contrary, most mothers find nursing physically and emotionally pleasurable.

To break the hold of the baby on the teat, the mother can insert the tip of a finger between the baby's gums and the areola and then pull the teat away or move the baby away or both. If the breast is too full at the beginning of nursing and the areola is firm and noncompliant, it will be difficult for the baby to latch on will be difficult and the nipple may be bitten and injured by the baby's gums. The extreme state of breast fullness is called engorgement, and the breast is often painful and reddened. The mother needs to soften the breast by expressing some milk either manually (see Figure 6.3) or with a breast pump. Hand expression is an important, readily learned, instantly available skill. Engorgement also suggests that the baby is not being put to breast on demand, so more frequent nursing may be needed.

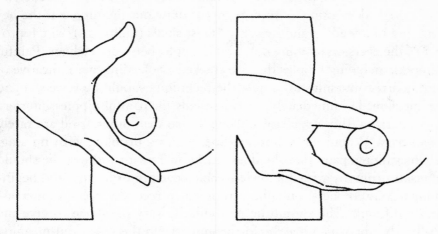

FIGURE 6.3   Expressing milk with the hand

Most women who are breast-feeding a baby for the first time will benefit when getting started from the help of a knowledgeable and experienced coach. Having such a coach can mean the difference between success and failure. Before labor the woman should make certain that such coaching will be available, either from the staff of the institution (hospital, HMO, or birthing center) or from a privately arranged source, for example, a friend or lactation consultant. The local chapter of La Leche League is another resource (see Appendix).

There is no need for a mother to drink extra fluids while nursing. She need merely drink when she is thirsty, as she does when she is not nursing. Guidelines for a healthful diet are provided in Chapter 2 (see p. 88). Following these guidelines will provide both mother and baby with sufficient vitamins, so vitamin supplements are unnecessary. Mothers who are anemic after delivery may need additional iron.

Nipples are best left to air dry, and creams and ointments should be avoided. Friction from a bra or other clothing should be minimized, particularly early on. Tea strainers or similar porous shields can be helpful. Soft, nonirritating breast pads will protect clothing from becoming wet and will not injure the nipples.

True inverted nipples are uncommon (see p. 68). They can generally be corrected by using a breast pump to draw out the nipple at the beginning of a feeding and by using breast shells (milk cups), which promote the eversion (coming out) of the nipple, between feedings. Painful nipples, including nipples that are cracked or bleeding, are indicative of an incorrect nursing technique; the technique should be reviewed and changes made immediately. Breast shields for painful nipples interfere with nursing (those made of silicone less so than others) and are rarely necessary. Whenever a mother experiences a problem with nursing, such as nipple pain, that she does not know how to address, she should consult promptly with a knowledgeable coach in order to avoid beginning a spiral of lactation failure from which recovery becomes increasingly difficult. She should be particularly wary of advice to give the baby a bottle, which may be forthcoming from the most well-meaning people, including grandmothers, for doing so can spell trouble for nursing.

Under special circumstances that do require supplementary feeding, the current recommended approach makes use of feeding devices other than an artificial nipple, which can confuse the baby and make return to the breast difficult. An example is a device known as a *supplementer,* a thin, plastic tube taped to the breast and ending at the nipple. A syringe with milk is attached to the upper end of the tube. The baby is put to the breast, with the nipple end of the tube along with the teat in the baby's mouth. Milk is injected through the tube into the baby's mouth.

A tender lump in the breast signifies a blocked milk duct. The overdistended milk glands behind the blockage may allow substances to leak into and irritate the overlying skin, causing redness and other signs of inflammation, including fever, chills, and generalized achiness. Continued nursing on that breast is crucial to draining the blocked region. As with sore nipples, a blocked duct also suggests faulty nursing technique, and a review with an experienced coach is in order. Streaks of redness that spread out from the tender area signify infection of the breast with bacteria, for which antibiotics will be needed. Tender nipples, even those without visible change, may also result from *Monilia* (yeast) infection, for which specific treatment is available.

If a baby is jaundiced during the immediate newborn period (see pp. 270–272), it is important to continue nursing without interruption and *not* to offer the baby extra water. Breast milk is effective in eliminating jaundice. In the less common condition of jaundice that persists and even increases after the newborn period, fatty acids in breast milk may play a role. Usually no treatment is required and the jaundice will clear on its own. Alternatively, if breast milk is determined to be a factor, stopping nursing for several days while pumping to maintain milk production will allow the baby to clear the excess bilirubin, as will heating expressed milk to fifty-six degrees Celsius and feeding it to the baby after it cools.

During the first three months an overactive let-down reflex may result in very strong sucking and hurried nursing, intense hunger, spitting up, passing excessive amounts of gas, and fussiness, on the part of the baby, and pain when the milk is initially ejected, on the part of the mother. After the first three months this same condition may result in the baby's not nursing well, refusing the breast, nursing frantically for a short time, then screaming and arching the back, sucking the thumb or pacifier, and failing to gain weight as expected. Whenever any of these symptoms occur, the mother should get help quickly; most of the time, careful listening and observation can unearth an explanation and nursing can be put back on track.

Canadian nurses Jan Riordan and Kathleen Auerbach, in their book *Breast Feeding and Human Lactation* (see Appendix), make several practical suggestions for handling overactive letdown.

1. Give one breast only per feeding and use that same breast again if nursing is wanted within one hour. Express milk from the other breast if it is uncomfortably full.
2. Position the baby on top of the breast or on the side facing the breast, with the mother leaning back and supported by a reclining chair (using gravity to slow the stream).
3. Make a special point of relaxing before nursing.
4. Allow the initial forceful spray of milk to escape onto a cloth or towel.
5. Burp the baby frequently.
6. Avoid pumping or expressing milk unless absolutely necessary.

Breast-feeding is possible in many special situations, such as when the baby is premature or has cleft lip and palate. Before writing off breast-feeding, the mother should check on the experience of others. Even relactation (starting milk flow when none exists) is possible. A knowl-edgeable coach and a determined mother are the ingredients for suc-cess.

Women who work outside the home or who must be temporarily separated from their babies for any reason can pump their breasts, store the milk, and feed it to their babies later. Today's pumped, refrigerated milk can be tomorrow's lunch. A variety of pumps are available for rent as well as purchase. Several popular models are listed in the Appendix. Employers who provide lactation rooms often also make pumps avail-able. Hand expression is as effective as pumping mechanically and in-stantly available.

Riordan and Auerbach also have some good pointers for pumping at work.

1. Pump (or express) three times at work.
2. Practice pumping one week before returning to work.
3. Use pumped milk stored in the refrigerator within three days. If freezing the milk in a refrigerator freezer, place it in the coldest area (as far from the door as possible) and use it within one month. Milk frozen in a deep freeze is good for six months.
4. Consider giving the milk in a cup after the baby is three months old to prevent the baby's becoming confused between the human and manufactured nipple.

Women who choose not to breast-feed and experience breast discom-fort from fullness can take measures to reduce milk production (which usually stops in several days in the absence of nursing), including wear-ing a bra for support, wrapping the breasts, applying ice, and taking pain relievers, such as ibuprofen.

Use of Drugs During Breast-Feeding

Generally, mothers who need to take medications can find medications that will be safe for the baby should some be secreted into the milk. Al-most all drugs listed as safe *during* pregnancy (see Tables 3.1 and 3.2, p. 128) are safe during breast-feeding, and several drugs listed as unsafe during pregnancy (because of their effects on fetal development) are safe during lactation, for example, angiotensin converting enzyme inhibitors for hypertension, antithyroid drugs, valproic acid, phenytoin, carbamezapine, anticholinergic drugs, and hypoglycemics (for diabetes). Tetracycline antibiotics remain worrisome because they are incorporated into growing teeth and bone. Table 6.1 lists drugs that may pose problems for nursing mothers.

BOTTLE FEEDING

This discussion of bottle feeding is short compared with that of breast-feeding, which is the preferred way of feeding. For a variety of reasons, some beyond their control, many women will choose to bottle feed their babies. I recommend that mothers who have chosen to bottle feed nonetheless read the section on breast-feeding because much of that discussion applies to both methods of feeding and will not be repeated here.

Even though cow's milk formula lacks the advantages of human milk, such as germ-fighting antibodies and white blood cells, most babies will thrive on it. In the sanitary conditions that prevail in the United States the biological advantages of human milk are less critical to infants than they are in underdeveloped areas of the world. For babies who are intolerant of cow's milk, substitutes will be required.

Formula is packaged as a powder or evaporated-milk liquid (the least expensive option, requiring the addition of sugar as well as water) that is reconstituted with water, or as a convenient, ready-made (and more expensive) drink in recyclable bottles. Directions for storage and, if needed, preparation are provided on the package. Cans of formula base with measuring scoops make single bottles of formula. Left-over base can be covered tightly with plastic wrap and stored in the refrigerator for forty-eight hours. Bottled formula can also be kept safely in the refrigerator for forty-eight hours. A bottle can stand at room temperature for an hour without spoiling and can go back in the refrigerator if unopened. Once opened, however, formula should not be kept for more than an hour (half an hour in a hot climate) and should not be returned to the refrigerator.

Bottles should be made of glass or plastic (or liners in disposable systems) that does not contain the chemical bisphenol-A, which has produced adverse effects in laboratory animals. Bisphenol-A leaches out when glass or plastic made from polycarbonates is boiled. In a *Consumer*

TABLE 6.1   Drugs That May Be Unsafe During Nursing

Antacids which reduce formation of stomach acids, for example cimetidine: although there have not been any reports of problems, could have the same effect on the baby. It is safer to use antacids which neutralize already formed stomach acid, are not absorbed into the body, and are not excreted into milk, the Maalox category of drugs available without prescription.

Beta-adrenergic-receptor antagonists for hypertension (for example, atenolol): may be a problem in the first few feedings, especially in premature babies

Ergotamines for migraine.

Lithium: freely passes into milk. If it must be used (alternatives are usually available), monitor blood levels in infant.

Metronidazole: although no ill effects have reported, if given as a single-dose treatment, consider holding feedings and discarding expressed milk for 12 to 24 hours.

Oral contraceptives (birth control pills): may interfere with milk production especially in the first six weeks. Progesterone-only pills are less likely to have this effect.

Sulfonamide antibiotics: may exacerbate existing jaundice (See p. 270)

Quinalone antibiotics (e.g., ciprofloxacin): although no reports of problems, concern remains about inflammation of cartilage. If used, monitor infant for limited use of and tenderness of joints

Tetracycline antibiotics: incorporated into teeth (staining them) and bone.

Alcohol passes freely into milk as do the constituents of tobacco smoke. A 1991 study in the *New England Journal of Medicine* showed that the odor and taste of milk containing alcohol is significantly changed and that babies consume less of it. There is speculation that teenagers may develop their first taste for cigarettes from early exposure to breast milk of mothers who smoke.

Even "safe" drugs pass to the baby during lactation and may cause symptoms such as diarrhea, poor feeding, sleepiness, and fussiness. Depending on the severity of these symptoms, the drug may have to be stopped or a substitution found. Of course, a conservative approach is always best: use drugs only if necessary.

Regarding the safety of herbs taken by a mother, there is no good date upon which recommendations can be based.

For references and resources on breast-feeding, please see Appendix.

Reports survey, the most widely available, safe plastic products cited were Playtex and Avent disposable liners, Evenflo Tinted Angled Nurser, Evenflo Tinted Pastel Nurser, and Gerber Fashion Tint. Evenflo glass bottles are also considered safe. If a bottle or liner is not mentioned here, call the manufacturer at the number listed on the product for more information. For updated information, check the free web site www.ConsumerReports.org.

Reusable bottles and nipples should be washed with hot water and soap. Sterilization is unnecessary if the water supply is safe.

VITAMINS AND MINERALS

Like people of all other ages, babies require vitamins. Breast milk contains all the vitamins and iron a baby needs. Vitamins and iron are added to commercial formulas, so there is no need to give additional drops of vitamins or iron, as is common practice. Nursing mothers must have an adequate vitamin intake themselves, which can usually be ensured through diet alone.

Vitamin K is necessary to the production of blood-clotting factors; without it, there can be bleeding throughout the body. Newborns have only small amounts of this vitamin and require about a week to make enough on their own to facilitate normal clotting. Therefore, vitamin K is routinely administered by injection at birth to boost its level immediately.

Fluoride is of proven benefit in preventing dental cavities. Populations of children exposed to fluoride, either in the water supply or as supplements, show a 50 percent reduction in cavities. Fluoridation of water has proved to be one of the most effective of public health measures. Fluoride is incorporated into growing teeth and can also be applied to the surface of teeth with a fluoridated toothpaste or a special fluoride solution. Since fluoride passes poorly through breast milk and is not added to prepared, ready-to-use infant formulas, parents need to give it directly to their babies. If the town water supply is fluoridated and that water is used to prepare formula, additional fluoride drops are not necessary. When to begin fluoride supplements has not been fully established. In the absence of data, opinion ranges from birth to six months, with the latter being favored by authorities on breast-feeding. Too much fluoride stains the teeth. As the breast-fed baby grows older and takes more town water, directly or in foods, the supplements should be tapered off, and by one year they are probably not needed. A doctor or nurse can give advice about obtaining fluoride drops and determining doses.

BURPING, HICCUPS, AND SOLID FOODS

Babies regularly swallow air with feedings and usually *burp* it up. Sometimes, when they appear uncomfortable because their stomachs are too full, burping provides relief. Since air rises, the upright position best facilitates burping, traditionally assisted with a gentle pat on the back. Along with burping, many babies bring up (spit up) some milk, which may exit through their noses as well as their mouths. Spitting up should not be of concern. It is likely that whenever a baby burps, some milk enters the esophagus (food tube). Since the distance from stomach to mouth in a baby is only a few inches, it does not take too much extra force to bring the milk all the way up and out. However, to decrease spitting up, parents can burp the baby midway through a feeding and stop feeding as soon as the baby slows down, so the baby does not get more milk than he or she can hold.

Babies also *hiccup*. They even have hiccups in utero, which mothers can often distinguish from kicking. Hiccups seem to bother babies little if at all, and most will merrily hiccup their way to sleep. There is no need for concern.

Babies have no need for *solid foods* for at least the first four months, preferably six. They certainly do not need to be given solid food until they are able to take it from a spoon. There is no evidence that the earlier introduction of solid foods reduces the number of nighttime awakenings.

SLEEPING

Sleeping patterns vary widely, and babies give plenty of clues about their schedules. Most babies sleep twenty of twenty-four hours in the first week or two and slowly taper off to sixteen to eighteen hours by the end of the first month. Some infants have predictable sleep-wake patterns; other babies are much more irregular. Some sleep more at night; others catnap during the day in a variable pattern. Most infants do not sleep through the night until age four or more months, although there is always the exception who sleeps through within the first one to two weeks. Many infants seem to mix up nights and days during the first several weeks of life. The introduction of solid foods does not affect the age at which babies sleep through the night.

Light and noise do not usually bother infants, but a baby who startles easily or is a restless sleeper may need a dark and quiet spot. The best recommendation regarding sleep position is to place the baby on the back (supine) or side until six months of age. Recent studies have demonstrated that these positions help prevent sudden infant death syndrome (see p. 271). There are two temporary and reversible consequences of these safer sleep positions: flattening of the back of the head and a delay in crawling, rolling over, creeping, and pulling up to a standing position. In both cases the benefits far outweigh the costs.

If a breast-fed baby is fussy and wakeful and the mother is drinking beverages that contain caffeine (coffee, tea, cola drinks), prudence suggests she stop, since caffeine reaches the baby through breast milk and can act as a stimulant to keep the baby awake, active, and irritable.

CRYING

Crying is an infant's major means of communication and expression. It can mean "I'm hungry," "I'm tired," "I'm uncomfortable," "I'm letting off steam," or "I'm bored." Not all crying can be readily explained, and, of course, babies cannot be asked about their inner experiences. Many babies will cry without obvious cause for up to several hours a day, often in the late afternoon and early evening (one hopes not in the middle of the night). Do what you will—feed, change, rock, swaddle, hug, coo—nothing works for long. Interestingly, babies show this common behavior across all cultures and child-rearing practices, meaning that the source probably lies within the infant rather than with the environment. (In other words, it's not your fault.)

An extreme degree of inconsolable crying (even screaming), when a baby seems truly miserable, is known as *colic*. Colic has been ascribed to intestinal cramps or to letting off tension, but its cause is not known. Cow's milk allergy may be a factor for some babies. When babies cry, they swallow air, which rumbles through their stomachs and intestines and is passed through the rectum. This air may contribute to intestinal cramps, leading to still more crying, more air swallowing, and so on. But, again, no one knows for sure if this is what happens when a baby has colic.

When all else fails, the parents may have to let the baby cry it out. One parent picks up and comforts the baby every fifteen minutes. If the crying continues, the parent puts the baby back to bed, closes the door, and covers his or her ears. If the crying is driving the parents up the wall, they can ask someone else to take over while they go for a walk. A rested person with a fresh point of view may be able to figure out a few tricks that have eluded the frazzled parents—little ways of working around a baby's individual quirks.

There are few forces on earth that can make one feel more inadequate or so undermine one's self-confidence as the crying of a baby who cannot be comforted. If your baby has colic, don't be surprised if you feel helpless, incompetent, or guilty in dealing with this behavior—you are not alone. You can reassure yourself that as far as anyone can tell, colicky crying leaves no permanent physical or emotional scars. And the best piece of news—even the worst colic does not go on forever. By three months, four at the outside, it is only a memory. (See the Appendix for books on babies in the first year.)

BATHING

Young babies do not need baths; they are not dirty at birth. *Vernix* (see p. 238), which coats the skin in utero, is healthy for the skin and may protect it against infection. Vernix that accumulates in the skin folds can be spread around and rubbed in like lotion. The baby's bottom should be washed with warm water on a soft cloth.

Traditional practice directs that until the stump of the umbilical cord falls off, the baby should be given a warm-water sponge bath and not immersed, presumably to prevent infection of the cord. To my knowledge this precept has never been critically studied.

The bathing procedure is simple. Wash the eyelids with a clean cloth or cotton ball. A cotton swab can be used to remove visible earwax, but should not be used to dig into the ear canal. (Earwax is normal. It becomes a problem in babies only when it blocks a doctor's or nurse's view of the eardrum when *otitis media* is suspected.) Use a mild soap to wash the baby from neck to feet, soaping the creases in the neck, under the arms, and in the groin. Wipe a girl's genitals from front to back to minimize the chance of a urinary tract infection. (This practice should be followed by the girl herself later in life when she begins using toilet tissue.) Use mild shampoo or soap for the scalp. Remove head scales (cradle cap, or *seborrhea*) by rubbing with a cloth. If the scales are particularly resistant, soften them first with some baby oil. Rub hard if necessary to get them off.

A baby bathtub or a standard bathtub filled with water to three inches can be used. The infant should be supported with one arm. *An infant should never be left alone or unsupported in the water.* Since babies usually enjoy being bathed, a bath is a nice time for socializing and a useful diversion during fussy periods.

The *umbilical cord* stub should fall off on its own in seven to fourteen days. It should not be pulled off. Until the cord falls off, the diaper should be rolled down under the navel. The effectiveness of the common practice of dabbing alcohol on the stump at each diaper change has never been proved. Redness that extends beyond the rim of the skin around the base of the cord could be a sign of infection, and the doctor should be called promptly. Following the separation of the cord, the umbilicus (belly button) may be wet and red, and the raw stump left behind may bleed when touched. This area will usually heal within a few days. If it does not, the doctor or nurse can treat it by applying dried silver nitrate on the tip of what looks like a long matchstick.

DIAPERING

The baby should urinate and have a *bowel movement* within twenty-four hours. The first stool, called *meconium*, is black and sticky, almost like tar. The appearance changes first to a seedy yellow, then, after the mother's milk comes in, to a golden yellow with the consistency of scrambled eggs.

Bowel patterns vary from infant to infant. Some babies will have a bowel movement with every feeding; others will have only three or four a week. Breast-fed infants are notorious for skipping days, and may even go a week between stools. The stool pattern may change dramatically after the first few weeks, from six stools a day to one every other

day. The all-time record holder in my practice went three weeks between stools and was perfectly well!

Babies may strain and turn brick red when passing stools, but their
discomfort usually lasts no more than a few minutes. None of this
straining means that the baby is constipated. *Diarrhea* is characterized
by frequent, watery, sometimes foul-smelling, sometimes green, loose
stools. The doctor should be called if the baby develops diarrhea. (The
green color comes from bile that has not undergone processing because
of the rapid passage of the stool through the intestine.)

A baby boy's *foreskin* will not retract completely at birth. Retractabil-
ity increases with age and is usually not complete for several years. During baths it is not necessary to retract the foreskin over the head of the
penis for cleaning. Periodically, the foreskin can be tested gently for re-
tractability, but it should *not* be forced.

A *circumcision* takes about ten days to heal. The area should be washed
at each diaper change with a cotton ball soaked with warm water.

There is no medical or hygienic argument for circumcision (except
some reduction in the already low risk for urinary tract infection), and
there are risks associated with the procedure, including bleeding and
trauma to the penis and infection. I advise against it. If the procedure is
done for religious reasons, a local anesthetic can be injected at the base
of the penis to minimize pain. Feeding the baby sugar water also reduces pain.

Pink urine is common during the first few weeks, particularly in baby
boys. The pink stain, lighter in color than blood, is often noticed on the
diaper but is no cause for alarm. The color comes from urate crystals
and is of no special significance.

A baby girl may have a *pink-tinged vaginal discharge* during the first
ten days. This is caused by the withdrawal of stimulation of her uterus
by maternal hormones that passed to her body via the placenta.

Babies of both sexes may temporarily have *swollen breasts* and nipple
secretions caused by the transfer of hormones from the mother across
the placenta. This swelling disappears in seven to ten days.

An accumulation of *mucus* in the corner of the eye, particularly on
awakening, is very common. It results from a transient partial blockage
of the duct that drains tears from the eye into the nose and can be
wiped away with a moist washcloth or cotton ball. Redness of the
whites of the eye (except for red spots present at birth, mentioned on

p. 241) signifies infection *(conjunctivitis)* and should be reported to the doctor or nurse.

Diaper rash is the almost inevitable result of using diapers, a price we seem willing to pay for the convenience of dry sheets, clothes, and laps. For an infant, wearing wet diapers is analogous to an adult's having a wet bathing suit on most of the day. Since infants vary in their susceptibility to rashes, care of their bottoms can be individualized.

The following procedures will help prevent rashes and clear up rashes in progress.

1. Change diapers as soon as they are wet, or at least every two to four hours, including a change at night. Gently rinse the skin with clear water, allowing it to air dry as much as possible.
2. Avoid overnight use of plastic pants over a cloth diaper. Instead, use a triple diaper made of cloth diapers and a rubber pad to protect the bed.
3. In washing cotton diapers, use an extra rinse with diluted vinegar added.
4. The super disposable diapers bind with water and don't merely absorb it, thereby providing a drier environment for the skin.
5. There is evidence that disposable diapers are less likely to cause a rash.
6. Use nonprescription ointments to protect the skin. They work better as prevention than as treatment for established rashes. Zinc oxide, A and D, Desitin, and Vaseline Intensive Care will all do. Air exposure will also reduce rash.
7. Check with the doctor or nurse about any rash that resists efforts to clear it up. Medicated creams or ointments may be required.

PREVENTING EYE INFECTION

All fifty states mandate by law the treatment of the newborn's eyes to prevent infection. Most states follow the standards of the Centers for Disease Control in allowing a choice between silver nitrate and an antibiotic ointment (erythromycin or tetracycline), but some states restrict treatment to the traditional silver nitrate solution.

A drawback to using silver nitrate is the resulting swelling of the eyelids that interferes with opening the eyes and early eye-to-eye contact with the parents. A second limitation of silver nitrate is its ineffectiveness against infection with chlamydia (see p. 134), which has replaced gonorrhea (see p. 137) as the most common cause of conjunctivitis in the newborn. Erythromycin ointment has none of these problems and for this reason is the preventive treatment of choice. Whether silver nitrate or erythromycin is used, treatment can safely be delayed for at least an hour to permit uninterrupted contact between baby and parents. Antibiotic ointment does not cause as much inflammation and is preferable to silver nitrate for this reason. Parents should inquire about this before birth.

METABOLIC TESTS, INCLUDING PKU

There are a number of diseases of metabolism detectable in the blood of newborns. Although all fifty states require testing for PKU (*phenylketonuria*) and several other of the most common metabolic disorders, including levels of thyroid hormone, there is great variation among the states in the number of diseases tested for, and in many states some very important but less common diseases are passed over. One such disease, affecting about 1 baby in 10,000, is MCAD (*medium chain acetylCoA dehydogenase deficiency*), which, if untreated, can cause neurological damage and death. To test for these disorders a technology called *tandem mass spectrometry* is used. Cost has limited its widespread application. Be sure to check on the screening program available in your state. If it is incomplete, ask for private testing. To learn more, check the web sites tylerforlife.com and neogenscreening.com.

TESTING NEWBORNS FOR DRUG EXPOSURE

Unfortunately, the most common toxic influence to which babies today are exposed before birth is illicit drugs taken by a drug-dependent mother. These include crack, cocaine, marijuana, and heroin. Some hospital nurseries are adopting a policy of testing infants for exposure to such drugs so that treatment and preventive measures can begin right away. A common source of samples for testing is meconium, the stools formed before birth, because it provides a months-long record of in utero drug exposure.

HEARING TESTING

Although not widely available at this time (largely because of cost), there is a growing consensus that newborns should have their hearing tested. About two babies per thousand have hearing loss. There is a premium in identifying them early so they can be fitted with hearing aids. Failure to do so can adversely affect their development.

SIGNS OF ILLNESS

The following signs of serious illness should prompt an immediate call for medical attention.

A fever above 100.5 degrees Fahrenheit (see the following discussion)

Diarrhea (frequent watery, foul-smelling, loose stools)

Continuous vomiting at feedings, or vomiting that shoots out several feet from the baby (remember, however, that simple burping may sometimes be projectile)

Weak or absent sucking

Decreased activity and body tone (floppiness)

Blood in stools or in vomitus

Labored breathing

Persistent or unusual crying

To take the baby's temperature, use a *rectal thermometer*. Shake it so that the mercury column falls below 98.6 degrees Fahrenheit, and grease the bulb end with petroleum jelly taken from the jar on a tissue (to avoid contaminating the jar). Lay the baby face down across your lap and gently insert the thermometer about one inch into the rectum, holding the thermometer between index and middle fingers with palm down to grasp and hold the buttocks together. This allows you to move with the baby if the baby wiggles, which prevents the thermometer from breaking. Keep the thermometer in place for three minutes, then wipe it off with a tissue to read it.

JAUNDICE

During the first week the baby needs to be checked daily in natural light for jaundice, a yellow color of the skin and the whites of the eyes. Some degree of jaundice is common and is considered normal. Any yellowness darker than just visible (as dark as the color of lemon peel or egg yolk) should be reported to the doctor or midwife.

Jaundice is produced by the buildup of a chemical called *bilirubin*. Normally present in all humans, bilirubin is a breakdown product of hemoglobin (the oxygen-binding protein) from red blood cells that have died. The bilirubin is carried by the blood, bound to albumin (a circulating protein), to the liver, where, after processing, it is delivered into the bile for elimination through the intestine. The newborn's liver normally takes a few days to reach peak efficiency in processing bilirubin. In addition, a newborn's red blood cells are rapidly reducing in number to accommodate the blood to life outside the uterus, thus liberating more hemoglobin and, hence, more bilirubin. For both these reasons, the newborn is apt to develop jaundice. If any other disorder that increases red blood cell destruction is present, such as maternal antibodies against fetal red blood cells, as in Rh D, or maternal antibodies to type A or B fetal blood (see p. 16), the likelihood of jaundice is even greater. Jaundice is also more likely if the mother has taken sulfonamide antibiotics late in the third trimester. These drugs cross the placenta and bind with albumin in the fetus's blood, displacing bilirubin, which is then free to be distributed among various body tissues, including the skin and whites of the eyes, where it is recognized as jaundice.

Bilirubin in the blood above a certain level can injure the brain, especially in a premature or sick baby. Hence, jaundice needs to be assessed and treated if excessive. Although full-term babies normally develop jaundice, only a small percentage require therapy. Experienced midwives and doctors can estimate the degree of jaundice simply by looking. If the level seems high, an exact measurement of bilirubin can be made on several drops of blood obtained by pricking the heel.

The garden-variety physiological jaundice in infants makes its appearance on the second or, more likely, the third day, peaks on day four or five, and is pretty much gone by day seven. If jaundice occurs during the first twenty-four hours, the doctor should be contacted right away, for the level is more likely to move quickly into the dangerous range.

The mainstay of treatment of jaundice is light (phototherapy). Light activates a chemical in the baby's skin that breaks down bilirubin. The infant is placed naked, with the eyes covered, under one or two special fluorescent lights for as long as it takes to lower the bilirubin or is wrapped in special light-emitting blankets, with the eyes uncovered. Nursing can continue while the baby is under the lights. Phototherapy can be given in the home as well as in the hospital.

Borderline levels of jaundice can be treated by exposing the baby to natural sunlight near the window at home. In babies whose severe jaundice is not controllable by phototherapy, bilirubin is removed by withdrawing blood bit by bit and replacing it with donor blood having a normal level of bilirubin, a procedure known as *exchange transfusion*.

There is no evidence that giving extra water will decrease jaundice, and water supplements will interfere with breast-feeding.

A form of jaundice related to breast milk and what to do about it is discussed on page 256.

PREVENTING SUDDEN INFANT DEATH SYNDROME

Although the devastating death of a baby from *sudden infant death syndrome* (SIDS) usually occurs several months after birth, preventive measures can start right at birth. The most important step is positioning the infant on the side or back, not on the stomach (see Sleeping, p. 262). Although this position affects the shape of the baby's head (see Appearance, p. 240) and the timing of turning over and crawling, these effects are temporary and reversible. Parents should also learn infant resusscitation.

In 1998, Peter J. Schwartz and Marco Stramba-Badiale and their colleagues at the University of Padua in Italy reported an association between an abnormality in the electrocardiograms of newborns (a prolonged corrected QT interval) and the later occurrence of SIDS. This abnormality is known to predispose the infant to ventricular fibrillation, a lethal condition in which the heart beats extremely quickly and ineffectively. Because ventricular fibrillation resulting from a prolonged QT interval is preventable with drug therapy, at least in adults, performing electrocardiograms on all newborns to identify this abnormality may become a standard procedure. Studies will be required to test the effectiveness of this promising approach. If there is a family history of prolonged QT, the newborn should have an electrocardiogram. Also, because this heart rhythm dysfunction is genetically based, gene therapy may someday provide a permanent cure.

AUTOMOBILE SAFETY

As discussed in Chapter 3, car safety is a critical issue for riders of all ages, but especially for infants and children, since automobile accidents are a leading cause of death and disability in this age group. Even in the absence of a crash, infants and children are at risk from the swerving and stopping of a car. In many of these situations the child is thrown from the car. Until they are four years old and weigh forty pounds, children require *special safety devices*. (After this age the car's lap and shoulder belts can be used.)

In general, rear-facing devices are better for infants; car seats that hook over seat backs are unsafe. Car seats must protect children from both front and rear crashes, cushioning them and keeping them from being thrown free. In addition, car seats must have a head restraint to protect against whiplash and have restraining belts at least 1.5 inches wide to hold the upper parts of the child's body. Any seat constructed of easily bent, bare metal or flimsy strapping, padded only with thin sponge rubber, or containing sharp or pointed hardware is unsafe and should be avoided.

In 1982 the U.S. government established guidelines for child and infant car restraints. Many states have passed laws requiring the use of restraints that meet the federal guidelines until children are large enough and old enough to use the belts that come with the car.

Whenever infants are transported in a car, even on their first ride home from the hospital, a specially designed restraint should be used. It should be installed and used according to the manufacturer's instructions. The backseat is safer than the front, and the center of the car is safer than the sides. Everyone else in the car should use seat belts, too (whether or not airbags are installed). In a crash, unrestrained passengers can literally crush others as well as hurt themselves. An infant should not be held by an adult in a moving vehicle. In a crash, the baby will be either released or crushed by the person holding him or her. A baby or child should not sit in the zone of expansion of an airbag; if this is necessary, the airbag should be deactivated. If for some reason the baby must be removed from the restraint in a vehicle, the vehicle should first be stopped.

If you insist on the use of restraints in the car right from the start, you will find it much easier to enforce this policy later when your child is old enough to protest. He or she simply will never have known anything different.

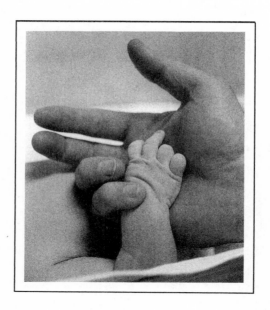

CHAPTER 7

Special Situations and Complications

Major Birth Defects

Major birth defects include the neural tube defects spina bifida and hydrocephalus (see p. 24) and other malformations of the brain; genetic syndromes, of which Down syndrome (see p. 46) is the best known; heart defects; abnormalities of the gastrointestinal tract (closure or faulty hookup of the esophagus [food tube], obstructions of the intestine or stomach, sealing off of the lower rectum and anus); diaphragmatic hernia (see p. 24); cleft lip and palate; and abnormalities of the urinary tract, for example, posterior urethral valves (see p. 243), and of the external genitalia. With improved (but still less than completely effective) methods of early detection in fetuses of genetic defects such as Down syndrome and trisomy 18 (see p. 25) and of open neural tube defects (see p. 29) and other malformations, therapeutic abortion (see p. 316), although not an attractive option, has resulted in fewer babies with these serious defects being born. (See Expanded AFP Test, p. 24; Amniocentesis, p. 27; Chorionic-Villus Sampling, p. 29; and Ultrasound, p. 32.) Folic acid supplements taken early in pregnancy (see p. 92) have proved effective in preventing open neural tube defects, further reducing the number of babies born with these kinds of malformations. However, there are other defects of the fetus for which detection methods are not yet available.

Except for the obvious circumstance of a major brain malformation, mental retardation and cerebral palsy are difficult to predict with certainty in a baby who appears neurologically damaged at birth. So often have doctors been proved wrong in such predictions and so often have parents been caused to worry needlessly that most doctors are staying clear of crystal balls on this question, and well they should. What has also become clear is that any difficulties the baby has during labor and birth are an infrequent cause of brain damage with resulting mental retardation or cerebral palsy. The vast majority of these disabilities originate from damage to the fetus's nervous system during pregnancy, well before labor. How they occur and how to prevent them is only partially understood.

Operations after and even before birth can correct many abnormalities (but not genetic defects such as Down syndrome) if not too much damage has occurred before birth. For example, if the normal flow of urine from the bladder into the amniotic fluid has been blocked, back pressure of urine may have damaged the kidneys to varying degrees. Relieving the obstruction at this advanced stage may not restore kidney function to the point necessary to sustain life. In an effort to avoid such life-threatening complications, the new field of fetal surgery has developed (see Treating the Fetus, p. 153). At this time, in the early development of this specialty, operations are performed mainly to buy time for a definitive correction after birth. In the case of a bladder obstruction, the surgical intervention is to place a catheter through the abdomen of the fetus into the bladder to drain urine and relieve pressure on the kidneys. After birth the catheter is removed and the obstruction is corrected.

A limiting factor to definitive surgery in complex malformations of newborns has been the lack of adequate skin for transplantation to cover defects, necessitating multiple procedures spread out over many months or more. A promising new, as yet incompletely worked out, solution to this problem is obtaining biopsy-sized samples of skin (and other tissue) from the fetus identified to have a birth defect, growing the tissue in the laboratory, and then using the expanded quantity of tissue in the surgical repair after birth. (See New Contributions of the Fetus and Baby to Medicine in General, p. 156.)

The psychological impact on the parents of a baby with a major birth defect is profound. John Kennell and Marshall Klaus, in their book

Bonding, which I cite several times, aptly say, "When a baby is born with a malformation, it is a crushing blow to everyone who shares in the event." The successive stages of adjustment for parents include shock; disbelief (denial); sadness, anger, and anxiety; equilibrium; and reorganization. Recommendations for parents in dealing with this most difficult of adjustments are seeing the baby as early as possible; recognizing what is *normal* about the baby as well as what is not; avoiding use of tranquilizers; receiving care by a special nurse in a special place in the hospital away from mothers with normal babies; sharing prolonged contact with the baby; meeting singly and jointly with the physicians involved in the baby's care and, later, jointly participating in phone calls so that both parents hear (and then can discuss) the (same) report from the doctor; openly communicating with each other; and keeping the family together (there is a high risk of divorce in these stressed marriages), best accomplished initially by "working hard to bring out the issues early and by encouraging the parents to talk about their difficult thoughts and feelings as they arise" (Kennell and Klaus).

BREECH PRESENTATION

Breech (buttocks-first) birth has been a source of concern for centuries because of increased risk to the baby during labor and delivery. Through modern obstetrical techniques, the risks have been greatly reduced. It is now reasonable to expect a successful birth, whether vaginally, or, as is more common, by cesarean section.

There have been major shifts over the past fifty years in the approach to delivery of breeches. With improved techniques of surgery and anesthesia by the 1960s and 1970s, the overall results of cesarean section were found to be superior to vaginal delivery in terms of death and injury, and cesarean section came into widespread use. Then, in the late 1970s, researchers revisited this question and found that in most cases frank breeches (see description below) could safely undergo a trial of labor, with cesarean section done only if necessary rather than routinely. The neonatal death rates in the cesarean-delivered and vaginally delivered infants were found to be essentially the same, nearly zero, in the university hospital settings where the studies were performed. None of the studies, however, had a randomized control design (see p. 5), which limited their value and left important questions unanswered.

Despite some efforts to reverse it (see discussion of National Institutes of Health report in Cesarean Birth, p. 213), the upward trend in C-sections has persisted. Spurred by the medical malpractice climate that began in the 1970s and the lack of randomized control studies addressing the question of safety, most obstetricians now perform C-sections in the case of breech presentations without exception. Given the very low risk associated with cesarean sections, it is hard to defend against the claim that any problems that occur in a breech baby delivered vaginally could have been prevented had a cesarean section been performed. Faced with this medical-legal reality, most physicians have simply abandoned breech vaginal delivery (and in so doing have lost the skills needed for doing it). Today, well under 20 percent of all breeches involving only one fetus are born vaginally. Fortunately, and at long last, we should soon have better answers to the question of the safety of breech birth from a well-designed randomized study now under way in Canada.

About 3 to 4 percent of term pregnancies are breeches. The more premature the baby, the greater the chance of a breech. All babies are breech at least some of the time early in pregnancy, as the fetus is in a sea of fluid and can turn every which way. As the fetus grows, it occupies more of the intrauterine space relative to the quantity of fluid, and there is less room for turning. After thirty-six or thirty-seven weeks, it is unlikely that the fetus will flip (or float) over by itself. Without manipulation, a breech near term stays a breech.

Prematurity is not the only factor associated with breech presentation. In twin pregnancies (p. 317) one twin is likely to be breech and the other vertex (head down), the most efficient way to pack the uterus. Breeches are also more common with various birth defects. A baby with Down syndrome (p. 46), for example, is twice as likely as a normal baby to be a breech. Breeches are more common in the presence of hydramnios, with its superabundance of fluid (p. 295), and in women who have had many pregnancies. Sometimes more than one factor is operating, for example, when prematurity and a congenital defect are associated. In about 80 percent of breeches, however, there is no known cause.

There are three common types of breech presentations. In a *frank breech*, the thighs are flexed on the abdomen and the legs are straight or

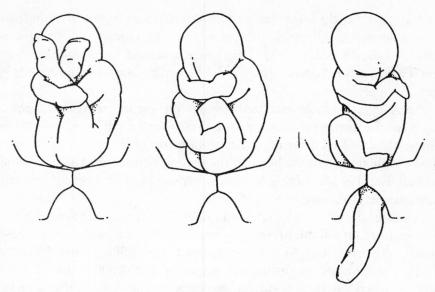

FIGURE 7.1   Three types of breech presentation: frank breech, complete breech, incomplete breech

near straight at the knees. This position makes it very difficult for the fetus to turn over on its own, since the legs serve to hold the rest of the body in place. Thus the frank breech is the most common type of breech, as in the other breeches the fetus is more likely to flip.

In a *complete breech*, the thighs are flexed at the groin but the legs are bent at the knees. In an *incomplete breech*, one or both hips are not flexed (they are straight) and one or both feet or knees lie below the level of the buttocks of the fetus. This type of breech is also called a footling breech because usually one foot is lying low. (See Figure 7.1.)

The frank breech accounts for 38 percent of all breeches weighing less than 2,500 grams (about 5 pounds) and 51.0 to 73.0 percent of those weighing over 2,500 grams. The corresponding figures for complete breeches are 12.0 percent and 11.5 percent, respectively. For incomplete breeches, the figures are 50.0 percent and 20.0 to 24.0 percent.

The frank breech is the only type in which the inlet to the pelvis is filled as well or nearly as well during labor as in a normal, headfirst presentation. When a foot or leg is adjacent to the buttocks, as in a complete or footling breech, the fit is not nearly as good. Because of this incomplete fit, the umbilical cord is much more likely to slide (pro-lapse) around the buttocks and enter into the vagina (see Prolapse of the Umbilical Cord, p. 315). The consequences of a prolapsed cord can be serious; at worst, the fetus can die if cord compression interrupts its blood supply.

An X ray, CT (computerized tomography) scan, or MRI (magnetic resonance imaging) to measure the dimensions of the woman's pelvis; and ultrasound to determine the relationship of the fetus's head to its body (only flexion of the head on the chest is considered a safe position) are all useful in identifying breeches that can be born vaginally, assum-ing that no problems develop in labor.

A consensus has developed that vaginal birth is reasonable to consider for fetuses in the frank breech position with heads flexed to their chests whose estimated weight is between 2,000 and 3,800 grams. Cesarean birth is safer when the estimated weight is over 4,000 or under 1,500 grams, when the head and neck are extended, and when the woman's pelvis is judged small. (Despite this consensus the data on the superior-ity of C-section for babies weighing less than 1,500 grams are weak.) The best results achieved to date demonstrate that in breeches for whom a trial of labor is considered appropriate, about 45 percent can safely deliver vaginally, whereas 55 percent will need a cesarean section, significantly fewer than the figures of two decades ago.

An interesting recent insight is that the squatting position may offer significant advantages in the vaginal delivery of a breech baby because the volume of the birth canal increases as much as 28 percent when a woman squats. No studies have been done yet to test the effects of this finding in breech birth.

Vaginal breech delivery is carried out in the hospital with the services of four physicians:

The *obstetrician in charge*
An *assistant obstetrician*, who is especially important if forceps are used to guide the birth of the head
The *anesthesiologist*, in case a C-section is required
The *pediatrician*, to attend to the needs of the baby

The birth of the head of a breech is the critical event. In vertex birth, the head, which is the largest part of the baby, leads the way and is born before the rest of the baby. Once the head has cleared, it is unusual for any other part of the baby to get stuck (with the exception of the shoulders; see Shoulder Dystocia, p. 315). But in a breech, the head is the *last* part of the body to be born. Thus, passage of all but the head is no guarantee that the head too will pass. If the head gets stuck, the cord will be compressed between the head and the wall of the birth canal as long as the head remains stuck, so time is of the essence.

Forceps are often used in delivering the head to protect it and avoid undue traction on the neck. Four obstetrical hands are needed, two to apply the forceps and two to support the baby's body. With one hand, the assistant obstetrician supports the baby's trunk and arms with a towel and pulls upward; the legs are supported and pulled upward with the other hand. The obstetrician in charge inserts the forceps into the vagina over the sides of the baby's head. The forceps bend downward at the perineum, and the handles lock below the baby. As the forceps exert downward traction on the head, the assistant obstetrician pulls upward on the body until the head clears the perineum.

In a cesarean section for a breech presentation, the ideal incision, in terms of avoiding cesarean sections in future pregnancies, is a *lower-segment transverse incision* (see Cesarean Birth, p. 213) However, when the fetus is premature, the lower, nonmuscular part of the uterus may be underdeveloped, forcing the obstetrician to make a vertical incision, thereby destining the woman to cesarean sections in subsequent pregnancies.

Because of the many issues surrounding the care of breeches, identifying these babies prior to labor is important so that adequate plans for birth can be made. Clues to the presence of a breech on examination of the uterus include feeling the head high in the abdomen and hearing the fetal heart tones *above*, rather than below, the umbilicus.

One way to avoid the problems associated with breech birth is to convert (turn) the breech to a vertex presentation before labor begins. In the procedure known as *external cephalic version*, the attendant positions one hand on the woman's abdomen over the fetus's head and the other over its buttocks. The hands are moved in opposite directions, one toward the woman's head and one toward her feet, as the baby is gently repositioned 180 degrees. The fetus is turned through the shorter of the two possible arcs, determined by the side the head is on, so that the head takes the shortest route to the pelvis. The maneuver takes a few minutes to perform.

The fetal heart rate is determined at the beginning and end of the procedure, and some doctors check it midway through as well. A marked increase, decrease, or irregularity of the rate is a sign of fetal distress and is an indication for the immediate return of the fetus to its original position. To further increase the safety of the procedure, the fetus and the placenta are checked by ultrasound before and after the turning. Drugs are given to the woman to relax the uterus (see p. 312 on tocolytics). Because the maneuver is associated with an increased chance of bleeding across the placenta from the fetus to the woman, the woman's blood is usually checked before and after the maneuver for the presence and number of fetal cells. If significant hemorrhage has occurred, the fetus is closely monitored for signs of distress that might necessitate an emergency C-section. Women with Rh (D)-negative blood are given D immunoglobulin to prevent their sensitization to Rh (D)-positive fetal blood cells (see discussion of blood types and Rh D factors on p. 16).

Following a successful turning, a woman is asked to stay in an upright position for the rest of the day. If necessary, the procedure may be repeated once. If the fetus does not stay in the vertex position after two attempts following the thirty-seventh week, no further efforts at version are made. The expected success rate is about 65 percent at the thirty-seventh week and does not increase subsequently. About 90 percent of successfully turned breeches will remain in the new position until labor begins. Since there is a higher rate of reversion earlier, thirty-seven weeks is considered the optimal time to do the procedure.

Reported complications of turning a breech manually, all uncommon, include the death of the baby (presumably due to twisting and entanglement of the umbilical cord), placental abruption (see Placenta Previa and Placental Abruption, p. 303), and rupture of the uterus. There are no good statistics on these complications, and they are considered rare. Nevertheless, many obstetricians do not subscribe to the notion of turning a breech and will not perform the procedure. Also, not all obstetricians are experienced with the procedure. If your obstetrician is not comfortable with it and you remain interested, ask for a consultation with a physician with experience and interest.

A recent report from China described effectively turning a breech by stimulating an acupuncture point in the foot (designated as BL67 and located beside the outer corner of the fifth toenail) with heat created by burning a leaf called *moxa* (the Japanese term for the plant *Artemisia vulgaris*), a procedure known as *moxibustion*. The treatments are self-administered for one to two weeks. The report stated that twice as many breeches in the treatment group turned, compared with the control group.

CARPAL TUNNEL SYNDROME

Hand pain is common in pregnancy, and *carpal tunnel syndrome* is a leading cause. This disorder results from pressure on the nerve (the median nerve) that supplies the side of the hand on which the thumb is located. The nerve is compressed as it passes through the narrow space in the wrist known as the carpal tunnel. The resulting symptoms, which are felt in the thumb, index and middle fingers, and half of the ring finger, are pain, numbness, and, in more advanced cases, weakness. Carpal tunnel syndrome is more common in pregnancy because of fluid accumulation in the inner spaces of the wrist.

Pain varies in intensity, from merely annoying and interfering with sleep, to intolerable in a small minority of women. Although pain is centered in the hand, aching can be felt as high up the arm as the shoulder.

In most cases, complete improvement occurs after delivery. During pregnancy, symptoms can be relieved with analgesics (pain medicines) and by splinting the wrist with the hand bent upward for part of the day or at night. If these measures are inadequate, the carpal tunnel syndrome can be corrected by a decompression operation performed under local anesthesia.

DEATH OF A FETUS OR BABY

Although most miscarriages occur during the first trimester, fetal death can occur at any time right up to and during labor itself. Causes late in pregnancy include intrauterine growth retardation (see pp. 296–298), accidents involving the umbilical cord (see Prolapse of the Umbilical Cord, p. 315), preeclampsia (pp. 307–309), poorly controlled maternal diabetes (pp. 288–289), smoking by the woman (pp. 142–143), or placental abruption (p. 304). Recently an association has been found between fetal deaths and mutations in the woman's genes that encode for blood-clotting proteins (see Venous Thromboembolism and Phlebitis, p. 321). Many deaths late in pregnancy are unexplained.

Deaths that occur before birth are called *intrauterine deaths* or *still-borns*. Fetal death after the eighteenth or twentieth week is usually suspected by the woman when she no longer perceives fetal movement. The absence of growth of the uterus is another clue. Death is confirmed by failure to detect the fetal heart tone either by fetoscope or by ultrasound; by a decrease, loss, or failure of increase of chorionic gonadotropin; and by lack of fetal growth as determined by ultrasound.

There are good reasons to bring about delivery promptly if a fetus has died and labor has not occurred. Women commonly experience severe psychological problems when they carry a dead fetus. Also, especially after several weeks have passed, absorption of the dissolved fetal tissue into the woman's blood can cause widespread and harmful clotting of her blood.

If death occurs in the third trimester, labor can often be induced with oxytocin (see p. 195). In the second trimester, when the uterus is relatively unresponsive to oxytocin, there are several choices. A dilatation and evacuation, or D & E, may still be effective. Alternatively, uterine contractions can be stimulated by prostaglandins (see 197), which can be administered as a vaginal suppository, by injection, or intravenously.

If the fetus cannot be delivered through the induction of labor because of some mechanical problem (such as a placenta previa or cephalopelvic disproportion), a cesarean section (pp. 213–220) may be necessary.

After the birth of a stillborn child, the risk of future stillbirths, postnatal death, and disabilities in surviving infants is more than doubled. In the case of two stillbirths, the combined risk increases fivefold and affects one-third of subsequent fetuses. The more that can be learned about a stillbirth, or early fetal death, from autopsy study, postmortem X-ray and ultrasound studies, and chromosomal analysis, the more information can be given to the parents to guide them in future pregnancies.

Emotional Effects of Pregnancy Loss

The guiding principles in coping with a fetal or infant death are recognition of the reality of the situation; full communication of feelings, beliefs, and fantasies; and acceptance of support from others.

Parents are encouraged to look at, talk to, and hold the dead baby, even one with deformities, as well as to be alone with him or her if they so wish. Photographs may be useful for later recall, to help make the unbelievable real again. Saved locks of hair or items of clothing serve the same purpose. If the baby was born alive, naming the child can help make the reality concrete. Crying is a healthy expression of emotion.

The decision to obtain an autopsy and chromosomal studies must be made quickly. Both procedures are desirable to obtain information about the cause of death (and thereby remove fantasies about it) and to provide important information for future pregnancies. If a death occurs out of the hospital, it should be reported to the medical examiner, who may request an autopsy as a matter of course. The parents should expect that the attendants will share the findings of the autopsy with them as soon as they are available.

Parents are encouraged to hold a simple funeral, memorial service, burial, or cremation. The funeral as a rite of passage serves to solidify the reality of the death and allows the couple to experience the sympathy and support of friends and relatives. Funeral services for infants are generally not expensive.

Bereaved parents need to be aware of the common physical and psychological elements of normal grieving. These include headache, muscle tightness, and chest pain; the welling up of intensely sad feelings, especially during the first few weeks and for up to a year or more after the death; a recurrent bizarre experience of believing that the baby is still alive; and feelings of anger directed toward themselves, each other, birth attendants, and others. In one typical study, over 50 percent of parents who had lost a baby described experiencing anger, guilt, irritability, loss of appetite, preoccupation with the death, difficulty in sleeping, and intense sadness.

Parents are advised to spend time talking with each other about their feelings. Many will find that they need to discuss the events surrounding the death many, many times before resolving their grief. The wound may be opened again by experiences that remind them of the loss, such as an anniversary, the birth of a friend's baby, or the sight of the hospital.

Bereaved parents also need to pay careful attention to the needs of their living children. It does not help to hide sad feelings from children. Parents' honesty about their feelings helps children deal with the feelings they are having. Parents should listen carefully to a child's re-actions, reaching for the deeper meaning underlying the words and be-havior. Often, young children will see themselves as the cause of the death. Such self-blame is not unlike that of the parents, who com-monly search their own actions and thoughts for a possible cause of the death, such as initial feelings of ambivalence toward the pregnancy, failure to stop smoking, or a cavalier approach to nutrition or other preventive issues. Parents need to acknowledge the child's feelings, whatever they may be, without criticism, while supplying necessary corrective information: "It may feel that the baby died because you didn't want us to have him, but the way you felt had nothing to do with it, nothing at all."

Ideally, the parents should meet with the birth attendants at the time of the death and several days later. Questions about procedures at the time of birth and their effects—what was done or not done—should be answered fully. Other family members should be welcomed to the sec-ond meeting if they want to be there. A third meeting to review the death and mourning can be planned for three to six months later. When the results of the autopsy are received, they should be shared promptly with the parents, providing yet another opportunity for the parents to ask questions.

Support groups for bereaved parents exist in many communities and can be a great help. Childbirth-education organizations, such as the lo-cal affiliates of the ICEA, can direct parents to such groups.

Many hospitals now offer bereavement teams, which can include a nurse, neonatologist, social worker, pathologist, and psychiatrist. These multidisciplinary teams supplement the support provided by the birth attendants.

Parents are usually advised not to plan another baby until they com-plete their mourning, which means waiting, on average, six months to a year before conceiving another child. Women in particular may have an intense desire to have another baby immediately in the belief that their pain and feelings of emptiness will thereby be relieved. It is generally considered preferable not to act on such impulses, but to wait and plan for a new baby who can have an identity of his or her own and not be-come simply a replacement for the baby who was lost. However, indi-vidual differences in psychological makeup and physical factors such as advancing age of the parents will play a role in these decisions. While respecting and considering the advice of others, including the experts, parents need to trust their own instincts and judgments.

DEPRESSION

Postpartum blues (see p. 226) are so common as to be considered normal; about 80 percent of mothers are affected during the first several weeks after birth (see p. 224 on postpartum emotions). Clinical depression, which usually appears after one or two months, affects 10 to 15 percent of women. That so many women experience the blues or depression is further evidence, if any were needed, of the huge impact of pregnancy and the birth of a child on the parents.

The warning signs of depression are unexplained feelings of sadness or irritability; loss of interest or pleasure in activities once enjoyed; thoughts of death or suicide; changes in weight or appetite; changes in sleeping patterns (too much or too little); feelings of guilt, hopelessness, or worthlessness; inability to concentrate, remember things, or make decisions; fatigue or loss of energy (exacerbated by the normal interruptions of sleep during the first few months); and restlessness or decreased activity levels.

Excessive anxiety is often a tip off to depression (and other serious illnesses, such as panic disorder, obsessive-compulsive disorder, bipolar disorder, post-traumatic stress disorder, and psychoses—all of which may be triggered following childbirth). Anxiety may be manifested in a mother's constantly checking to see that her baby is still breathing (indeed, *still living*), frequent calls to the pediatrician, and difficulties with breast-feeding.

Factors that increase the risk for depression, in addition to the major factor of just having had a baby, are a personal history of depression before childbirth, a previous bad birth experience, illness of the baby (also see Major Birth Defects, p. 275), a history of major mood disturbances during menstrual cycles (severe PMS), recent death of the woman's mother, and marital problems. Women who are depressed after childbirth are more likely to have thyroid problems and their thyroid function should be checked.

As with many psychological problems, often the person with depression is blind to symptoms that are obvious to everyone else (and without input from others may never know that something is wrong).

It is both telling and fortunate that in prenatal classes women typically appear to tune out discussions of depression, whereas men are often all ears. Husbands and other family members are relied on to recognize depression and help the depressed woman get the care she needs.

Fortunately, treatments for depression, both drugs and counseling services, have never been better. Both types of treatment are necessary. Help at home is also key in taking both the psychological stress and the physical workload (including housework) off the mother. She will need time for herself—to be alone, to sleep—with the assurance that her baby is being well cared for. One suggestion for women who have stopped eating and lost weight is to leave bowls of trail mix in each room for grazing.

(See Appendix for reference on depression.)

DIABETES

Although diabetes and pregnancy do not mix well, attentive care can do much to reduce risks to the woman and to the developing fetus. Pregnancy intensifies the metabolic derangement in this disorder in women who already have it, and pregnancy can bring out diabetes in a woman with an underlying predisposition to it, even if she has not previously shown signs or symptoms of the disease. During pregnancy these women may develop symptoms typical of diabetes, such as weakness, increased thirst, and increased urination.

The adverse effects of untreated or inadequately treated diabetes on pregnancy include increased risk of preeclampsia and eclampsia (see pp. 307–309); increased susceptibility of the pregnant woman to infection; increased size of the fetus, which may complicate delivery (see Shoulder Dystocia, p. 315, and the following section, on disproportion); increased incidence of polyhydramnios (see pp. 295–296); and increased incidence of congenital abnormalities (birth defects).

The good news is that with careful control of blood-glucose levels with insulin therapy initiated early in pregnancy (the earlier the better), aided by home blood-glucose testing, the course of pregnancy for many women with diabetes will not be significantly different from that for women without this disease. Ideally, plans for care should begin before pregnancy occurs (see Before You're Pregnant Dos and Don'ts, p. 12).

The less tight the control of blood glucose, the more likely adverse consequences will occur. Interventions, such as cesarean section, should be made based on indications that apply to any pregnancy, rather than simply because a woman has diabetes. Women with diabetes should have their urine checked for infection more frequently than should women without this disease.

Women with long-standing diabetes are at increased risk during pregnancy for deterioration of kidney and eye function and may require treatment for these problems. Some women may demonstrate the first signs of kidney and eye problems during pregnancy. Women with diabetes should discuss the risks to them *before* becoming pregnant. For some, pregnancy is not a good idea at all; for others, continuation of a pregnancy can be a danger. (See pp. 15–16 on tests for diabetes.)

DISPROPORTION

Cephalopelvic disproportion (CPD) refers to the inability of a fetus to fit through the woman's pelvis. This condition is suspected when the cervix fails to dilate as expected or the baby does not descend in the birth canal after an adequate trial of labor, sometimes augmented with oxytocin stimulation.

As might be expected, labors complicated by CPD are long, hard, and frustrating. The lack of progress is discouraging to the woman, her partner, and all those attending the birth. A common physical finding associated with CPD is *caput succedaneum*, or localized swelling of the baby's scalp from constriction by the cervix (see p. 176). Once CPD is diagnosed, the attempt at vaginal delivery is discontinued, and a cesarean section (see pp. 213–220) is carried out.

ECTOPIC PREGNANCY

An *ectopic* pregnancy is one in which the fertilized egg becomes implanted outside the uterus. The word derives from the Greek *ex*, meaning "out of," and *topos*, meaning "place." Most ectopic pregnancies are located in the fallopian tubes (named after the sixteenth-century Italian anatomist Gabriele Fallopius), but they can occur at other sites as well, including the ovary, the outside of the uterus, or within the abdominal cavity. Various studies have shown a frequency of ectopic pregnancies ranging from 1 in 64 to 1 in 230 pregnancies. All sexually active women of childbearing age should know the common symptoms of this disorder.

The most common symptoms of ectopic pregnancy are lower abdominal pain and vaginal bleeding. Often the menstrual pattern has been irregular, suggesting pregnancy. Pain occurs as the embryo distends and erodes through the fallopian tube, especially when it actually breaks through the walls of the tube. The free blood in the abdominal cavity can irritate the diaphragm, producing pain in the shoulders when the woman breathes.

Because the growth and development of the ectopic embryo and placenta are eventually halted, hormonal support of the pregnancy is also halted, and growth of the endometrium (inner lining of the uterus) is affected. The endometrium is shed and is recognized as vaginal bleeding. The pattern of this bleeding is usually different from that of a normal menstrual period; it is later, usually lighter, and more like spotting than like a regular flow. Nonetheless, it is easy to mistake this bleeding for a normal period. As will be discussed, bleeding caused by an ectopic pregnancy can also resemble that seen in a miscarriage (pp. 298–303), a condition with which an ectopic pregnancy can easily be confused.

There is usually little difficulty in diagnosis when a major rupture occurs in a woman who knows she is pregnant. Besides vaginal spotting, symptoms include sudden sharp, stabbing, one-sided lower-abdominal pain; shock (signified by light-headedness, dizziness, pallor, and sweating, along with rapid pulse and falling blood pressure); tenderness in the abdomen, and severe tenderness when the cervix is moved; a tender mass on one side of the uterus; and a soft swelling caused by pooled blood felt behind the cervix on rectal examination. A woman with these classical symptoms should be wheeled straight to the operating room.

Most ectopic pregnancies, however, are more subtle during the early phase of rupture. Over a period of days to weeks symptoms of mild lower-abdominal pain, vaginal spotting, and tenderness on pelvic examination develop in a woman who may or may not know that she is pregnant. Any combination of these findings may be present in any degree of intensity. Women and their medical attendants must keep the possibility of an ectopic pregnancy foremost in their minds if a diagnosis is to be made early. It is often difficult to distinguish ectopic pregnancy from appendicitis and other conditions.

Determining whether a woman is pregnant is the first step in establishing whether her symptoms could be related to an ectopic pregnancy. If it is determined that the woman is pregnant and an ectopic pregnancy is suspected but not verifiable, the next step is to measure blood human chorionic gonadotropin (HCG; see Pregnancy Tests, p. 53).

Because in pregnancy the level of HCG normally doubles every three days, if it doesn't (taking the shape of a flattened curve) or if it declines (a falling curve), a pregnancy in trouble, which may be an ectopic pregnancy, is suspected. Thus, serial measurements are often made to determine the normalcy of a pregnancy when signs and symptoms such as spotting and pain raise doubt.

By five to six gestational weeks, ultrasound examination can detect a fetal sac in the uterus or fallopian tube. In a pregnant woman an intrauterine sac argues against an ectopic pregnancy, whereas its absence argues for it, even if the tubes appear normal. Because ultrasound cannot detect an intrauterine pregnancy younger than five to six weeks, it is not useful as a diagnostic tool in ectopic pregnancies suspected before this stage. (In very rare cases—1 in 5,000—intrauterine and tubal pregnancies can coexist. Thus, although the presence of a fetal sac in the uterus argues against an ectopic pregnancy, it does not completely exclude it.) Ultrasound is also useful in detecting fluid behind the uterus, which is blood from a leaking ectopic pregnancy.

Beginning at five to six weeks of gestation, direct visualization of a fallopian tube with a laparoscope (passed into the abdomen through the umbilicus) can identify an ectopic pregnancy. (The laparoscope is a flexible, pencil-thin tube with a light at one end, through which light beams are transmitted in bendable fiber-optic channels.)

Another diagnostic measure is the identification of blood in the pelvic cavity using aspiration with a needle passed through the vaginal wall just behind the cervix. The existence of such blood is strong evidence for a ruptured ectopic pregnancy in a woman who is pregnant.

Even with these advanced diagnostic approaches and heightened awareness, an ectopic pregnancy can escape early detection and become an urgent problem. Ectopic pregnancies that occur in the part of the fallopian tube contained within the wall of the uterus, so-called *interstitial pregnancies*, are particularly treacherous. About 2.5 percent of ectopic pregnancies in some studies were of this variety. Because of the site of implantation in interstitial pregnancies, no mass is present in the tube, and the uterus enlarges much as it would in a normal intrauterine pregnancy. Because of the strength of the wall of the uterus in contrast with that of the tube, rupture of the pregnancy is likely to occur at a more advanced gestational age, between the end of the second and the end of the fourth month. When rupture does occur, the bleeding is likely to be heavy and immediate attention is required.

The treatment of an ectopic pregnancy depends on its location, size, and whether rupture has occurred. The very smallest ones may dissolve on their own, evidenced by declining levels of pregnancy hormone and disappearance of the sac as revealed by ultrasound examination. An ectopic pregnancy that persists can often be successfully treated with the drug *methotrexate*, which is also used to treat some tumors and immune disorders. Larger ones will require a surgical procedure; the location and size of the pregnancy determine which surgical procedure will be performed. Ectopic pregnancies near the open end of the tube grow under its surface, not in the central lumen, or core, and can often be removed without cutting through the tube. Those nearer to the uterus, which usually grow within the lumen of the tube, must be cut out; afterward, the surgically severed ends of the tube are reconnected. In an interstitial ectopic pregnancy, the uterus itself may have to be removed (hysterectomy) along with the tube and the products of conception. The choice of surgical method also depends on the location and size of the ectopic pregnancy and on the associated blood clot; surgery is performed either under visualization with a laparoscope, with its various mechanical attachments (pincers, etc.), or through a lower-abdominal surgical incision. Recovery from a laparoscopy is usually easier and quicker.

During an operation for a ruptured ectopic pregnancy every effort is made to preserve the tube, although its ability to transport a fertilized ovum successfully will be reduced and the likelihood of its again harboring an ectopic pregnancy will be increased. However, with an advanced ectopic pregnancy it is often impossible for the surgeon to remove the products of conception without also removing the tube itself.

Rh D-negative women should be given D immunoglobulin at the time of treatment for an ectopic pregnancy to prevent sensitization to D blood type and resulting risk to subsequent pregnancies (see pp. 16–19).

An ectopic pregnancy may have all the symptoms of a miscarriage, but it is important to distinguish between the two conditions. Sometimes it is not possible to make this distinction using currently available tests. Therefore, if a D & C is done because of a suspected incomplete abortion (miscarriage) or to interrupt a pregnancy, it is important to submit the curettings (scrapings) to a pathologist for examination. The absence of fetal tissue strongly suggests (but does not by itself prove) an ectopic pregnancy and should prompt a search for this disorder. Some ectopic pregnancies are discovered in this way.

The cause (or causes) of an ectopic pregnancy is often not certain in an individual case, but several factors are known to predispose a woman to this condition. These factors are associated with changes in the structure and function of the fallopian tubes. Prior infection of the tubes (salpingitis), most commonly from chlamydia or gonorrhea (pp. 134–137), is perhaps the most common causal factor. The practice of vaginal douching in women who carry chlamydia is also associated with ectopic pregnancy. The fallopian tubes can be malformed, with narrowing, blind pockets and misplaced openings. They can be scarred and stunted from prior inflammation within the abdominal cavity (such as that caused by a ruptured appendix). Uterine tumors, such as fibroids, can block the entry of the tube into the uterus and predispose to tubal implantation. The failure of a previous operation on the tube to restore its ability to carry fertilized eggs as well as sterilization procedures (having the tubes tied) can also set the stage for an ectopic pregnancy. Finally, the woman who has had one ectopic pregnancy is at increased risk for another; her subsequent pregnancies have about a 10 percent chance of being ectopic.

Women at increased risk for ectopic pregnancy should be monitored closely and should get in touch with their doctors when they intend to conceive. Monitoring includes early diagnosis of pregnancy through hormonal testing, serial measurements of the human chorionic gonadotropin (HCG), ultrasound, and increased awareness of the earliest signs of rupture.

The earlier an ectopic pregnancy is recognized (ideally, even before symptoms occur), the better. Surgery done before rupture not only spares the woman a potentially life-threatening condition and much inconvenience, but also offers a better chance of leaving an intact and functioning fallopian tube. The issue of ectopic pregnancy is closely tied to that of infertility. Infertile women are at increased risk for ectopic pregnancies, and women who have had an ectopic pregnancy are at increased risk for infertility.

Tubal problems that contribute both to infertility and to ectopic pregnancy can sometimes be repaired by microsurgery. When such measures fail or cannot be performed, the defective tubes can be bypassed altogether by using *in vitro fertilization* and embryo transfer. In this technique, the egg is removed just before ovulation through use of a laparoscope and fertilized with the sperm in a test tube. The resulting fertilized ovum is then implanted in the uterus, and the pregnancy proceeds normally.

Although the problem of ectopic pregnancy can be dealt with today much more effectively than in the past, its prevention is a major unresolved issue that is growing in importance. Furthermore, from the point of view of achieving and preserving fertility, present-day treatment is less than ideal. Finally, an ectopic pregnancy can involve all the emotions associated with a pregnancy loss (see pp. 284–287).

GALLSTONES

During and after pregnancy there is an increased incidence of symptoms from stones in the gallbladder. These symptoms include attacks of crampy upper-abdominal pain, more often on the right side and sometimes radiating to the right shoulder, often accompanied by nausea and even vomiting. (Thus gallstones and gallbladder inflammation are considerations in evaluating pain in the upper abdomen; see p. 75). In addition to the obvious discomfort and inconvenience of such symptoms, there is a risk that a gallstone will actually block the bile duct and interfere with the flow of bile, a more serious problem.

There is now good evidence that during pregnancy the gallbladder is less effective in emptying itself of bile and thus increases in size. The bile pools and thickens, forming sludge and stones, which usually (particularly the sludge) go away after delivery. It is preferable to postpone surgery to remove symptom-producing stones (and the diseased gallbladder) until after the baby is born. If that is not possible, a laparoscopic (through the umbilicus) removal of the gallbladder can be accomplished in the first trimester; in the second and third trimesters, open abdominal surgery is required because of the size of the uterus.

HYDATIDIFORM MOLE

Hydatidiform mole (also known as *gestational trophoblastic neoplasm*) is a rare, usually benign but sometimes malignant tumor of the placenta. In the United States moles complicate 1 in 1,500 pregnancies. In Japan the figure is 2 per 1,000. Moles that occur in association with fetal tissue are known as *partial* moles; moles that occur without fetal tissue are known as *complete moles*. Complete moles are associated with low dietary intake of vitamin A (carotene), maternal age over thirty-five years, and previous miscarriage. Incomplete moles also are associated with previous miscarriage. Moles may also coexist with viable pregnancies and cause symptoms before or after birth.

The most common early sign of a mole is vaginal bleeding, similar to that seen in a miscarriage, associated with a level of the pregnancy hormone higher than would be expected for the gestational age of the fetus. As a mole grows, its symptoms and signs also include marked nausea, elevated blood pressure, uterine enlargement out of proportion to the duration of the pregnancy, and the spontaneous passage of tiny, fluid-filled sacs, somewhat similar in appearance to grapes. Ultrasound shows a characteristic picture.

Treatment of a hydatidiform mole consists of removal of the abnormal tissue through a dilatation and suction curettage of the uterus. In some cases, the mole must be removed through an incision into the uterus reached through the abdomen (hysterotomy) or even by complete removal of the uterus itself (hysterectomy).

Following removal of a mole it is important to monitor the chorionic gonadotropin level. Until it disappears, the possibility exists that some of the mole remains or that cancerous changes in the mole have occurred. A cancerous mole, known as a *choriocarcinoma*, may be confined to the uterus (a *noninvasive mole*) or may spread to other parts of the body. Malignant moles are treated with a combination of surgery and chemotherapy.

HYDRAMNIOS AND OLIGOHYDRAMNIOS

Hydramnios means excessive amniotic fluid, and *oligohydramnios*, a relative lack of it. When the size of the abdomen is either larger or smaller than predicted, the relevant condition is suspected. The diagnosis is confirmed by ultrasound. The existence of one of these conditions is most often detected by an ultrasound exam done for some other purpose.

Both disorders are symptoms of an abnormality in the pregnancy that must be carefully evaluated. For example, congenital abnormalities of the fetus that interfere with swallowing or with production of urine can result in hydramnios or oligohydramnios, respectively. An explanation for these disorders is not always found, however, particularly when the increases or decreases in fluid are small and detected by ultrasound as an incidental finding.

If excessive, hydramnios itself represents a problem for the woman. If it interferes with breathing, it may need to be treated by withdrawing amniotic fluid through amniocentesis (see pp. 27–29).

Oligohydramnios presents hazards to the fetus, such as interference with development of the lungs, which do not then fill normally with air at birth; deformities of the arms and legs (because of severely restricted movement); and twisting or compression of the umbilical cord, which can interfere with the fetus's oxygen and food supply to the point of malnutrition and even death. Injecting salt solution into the amniotic cavity is a way of buying time for the fetus in trouble until it can be delivered.

INTRAUTERINE GROWTH DISTURBANCE

Intrauterine growth is of concern if the baby's birth weight is 10 percent less than that predicted for his or her gestational age. Using this definition, the growth of about 7 percent of fetuses is impaired. Prematurity alone is not synonymous with growth disturbance according to this definition, since premature infants may or may not have normal weight for their gestational age.

Several patterns of growth disturbance have been recognized, and some fetuses have more than one. With *asymmetric intrauterine growth retardation*, the length and weight of the affected fetus are reduced, but its head may or may not be small. The baby's mother is more likely than mothers of infants of normal weight to have been ill during pregnancy with high blood pressure, including preeclampsia (see p. 307), chronic kidney disease, or advanced diabetes. In some of these pregnancies growth failure appears related to impaired circulation in the uterus and placenta, so that the fetus is undernourished. A recent finding is an association between fetal growth failure and mutations in the woman's genes that encode for blood-clotting proteins (see Venous Thromboembolism and Phlebitis, p. 321). In many other cases the cause of the growth impairment is still unknown.

With *symmetric intrauterine growth retardation*, the overall growth of the fetus, including growth of the head, is stunted, usually because of illness in the fetus and unrelated to the health of the woman or of the placenta. The illness can be genetic or the result of an infection or toxin. Among the causes are chromosomal abnormalities (see p. 45), congenital rubella syndrome (see pp. 140–142), congenital cytomegalovirus infection (see pp. 135–136), fetal alcohol syndrome (see pp. 143–145), and fetal exposure to cocaine (see p. 145).

A third type of growth disturbance is known as *dysmaturity* or *postmaturity* (see pp. 306–307) because it occurs most commonly in fetuses whose gestations have exceeded forty-two weeks. These babies show signs of having regressed in nutritional status. Their length and head size are normal, but their weight is reduced. After birth, they look skinny, as though they have lost weight; their skin is loose, dry, and wrinkled; and they have little of the fine, long body hair (lanugo) of the normal newborn. Their nails are long, and their skin and nails may be yellow from staining by the fecal material *(meconium)* they pass into the amniotic fluid. This passage of meconium is itself a sign of the stress to which these fetuses are subjected. Their dysmaturity is the result of disease of the placenta, which is unable to supply them with necessary nutrients and oxygen. The cause of this condition is still unknown.

Fetuses with a growth disturbance are at greater risk for death before, during, and after labor. They are more likely to have difficulties as newborns and to require special attention. Some of these difficulties include low blood sugar, low blood calcium, and temperature instability.

The long-range outlook for these fetuses depends both on the cause of the disturbance and on the events surrounding birth and the immediate period following birth. For example, a baby with congenital rubella syndrome is at great risk for permanent physical disabilities, and a postmature infant who has suffered lack of oxygen compounded by meconium in the lungs (which interferes with breathing at birth) is more likely to have neurological difficulties. On the other hand, many babies who are small for their gestational age but have a normal head size do perfectly well. Head size seems important in predicting the outlook for these babies. A study from the Queen Charlotte Maternity Hospital in London showed that children who were small for their gestational age and had head growth that began to slow before twenty-six weeks of gestation demonstrated significantly lower scores in perceptual performance and motor ability at five years of age when compared with a matched control group of children who were normal for their gestational age. Head size was of greater predictive value than weight or length, a logical relationship given that head size corresponds to brain growth.

During pregnancy the growth of the fetus is assessed at each prenatal visit by measuring the size of the uterus. But the size of the uterus provides only indirect evidence on fetal growth, since it depends not only on the growth of the fetus, but also on the amount of amniotic fluid present as well as on other factors. Furthermore uterine size becomes measurable only after the first trimester and there is now evidence that low birth weight with premature births is associated with poor growth in the *first* trimester. However, uterine size is still a good overall indicator.

Ultrasound is the most accurate means of assessing fetal growth (see pp. 32–34) and is used when a concern about growth is raised or when the woman has an illness known to be associated with impaired growth. Ultrasound examination measures the diameter of the head, the circumference of the abdomen, and the size of other body parts. Ultrasound is also used to evaluate the maturity and health of the placenta. Serial ultrasound examinations of fetuses suspected of having growth disturbance can show how well growth is proceeding.

When growth disturbance is suspected, fetal well-being is monitored by tests such as the biophysical profile (see p. 161), umbilical artery wave analysis (see p. 162), and measurement of cord-blood oxygen and acidity (see Umbilical Cord Blood Sampling, p. 162). If the fetus is considered to be in jeopardy, early delivery is considered.

There is no effective intrauterine treatment for the fetus whose growth is impaired. Better understanding of growth retardation and its prevention and treatment are important research priorities.

MISCARRIAGE

A remarkably high percentage of pregnancies do not result in the birth of a live baby. Although fetal death can occur at any gestational age, most deaths occur early in the first trimester, often even before the pregnancy is recognized. Such deaths are referred to medically as *spontaneous abortions* (or miscarriage), to distinguish them from induced abortions.

The statistics on miscarriage are sobering. Overall, about 70% of pregnancies will result in the birth of a live child and roughly 30% will miscarry. In making this calculation, the presence of pregnancy is determined by measuring hormone changes. While pregnancy is not recognized clinically until 5 to 6 weeks after conception by signs such as a missed period and morning sickness, hormone changes (see Pregnancy Tests, p. 53) can detect it far earlier. Many pregnancies, about 22%, result in miscarriages before the woman knows she is pregnant and she does not even know that she has miscarried. After pregnancy is recognized, about 12% of pregnancies will abort with the typical symptoms described below. Loss rates are lowest, about 6%, in women who are pregnant for the first time and highest, 25 to 30%, after three or more losses.

The risk increases with the age of the woman. For example, a twenty-year-old has a 15 percent chance of her first pregnancy's ending in miscarriage; a twenty-five-year-old, 15 percent; a thirty-five-year-old, 25 percent; and a forty-year-old, 40 percent.

Genetic defects are the cause of most miscarriages. Of first trimester miscarried fetuses of less than eight weeks' gestation, 70 to 75 percent are estimated to have chromosomal abnormalities. Between eight and twelve weeks, 40 percent of spontaneously aborted fetuses are chromosomally abnormal. In all, about 60 percent of first-trimester miscarriages are estimated to have chromosomal abnormalities. We do not yet understand how these aberrations occur, but we know that they occur very early in embryonic development. Research on pluripotent stem cells (see p. 157) is expected to provide an understanding of the process and to point the way to preventive measures. Because in some instances the source of an abnormal chromosome may be one or both parents, chromosomal analysis of the parents may be part of the evaluation of recurrent miscarriage (see pp. 34–49 on genetics).

Another 20 percent of first-trimester miscarriages result from the joining of two recessive lethal genes, one from each partner. Each of us carries between six and ten such genes. If partners each carry one or more of the same recessive lethal genes, their mating carries a 25 percent chance for two such genes to combine. Such combinations lead to the death of the fetus. Chromosomal abnormalities and recessive lethal genes taken together account for approximately 80 percent of all first-trimester miscarriages.

Another 10 percent or more first-trimester pregnancy losses appear to be related to immunological factors. For instance, there is an association between early spontaneous abortion and the production by the woman, for unknown reasons, of antibodies to her own thyroid gland. *Antiphospholipid syndrome* involves production by the woman of antibodies directed against normal phospholipids in her own tissues and in those of the placenta and fetus. When these antibodies attach to the phospholipid receptor sites in the tissues, a destructive process, varying in intensity from woman to woman, is initiated. Why a woman's immune system does this is not known. In the woman this immunological attack can result in blood clots in veins (see Venous Thromboembolism and Phlebitis, p. 321) and destruction of platelets, the blood cells involved in blood clotting (see Platelet Disorders, p. 305). In the placenta, the result is both interference with function and impairment of nutritional support for the fetus, which can lead to early miscarriage, intrauterine growth retardation (see pp. 296–298), and, possibly, preeclampsia (p. 307). In the fetus, the antibodies can destroy platelets and heart tissue. A tip-off to this syndrome is a false-positive test for syphilis during the first prenatal visit (see p. 141). Many women with antiphospholipid syndrome are also diagnosed with *lupus erythematosis.*

There is no treatment for antiphospholipid syndrome. The anticoagulant drug heparin is given preventively to women who develop blood clots or who have a history of this problem.

An example of a hormonal explanation for recurrent miscarriage is *inadequate luteal phase,* in which, following ovulation and the formation of the corpus luteum during the menstrual cycle, insufficient amounts of progesterone are produced (for reasons unknown) to sustain an early pregnancy. Spontaneous abortion results. Hormonal treatment has been successful in this disorder. The study of immunological and hormonal factors in pregnancy loss appears to be a fruitful area for further research.

Infection of the fetus with certain viruses (for example, mumps and rubella) is a known cause of miscarriage, and infection is a major cause of spontaneous abortion in cattle. Recently, the common vaginal infection known as bacterial vaginosis (see p. 80) has come under scrutiny as a cause of miscarriage. Thus, it is quite plausible that other, as yet unidentified, infections could play a role in miscarriage in humans.

A recent insight into a possible cause of miscarriage has come from a 1999 study sponsored by the National Institutes of Health. The study showed that in most successful pregnancies the conceptus (fertilized egg in its early stages of development) implants (into the lining of the uterus) within eight to ten days after ovulation. After the tenth day, the later the implantation occurs, the higher the rate of pregnancy loss. How to make use of this finding is not yet clear.

Completing the list of causes of spontaneous abortions that occur in the second or third trimester are causes usually designated as environmental, referring to the environment of the fetus. Some of these factors are known, whereas others are merely postulated. Among the known factors are anatomical abnormalities of the uterus and cervix. Rather than consisting of one chamber, the uterus may form two chambers, ranging from partially to completely separate. This defect can be corrected surgically with a reasonable chance of success. Another well-known, but, fortunately, uncommon, problem is *incompetent cervix*. This disorder, actually more a cause of premature labor than of miscarriage (the lines are blurred), is characterized by painless dilatation of the cervix in the second trimester or early in the third, followed by rupture of the membranes and the subsequent expulsion of a fetus that is usually too immature to survive. The same course of events tends to be repeated in subsequent pregnancies. The surgical approach of sewing the cervix together early in pregnancy has not been successful. How to treat this problem remains unknown.

Much is known about the actual causes of miscarriage, yet humans continue to supply imagined ones as well. Rare is the woman who does not search for some additional cause—what she did or didn't do, what she felt or didn't feel—even though there is no evidence that individual behavior or feelings play a role in spontaneous abortion.

One noncause of miscarriage is sexual intercourse. So often one hears the lament, "If only we had not had intercourse, this would not have happened!" Although intercourse may be a factor in the *timing* of spontaneous abortion, it does not cause the abortion; the pregnancy would have aborted anyway, perhaps several days later, if intercourse had not occurred. *Intercourse cannot be said to cause miscarriage*, which is primarily a result of genetic abnormalities.

Other common noncauses of miscarriage are horseback riding, skiing, and car accidents. A fall, like intercourse, may affect the *timing* of a miscarriage, but won't be its cause. Ambivalence about being pregnant, for whatever the reason, can also lead to guilty feelings after a miscarriage, as can having considered an induced abortion to terminate the pregnancy. In these circumstances a woman might see herself as being punished for her feelings. Women worry about morning sickness and not having eaten well as a result (presumably leading to malnutrition of the fetus), having had a cold or flu, having drunk an alcoholic beverage either before or after finding out about the pregnancy, having taken acetaminophen (Tylenol) for a headache, and so forth. Having feelings of guilt is understandable and searching for rational causes only human, but the facts simply do not support any of these common worries as having anything to do with miscarriage. Drinking, smoking, and medications can affect the *health* of the fetus, but they do not cause miscarriage.

The onset of a miscarriage is heralded by vaginal bleeding. As long as the cervix has not dilated and fetal or placental tissue (sometimes referred to as the products of conception) has not been passed, the term used to describe the bleeding is *threatened abortion.* At this point there is no good way to predict whether the bleeding will stop and the pregnancy proceed normally, or whether an abortion will occur.

If crampy uterine pain occurs in addition to the bleeding, the chances of a miscarriage increase. If there is a gush of amniotic fluid and dilatation of the cervix, the miscarriage is inevitable. Once tissue is identified or the intact fetus in its sac is seen, a miscarriage has occurred (or is occurring). Continued bleeding and cramping lead to suspicion that parts of the pregnancy remain in the uterus, and these will have to be removed by dilatation and curettage (D & C), described in subsequent paragraphs.

Traditionally, women with threatened abortions have been prescribed bed rest. Yet bed rest has never been demonstrated to prevent miscarriage, nor is there any reason to believe that it could or would, now that we know that miscarriage results primarily from genetic abnormalities of the fetus. It is important to know what steps to take if threatened abortion progresses and tissue is passed before the woman reaches the hospital or doctor's office. Tissue should be placed in a sterile (or, at least, clean) receptacle and taken promptly to the hospital for study by a pathologist. If the miscarriage occurs in the hospital or doctor's office, the doctor will follow the same procedure. The purpose of the pathological analysis is to distinguish an aborted intrauterine pregnancy from an ectopic pregnancy (see p. 289) or a hydatidiform mole (see p. 295), both of which can cause similar symptoms. If bleeding stops and pregnancy continues, the condition is commonly referred to as the *cyclic bleeding of pregnancy*, a diagnosis that can be made only in retrospect. (We now know that one common explanation for this sequence of events is the spontaneous abortion of one twin of a twin pregnancy, in what is sometimes referred to as the vanishing twin syndrome [see p. 318].)

When there is uncertainty about whether a miscarriage has occurred or whether the uterus is completely emptied, ultrasound can be helpful; it can detect the presence or absence of the fetus and determine whether the fetus is alive. Failure of the uterus to continue to grow, loss of the associated signs of pregnancy (breast enlargement, etc.), and absence of the predicted increase in chorionic gonadotropin, the hormone commonly measured by the various tests of pregnancy (see p. 53) are other signs of a lost pregnancy.

D & C (dilatation and curettage) is the technique used to complete an incomplete abortion. When done to remove the contents of the uterus, a D & C is more accurately referred to as a D & E (dilatation and evacuation). Pain associated with the procedure is controlled by local or general anesthesia. Metal dilators of successively increasing diameter are inserted into the cervix to stretch the canal to the desired size. Next, a plastic tube (cannula) is passed into the uterus and then attached to a suction machine that draws out the contents of the uterus.

The common practice of routinely performing a D & C after an abortion has come into question with the realization that a high percentage of abortions are actually complete and require no further attention. The use of ultrasound and of measurements of HCG has improved our ability to make this determination.

All losses of pregnancy, whether through miscarriage or induced abortion, will arouse strong emotions in the woman experiencing them. If she can acknowledge these feelings and give herself time to rest or be with close friends, she will recover more completely.

PLACENTA PREVIA AND PLACENTAL ABRUPTION

Placenta previa refers to a low-lying placenta that partially or completely covers the inner opening to the cervix or is very close to the edge of the cervix. In this situation, the placenta will detach and tear as the cervix stretches before and during labor. Before the onset of labor, painless bleeding that stops of its own accord is the most common sign of placenta previa. In a typical case, the woman awakens in a pool of blood. Usually the volume of the initial episode of bleeding is not enough to cause symptoms of blood loss.

Placenta previa is now diagnosed by ultrasound. Once it is diagnosed, the pregnancy is considered at high risk, even when the bleeding has temporarily stopped. The woman is hospitalized and stays in bed up to the time of delivery. Because of the high risk of hemorrhaging in labor, delivery is accomplished by cesarean section after the fetus reaches a mature thirty-seven weeks' gestation. If hemorrhage recurs before thirty-seven weeks or fails to stop after the first bleeding, cesarean section is performed immediately as an emergency procedure.

The cause of placenta previa is not known. It affects about 0.5 percent of all pregnancies and is more common the more children a woman has had and the older she is. Previous induced abortions may also be a factor. Now that ultrasound is widely used in pregnancy, it has been observed that in the second trimester a significant percentage of placentas cover the inner opening to the cervix, but few remain that way until term. As the uterus grows, the positioning of the placenta shifts. There is no reason to repeat ultrasound examinations simply to follow the course of these early low-lying placental positions. With placenta previa the fetus (and later the baby) are at increased risk for a birth defect.

Placental abruption refers to a peeling away of the placenta from the uterus, with associated bleeding between the separated placenta and the uterus. It is the other major cause of bleeding late in pregnancy. The accumulated blood may be trapped within the uterus, or it may escape between the amniotic membranes, passing through the uterus and cervix into the vagina, where it is recognizable as vaginal bleeding. Other symptoms and signs are spasm (increased muscle tone) of the uterus; pain and tenderness; signs of shock due to blood loss (sweating, pallor, faintness, clammy skin, and so on); changes in the pattern of the fetal heartbeat or, in the case of fetal death, complete absence of the fetal heart tones. Since there are various degrees of abruption, the signs and symptoms also vary. At one extreme the fetus may die and the woman may be in profound shock from blood loss. At the other extreme, the woman may show no vaginal bleeding, the fetal heart rate may be normal, and only persistent uterine pain points to the problem. Sometimes partial abruption is totally without symptoms and is discovered only after the placenta is examined following birth.

Once the diagnosis of placental abruption is made, delivery should be accomplished promptly by cesarean section after the woman's blood volume is brought to a stable level.

Placental abruption occurs in less than 1 percent of pregnancies, and its cause is not known. It is reported to be more common in women with severe preeclampsia (see p. 307) and in the second born of twins. A recent finding is that mutations in the woman's genes that encode proteins involved in blood clotting are associated with this disorder (see Venous Thromboembolism and Phlebitis, p. 321). The risk for recurrence of placental abruption is about ten times the original expected rate.

PLATELET DISORDERS

Platelets are the blood cells that play an essential role in blood clotting. A fetus with insufficient platelets is at heightened risk during the stress of vaginal labor and delivery for bleeding into the skin or other organs. Particularly worrisome is bleeding within the skull. Low numbers of blood platelets (*thrombocytopenia*) in the fetus and newborn occur in about 1 in 5,000 pregnancies and most commonly result from the destruction of platelets after they are tagged by antibodies made by the woman and passed to the fetus across the placenta. In most cases these antibodies are produced by the woman's immune system because the fetus's platelet type (analogous to blood type, such as A, B, or O) is different from that of the woman and the woman's body reads fetal platelets in the circulatory system as foreign substances that need to be removed. Fetal platelets leak across the placenta in the same way as do other fetal cells. (See tests for blood type, p. 16, and testing of trophoblasts, p. 31.)

Women may also produce antibodies that destroy fetal platelets because they have illnesses that affect their own platelets as well, often with symptoms of easy bruising and bleeding. The only self-directed antibodies many women produce are antibodies to their platelets. Other women who make antibodies to their platelets also produce antibodies to other body tissues (see, for example, the discussion of antiphospholipid syndrome on p. 300). These women will require treatment during pregnancy.

When low numbers of platelets are suspected in a fetus because the woman has thrombocytopenia or has had a previously affected child, the fetus needs to be monitored closely by serial ultrasound examinations and platelet counts after blood is sampled by umbilical-cord puncture (see p. 162). If a fetus has a low platelet count at term, the current recommendation is to deliver by C-section, thereby minimizing physical trauma to the baby, or to treat the fetus before birth to raise its platelet count. Before birth the fetus can be treated with gammaglobulin (the antibody fraction of plasma) given by way of the woman and through the placenta or with transfusions of platelets into the umbilical blood vessels. Sometimes the therapies are combined. (Also see discussion on Treating the Fetus, p. 153.) Further treatment of the baby is usually required after birth, including transfusion of platelets and administration of gammaglobulin.

POSTDATE PREGNANCY

A pregnancy may extend beyond the average forty weeks because of an error in dating the time of conception (the pregnancy is actually forty weeks; it simply appears to be longer, and a review of dating data may correct the conclusion) or because for that woman and fetus a longer gestation is normal. The concern for pregnancies lasting longer than forty weeks is that a minority of fetuses will suffer progressive malnutrition and asphyxia (see p. 296 on intrauterine growth retardation), including stillbirth, all of which are related to failing placental function. Loss of amniotic fluid (oligohydramnios; see p. 295) can also create a problem. For these fetuses the intrauterine environment is no longer healthy and they would be better served by being born.

To protect the minority of fetuses who are at increased risk in a continued postdate pregnancy, standard practice, based on the best evidence available, is to induce labor in all women at the end of forty-one weeks. Between the expected date of delivery and the end of the forty-first week, the well-being of the baby is checked by nonstress and, if necessary, other tests, usually twice a week (see p. 160). Signs of ill health in the baby may lead to induction of labor or cesarean section.

PREECLAMPSIA AND ECLAMPSIA

Preeclampsia-eclampsia, also known as pregnancy-induced hypertension, is a common, multifaceted disorder of pregnancy. It occurs after twenty weeks' gestation, except in the case of gestational trophoblastic disease (see Hydatidiform Mole, p. 295) when the syndrome can occur in the first trimester as well. Its cause is unknown. Preeclampsia-eclampsia is characterized by high blood pressure and the presence of protein in the urine, with or without edema (swelling) of the legs, arms, and face. Despite nearly fifty years of research, preeclampsia remains a major contributing factor to illness and even to death of women and babies. It affects up to 6 or 7 percent of all pregnancies and can be superimposed on the ordinary kind of hypertension (high blood pressure) that some women have prior to becoming pregnant or that develops as pregnancy progresses.

Known risk factors for developing preeclampsia are first pregnancy, age over forty, African American background, family history of pregnancy-induced hypertension, chronic high blood pressure (hypertension), chronic kidney (renal) disease, antiphospholipid syndrome (see p. 300), diabetes (see p. 289), being pregnant with twins (see p. 317), and high levels of the normally present amino acid *homocysteine* (a genetic abnormality that can be treated with large doses of folic acid). An association between preeclampsia and mutations in genes that encode for blood-clotting proteins has been found (see Venous Thromboembolism and Phlebitis, p. 321).

Blood pressure and urinary protein levels are routinely checked during prenatal visits to detect preeclampsia early. When blood pressure rises above 140 (systolic) over 85 (diastolic), or if the systolic pressure increases 30 points over the prepregnancy level or the diastolic pressure increases 15 or more points, preeclampsia is suspected. A urinary protein level of two plus or greater, as measured by the dipstick method, or the excretion of more than 500 milligrams of protein in the urine over a period of twenty-four hours, is considered significant.

The accumulation of fluid (edema) (see p. 79) in the skin of a pregnant woman, especially in the hands and face, is a sign of preeclampsia. Although edema, especially in the legs, is normal in pregnancy, if it is accompanied by rapid, sudden weight gain preeclampsia is suspected.

Preeclampsia can also cause symptoms, varying in intensity, of upper-abdominal pain, nausea, and vomiting, usually with but sometimes without elevated blood pressure or protein in the urine. When these symptoms are present (see abdominal pain and nausea, p. 74), preeclampsia is a consideration, particularly when blood abnormalities constituting what is known as the *HELLP syndrome* are also present. The HELLP syndrome has three defining characteristics, from which the term *HELLP* is derived: *h*emolysis (destruction of red blood cells), *e*levated *l*iver enzymes in the blood (evidenced by inflammation of the liver), and *l*ow *p*latelet counts (also see Platelet Disorders, p. 305). The HELLP syndrome can lead to problems of its own. A 1999 study identified as one likely cause of the HELLP syndrome a genetic defect, shared by the fetus and the pregnant woman, in the processing of fatty acids. The thinking is that fatty acids that are not metabolized by the fetus accumulate in the woman's blood and are toxic to her liver because she cannot process them either. Measurement of liver enzymes, platelets, and uric acid can assist in distinguishing between preeclampsia and worsening chronic hypertension uncomplicated by preeclampsia.

The risks to the fetus of preeclampsia include intrauterine growth disturbance (see p. 296), stillbirth (see p. 283), placental abruption (see p. 304), and prematurity (see next section), when the baby is purposely delivered early to prevent other problems and safeguard the health of the woman. Risks to the woman include convulsions (known as *eclampsia* when occurring in the context of preeclampsia); hemorrhage into the brain, with possible permanent neurological deficits; loss of vision (usually temporary); hemorrhage into the liver; kidney failure; and, at the extreme, death. Tests of fetal health in late pregnancy (see p. 158) are used when preeclampsia is present. These tests help determine whether it is safe for the fetus for the pregnancy to continue.

The only treatment for preeclampsia is ending the pregnancy through birth of the baby, either through induction or by cesarean section. The results of studies of the effectiveness of taking aspirin during the second trimester in preventing preeclampsia in women at increased risk for this disorder are inconclusive. On the other hand, a high-calcium diet (including supplements) is effective in prevention. Preeclamptic mothers must be carefully monitored for seventy-two hours following delivery because eclamptic convulsions can occur during this time. In rare cases, convulsions occur after delivery when there were no signs of preeclampsia before labor and delivery. Headache, confusion, an increase in blood pressure, abdominal pain, nausea, and vomiting signal impending convulsions. If convulsions have occurred or seem impending, the standard treatment is magnesium sulfate administered intravenously.

It is frustrating that, despite much research, the cause of preeclampsia is still unknown. One feature of preeclampsia demonstrated in the studies of German physician Hans Schobel and his colleagues is a markedly increased tone (state of constriction) of the smooth muscles in the woman's arteries, resulting from excess stimulation of these muscles by the nerves that control them. How this hyperstimulation arises is a question to be addressed by more research.

A study organized by the National Institutes of Health has demonstrated that long before preeclampsia develops, there is a reduction in blood vessels of the chemical *prostacyclin*, which causes them to relax (dilate), in relation to the chemical *thromboxane*, which causes them to constrict. We are just beginning to get a handle on the biochemical basis for preeclampsia.

PREMATURE LABOR, BIRTH, AND BABIES

Premature birth, defined as birth before thirty-seven weeks, is one of the great unsolved problems in maternity care. Premature birth occurs in 11 percent of all pregnancies and is on the rise. In the United States, prematurity accounts for the majority of deaths of babies after birth and for nearly half of neurological disabilities in children, including cerebral palsy. The cost of caring for premature babies also adds greatly to dollar outlays for medical care. Fifty percent of premature births occur after spontaneous premature labor, 30 percent after spontaneous premature rupture of the membranes (see next section), and 20 percent after purposeful intervention to bring about birth for the health of the mother, baby, or both.

The immediate problems of the sickest and usually smallest premature infants include *respiratory distress syndrome* (difficulty in gas exchange because of fluid and protein accumulation within the small air sacs and collapse of the sacs themselves); difficulty in feeding as a result of weakness; increased incidence of jaundice and increased sensitivity to its effects (pp. 270–271); increased susceptibility to infection; congenital defects, including those of the heart; and danger of bleeding within the brain and the resulting development of hydrocephalus (dilatation of the fluid-filled cavities or ventricles in the brain). The care rendered to these frail babies itself carries certain risks: the blowing out of a lung overinflated by a respirator (pneumothorax), blindness or impaired vision related to oxygen therapy, scarring of the lungs as a result of treatment with a respirator, errors in dosages of drugs and fluids, and so forth. Precautions are taken to minimize these risks.

Decisions about treatment for the very smallest and sickest premature babies just after birth are complicated, often made quickly and under conditions of great stress. Every decision carries risks. If parents choose medical intervention and the baby grows into a child with disabilities, the parents must live with the consequences and responsibilities entailed by their decision. On the other hand, if life-support measures are never initiated or are discontinued, the parents will have to accept responsibility for deciding to let the baby die. To help parents make these decisions, professional organizations of neonatologists (physicians who specialize in the medical care of newborns) are developing guidelines for determining which premature babies are likely to benefit from an all-out effort to save them and which are not.

Births before thirty-two weeks account for most of the disabilities and high health-care costs incurred with prematurity. Even with remarkable improvements in the care of premature infants in neonatal intensive care units, many who survive have lifelong disabilities. Babies who in the past would have died now survive, but with increased risk of disability, and babies who in the past would have survived with disabilities now survive in good health. In effect, we have at great cost moved the cutoff point for survival to an ever-lower gestational age, and the developmental outcomes for the youngest premature babies are still a problem.

It is not always desirable to attempt to stop premature labor. In situations such as infection of the uterus and amniotic fluid, fetal distress, and unexplained vaginal bleeding, the fetus is, in effect, trying to escape from a hostile intrauterine environment. In other cases, stopping labor would be welcome if only we knew how to do so.

Attempts to prevent spontaneous premature labor have included the closing and reinforcing with suture material of an incompetent, or structurally weak, cervix (occurring in 1 in 200 to 1 in 1,000 pregnant women), use of progesterone hormones, nutritional interventions, bed

rest, uterine monitoring at home to detect ea
apy might still stop it, and trials of various dru
stop uterine contractions. A large trial to test the
terone is now underway under sponsorship of the
Child Health and Human Development.

A growing understanding of the role of maternal in,
ture labor holds promise for prevention and treatment. ₍   the
uterus is present in about 80 percent of early preterm birth   .c the antibiotics used to treat these infections have not proved effective. There
is also a known association between urinary tract infection, both symptomatic (see p. 73) and asymptomatic (see Urine Culture, p. 20), and
premature birth as well as preliminary evidence that antibiotic treatment may be protective. Of considerable interest is the recent finding
that one type of bacterial vaginal infection called bacterial vaginosis (see
vaginitis, p. 80), increases the risk of premature birth by one and one-
half to three times and that treatment of pregnant women with symptoms of this infection reduces the risk significantly. However, according
to a large 1999 study, reported in 2000, treating women without symptoms of vaginitis who on testing after the sixteenth week were found to
have bacterial vaginosis (solely as a laboratory finding) did not reduce
the rate of premature labor, whether or not the women were at increased risk for premature labor (for example, having had a previous
premature baby). Nevertheless, The Centers for Disease Control and
Prevention, having weighed all the evidence, including the limitations
of the studies performed to date, still recommends that women with
asymptomatic bacterial vaginosis who are at increased risk for premature labor be treated. The final word is not in on this subject. Other
vaginal infections associated with premature labor include those caused
by the microorganisms gonorrhea (see p. 137), chlamydia (see p. 134),
group B streptococcus (see p. 137), trichomonas, and ureaplasma.

An association between periodontal (gum) disease and premature labor has been identified, presumably mediated by toxins from bacterial
gum infections that reach the uterus by way of the woman's blood. This
finding may represent a major breakthrough in our understanding of
premature labor. Whether treating gum infections will prevent premature labor remains to be seen, but it seems reasonable at this time to
hedge one's bets by attaining and maintaining the best possible dental
health.

that help predict premature labor measure by ultrasound the length of the cervix (a length of less than 2.5 centimeters has a negative effect) and the presence in the cervix and vagina of a protein made in the placenta, *fetal fibrinonectin*, which is normally absent between about twenty to thirty-seven weeks. The crux of the matter, however, will be whether being able to predict premature labor will result in being able to prevent it.

Although the tocolytic drugs currently available (magnesium sulfate and ritodrine hydrochloride are those most commonly used) are not able to stop premature labor permanently, they can buy twenty-four to forty-eight hours of time. During this time cortisone can be given to the fetus by way of the woman to help the fetal lungs mature and thereby reduce the baby's risk of having breathing difficulties resulting from respiratory distress syndrome (RDS). The protective effect of cortisone is needed only if the fetal membranes are intact; if the membranes have already broken, there is less risk for RDS. Other benefits of prebirth administration of cortisone are the prevention of a severe and sometimes fatal inflammation of the intestine known as *necrotizing enterocolitis* and the prevention of brain hemorrhage and of a brain disorder known as *periventricular leukomalacia*, both of which can result in permanent damage. These three additional protective effects of cortisone apply whether or not premature rupture of the membranes has occurred. Cortisone injections are given twice, twenty-four hours apart, and their effect lasts for one week, which means that if birth has not occurred in seven days even though contractions are continuing, cortisone must be given again.

Under two conditions premature birth is brought about intentionally to preserve the health of both mother and baby: preeclampsia (see p. 307) and intrauterine growth retardation (see p. 296). The decision to deliver early balances the risks of prematurity against the risks of continued pregnancy. Fetuses in trouble are identified through various tests of fetal well-being, discussed elsewhere (see tests in late pregnancy, p. 158). Although prematurity is not prevented through this strategy, in the past twenty years the number of stillbirths (see p. 284) in the United States has significantly declined as a result of this approach.

Because of the complexities of preterm labor and birth, every effort is made to provide care in medical centers fully equipped to handle high-risk pregnancies. When a premature baby is born at a community hospital, he or she is transferred by a specially trained transport team that can stabilize the infant before and during travel. There is no basis for routinely delivering by C-section or for routinely using forceps in a vaginal delivery in cases of prematurity.

Premature birth presents an unanticipated challenge to parents that complicates the early parent-baby relationship. Kennell and Klaus have adapted their recommendations on bonding and attachment for parents and their premature infants. Before transport to a medical center and after stabilization in the nursery, parents should be allowed to see their baby, even if only briefly and through the window of an incubator. If possible, the father should follow the transport team so that he can see and report on what is happening to the baby and establish a communication link with the medical center. The mother should visit as soon as she feels up to it. During telephone contact with doctors or nurses, both parents should listen in so that both hear what is said. After the initial period of adaptation, parents should begin to touch and gently massage the baby, even in the incubator, and look for the baby's responses to them. As the baby's condition improves, the parents can hold him or her, covered, over the chest, skin to skin *(kangaroo care)*. (A study from Zimbabwe showed that, compared with premature infants raised in incubators only, groups of babies cared for this way gained weight twice as quickly, were able to leave the hospital earlier, and had fewer deaths.) According to recent studies at Stanford University, massaging the skin with an ointment extracted from sheep's wool reduces the incidence of infection, presumably by providing a protective barrier similar to the vernix that coats the skin of the full-term infant (see p. 238). Both reducing the volume of noise and playing soft music appear to be beneficial (see p. 151). Family members of all generations should be encouraged to view the infant through the window of the nursery so that they, too, will begin to feel a sense of attachment. If at all possible, the baby should be breast-fed. Breast milk, initially pumped and tube fed to the baby, is particularly valuable for a premature baby.

PRETERM RUPTURE OF THE MEMBRANES

Before the thirty-seventh week, if the amniotic membranes break—a situation known medically as preterm rupture of the membranes—the woman typically starts labor soon. For the minority of women who do not go into labor in this situation, infection is of concern because the protective barrier between the fetus and the vagina, with its normal bacterial flora, has been broken. Between thirty-four and thirty-seven weeks the discussion of premature rupture of the membranes at term (see next section) largely applies. If the membrane breaks before thirty-four weeks, giving antibiotics to the woman, and through her to the fetus, can delay the onset of labor, allowing the fetus more time to mature and reducing the risk of infection for both mother and baby. For fetuses younger than thirty-two weeks, giving cortisone in addition to antibiotics can reduce the risks of bleeding into the brain and inflammation of the colon. If signs of infection do occur, delivery of the baby is quickly accomplished.

PREMATURE RUPTURE OF THE MEMBRANES AT TERM

Premature rupture of the membranes (PROM) at term is defined as leaking of amniotic fluid from the vagina prior to the onset of labor and after thirty-seven weeks of gestation. Its cause is not well understood. Smoking (pp. 142–143) and infection (see pp. 180, 300) may play a role. The risk of breaking the barrier formed by the amniotic membranes between the sterile intrauterine environment and the vagina, where many bacteria normally reside, is that bacteria can enter the uterus, where they can initiate an infection of both fetus and woman.

In most full-term infants, labor follows within hours of the so-called breaking of waters. Seventy percent of women will be in labor in twelve hours and over 90 percent by twenty-four hours, with little to no risk to themselves or to their babies. Only 2 to 5 percent will not deliver within seventy-two hours. The most common practice in PROM is to induce labor (see p. 195) by twenty-four hours, if not earlier, and to avoid vaginal examinations after an initial sterile speculum examination (to confirm that rupture has occurred and to assess the status of the cervix) until labor is underway. If a woman wants to wait until labor begins on its own, for example, because she is planning a birth at home, where induction is not possible, she can do so safely, as far as is known, unless signs of infection—fever, pain, discharge—develop. To minimize the risk of infection she should avoid tub baths and intercourse.

PROLAPSE OF THE UMBILICAL CORD

Prolapse (or falling through) of the umbilical cord into the vagina is a true obstetrical emergency. The cord may be trapped and compressed between the baby and the cervix, cutting off blood flow between the placenta and the fetus. The fetus can be endangered and even die.

Prolapse of the cord is more likely when the fetus does not fit snugly into the lower part of the uterus. Circumstances in which this occurs include breech presentation (pp. 277–283), prematurity (pp. 309–313), twins (pp. 317–321), disproportion (p. 289), and situations in which the amniotic membranes rupture (or are ruptured) before the head or other presenting part has occupied the lower portion of the uterus near the entrance to the vagina.

Cord prolapse can be detected by feeling the loops of the cord protruding from the cervix into the vagina. The fetal heart rate is usually depressed. The immediate treatment for cord prolapse, which buys time while the C-section team is mobilized, is for the woman to get onto her knees with her chest on the bed (or table) and her buttocks up. This position uses gravity to shift the fetus higher in the uterus, away from the cervix, and may allow the cord to slide back into the uterus or at least take pressure off it.

To achieve the same objectives, the attendant can place a hand in the vagina to push the fetus up higher and work the cord back into the uterus. Because of the high likelihood of repeated prolapse, almost all babies in this situation are delivered by C-section.

A form of cord prolapse known as *occult prolapse* occurs when the cord is positioned between the baby's head and the lower part of the uterus but does not fall through the cervix. Occult prolapse is recognized by alterations in the fetal heart rate in relation to uterine contractions, known as a variable deceleration (see Principles of Electronic Fetal Monitoring, p. 164). Changing the woman's position may reverse this condition.

SHOULDER DYSTOCIA

The term *shoulder dystocia* is used when the baby's shoulders become stuck during delivery, preventing further progress through the birth canal. The upper shoulder is wedged under and behind the unyielding symphysis pubis (see Figure 4.3), and the lower shoulder is pressed against the woman's equally unyielding sacrum. The diagnosis is made if the contraction following the birth of the head fails to result in the birth of the rest of the baby. Although in the vast majority of cases shoulder dystocia can be managed by certain maneuvers, in extreme cases it can be fatal. Another danger is that traction on the baby's head to dislodge the shoulder may stretch and damage the nerves passing through the neck to the arm with a risk of permanent palsy. The size of the baby in relation to the pelvic outlet is the major determining factor. Large babies, such as those of diabetic or very overweight mothers, are at increased risk. There is no way to predict severe shoulder dystocia; if there were, cesarean section would be the recommended course.

The initial approach to shoulder dystocia is to slide the shoulder under the pubic bones by pulling the baby's head and neck (and, thereby, the shoulder) down while an assistant pushes on the uterus from above. If this does not work, the attendant can try several maneuvers to rotate the shoulder to the side of the symphysis, where resistance to exiting the canal is much less. Another approach is to reach in and grasp the lower arm and pull it out of the canal, thereby reducing the pressure of the lower shoulder on the sacrum so that it can be drawn out. Having the woman draw the thighs up onto her abdomen may help rotate the symphysis pubis up and over the entrapped upper shoulder.

The asphyxia associated with prolonged cord compression during shoulder dystocia may lead the infant to begin breathing movements prior to actual birth. In this case there is a danger that the infant will suck amniotic fluid and mucus from his or her mouth and upper airways into the lungs. For this reason, standard practice is to suction the baby's mouth as soon as shoulder dystocia is suspected.

THERAPEUTIC ABORTION

This discussion is intended primarily for pregnant women and their partners who have come to the decision to terminate a pregnancy because of a major abnormality of the fetus. It is largely with the option of therapeutic abortion in mind that women undertake the testing that identifies malformed or genetically abnormal fetuses that are untreatable (see Expanded AFP Test, p. 24, and Genetics and Your Pregnancy, p. 34).

The surgical approach to abortion, dilatation and evacuation (D & E), was described in the section on miscarriage (see p. 303). The medical induction of abortion centers on the use of prostaglandin (see p. 197), usually taken orally as the drug misoprostol, to cause uterine contractions and cervical dilatation. Misoprostol can be used in the first or second trimesters alone or combined with other drugs. In the first trimester misoprostol can be given with methotrexate, which destroys rapidly dividing trophoblastic cells (see Ectopic Pregnancy, p. 289). This combination is more effective than misoprostol alone. Misoprostol can also be used in combination during both the first and second trimesters with mifepristone (RU486), a chemical that blocks the action of progesterone, the female hormone whose presence is essential in supporting a pregnancy. By blocking progesterone, mifepristone causes the implanted embryo to separate from the uterus, and, like prostaglandin, softens the cervix and increases uterine contractions. Mifepristone is widely used in Europe and China, but its use in the United States has been hindered by antiabortion politicians and lobbyists despite FDA approval. Both mifepristone and prostaglandin can be used to induce labor after a fetus has died in utero (see Death of a Fetus or Baby, p. 283). Prostaglandin is also used to induce labor (see p. 197); misoprostol may also be effective for this purpose.

TWINS AND OTHER MULTIPLE PREGNANCIES

The thought of twins probably crosses the mind of every pregnant woman and her partner—and with good reason, for twins are not uncommon. Twins pose special problems in pregnancy and birth. About 4 in 1,000 births, regardless of the ethnic background of the parents, will involve *identical (monozygotic)* twins, those who originate from a single fertilized egg (ovum) that later separates into two similar embryos. The frequency of twins involving two eggs fertilized during a single ovulation, so-called *fraternal*, or *dizygotic*, twins, is more variable. The rate is higher in some families and increases with the number of pregnancies and the woman's weight and height. In whites, the incidence of fraternal twins is about 1 in 100; in blacks, 1 in 79; in Japanese, 1 in 155. Being a twin increases one's chances of bearing or fathering twins.

The drugs and hormones used to promote ovulation in cases of infertility are notorious in producing multiple ovulations and conceptions.

Following hormone treatment, multiple pregnancy may occur as often as 20 to 40 percent of the time. One study showed that after administration of the drug clomiphene to induce ovulation, 6.9 percent of the resulting pregnancies were twins; 0.5 percent, triplets (without fertility drugs triplets are born once in every 10,000 births); 0.3 percent, quadruplets; and 0.13 percent, quintuplets. Another study of clomiphene showed the incidence of occurrence of multiple fetuses to be 13 percent. In 1997 and 1998 the birth of septuplets (seven babies) and octuplets (eight babies) following the use of clomiphene made headlines worldwide.

The figures quoted for occurrence of twins have to do with percentages of babies born. Now that ultrasound is widely used during pregnancy, it has become clear that the frequency of twin fetuses is far higher than birth statistics indicate; in many cases, only one fetus survives to be born. According to studies of Charles E. Boklage, a developmental biologist at the East Carolina University School of Medicine, at least 10 to 15 percent of those of us who consider ourselves singletons (the sole offspring of our mother's pregnancy leading to our birth) actually started life as a twin. Our co-twin was lost to miscarriage early in pregnancy, while we survived, a phenomenon sometimes referred to as "the vanishing twin syndrome." We have long recognized that many women have vaginal bleeding in the first trimester without losing the pregnancy, what has been called *cyclic bleeding of pregnancy*. It now appears that the spontaneous aborting of one twin fetus accounts for some of these episodes of bleeding.

From the very outset, twin fetuses have more problems than singletons. The major problem is premature birth (see p. 309). Up to 50 percent of twins are born prematurely, and up to 10 percent of all premature babies are twins. In one study, the average gestational age of twins at birth was thirty-five weeks, compared with thirty-nine weeks for singletons. With triplets, the average age at birth was thirty-three weeks; with quadruplets, only twenty-nine weeks.

Twins are more than twice as likely as singletons to be affected with major (see p. 275) and minor birth defects. Because they are competing for nutrients, they are more vulnerable to malnutrition (see Intrauterine Growth Disturbance, p. 296), which may affect one or both fetuses. Because of the risk of what is called discordant growth, in which one twin is malnourished, surveillance of twins by ultrasound and other tests of fetal well-being are performed frequently.

Joining of the blood vessels in the placentas of monozygotic twins results in the mixing of blood and creates a setup for several unique problems. One twin can receive too much of the combined blood while the other receives too little. The twin with decreased blood volume can have retarded growth, hypotension (low blood pressure), and an underdeveloped heart. The twin with excess blood can be larger and at increased risk for heart failure, abnormal blood clotting, and jaundice. Both twins are at risk for death at birth.

If one twin dies in utero, the dissolving of its tissues can release chemicals that can cause the blood of the other twin to clot, often with serious consequences.

Women pregnant with twins are at increased risk for such complications of pregnancy as preeclampsia (p. 307), anemia, hemorrhage at delivery, and hydramnios (p. 295) and such complications of labor as premature labor (p. 309), prolonged labor, nonvertex fetal presentation (especially breech presentation; see p. 277), and prolapse of the umbilical cord (p. 315).

A woman with twin fetuses needs to eat for three people, not only for two. Her caloric intake should increase by 300 calories per day, and she should take sixty to eighty milligrams of supplemental iron. Her need for folic acid is also increased and can be met through diet or supplementation.

Issues with twins do not end when labor begins. A decision will have to be made about vaginal versus cesarean delivery. There is general agreement that cesarean section is the preferred route if the twin presenting first is in the breech position, because most breeches of twins who present first are of the footling type and cord prolapse (see p. 315) is a major risk. If both twins present headfirst, vaginal birth is a reasonable choice. If the twin who presents first is headfirst and the second twin is breech, it may be possible to turn the second twin to a vertex presentation after the birth of the first or to deliver it in the breech position. Not all physicians are skilled in vaginal breech delivery. If this option is important to you, you may need to do some doctor shopping. (See further discussion under Breech Presentation, p. 277.)

Ideally, the presence of twins should be identified before labor and delivery so that appropriate plans can be made. More help is needed at birth to deal with the unexpected, and more help is needed afterward to care for the babies.

Ultrasound is the best way to diagnose twins early in pregnancy; it can demonstrate separate gestational sacs as early as six to ten weeks. The increasingly routine use of ultrasound in pregnancies has resulted in a higher percentage of twin pregnancies being identified early.

A by-product of testing for alpha-fetoprotein in the second trimester (see Expanded AFP Test, p. 24) is the identification of twins, for the presence of more than one fetus is one cause of persistent elevated maternal alpha-fetoprotein levels.

Later in pregnancy twins are suspected when the size of the uterus is larger than would be expected on the basis of gestational age. This finding warrants an explanation that includes checking for twins with ultrasound. (Other explanations for a large uterus include an error in dating the pregnancy, hydramnios [p. 295], fibroid tumors of the uterus [p. 75], and, late in pregnancy, a large single fetus.)

Late in the second trimester and throughout the third trimester, it is possible to identify twins by palpation of the uterus and to hear two distinct fetal heartbeats. The heart tones can be heard equally well at two separate sites on the abdomen; each heart beats at a different rate, and may be recorded by two observers listening and counting simultaneously.

When twins are suspected of having open neural tube or other serious congenital defects (see p. 275), amniocentesis must be done on both sacs to determine whether one or both twins are affected. Similarly, if twins are at increased risk for chromosomal or gene abnormalities, both need to be studied by amniocentesis and cell culture or gene analysis (see Genetics and Your Pregnancy, p. 34).

Twins make more complicated the already difficult issue of therapeutic abortion. In conditions under which abortion might be performed for an abnormal fetus, as in the case of Down syndrome, the presence of a normal twin along with the chromosomally abnormal one creates a dilemma, because routine abortion procedures would lead to the loss of both. There are reports of selective termination of the life of an abnormal twin. In this ethically controversial procedure, the heart of the fetus is punctured with a needle guided through the uterus using ultrasound visualization, resulting in its death. The normal twin goes on to develop, be born, and survive without difficulties.

Rarely, a malformed and usually nonviable twin will threaten the survival of its normal mate. An example is a twin lacking its own heart and relying on its co-twin's heart to pump blood through a shared circulation. The normal twin's heart is at serious risk of failing as it attempts to do the work of two. A treatment for this disorder is discussed in Treating the Fetus (p. 153).

Although twins face many hurdles, if they are not born very prematurely most do fine. Women expecting twins should plan for more help at home in the early months. Not only will they want time to recover from the extra strain on their bodies, but twins take more time to feed, to bathe, and to enjoy. Once the adjustment has been made and the obstacle of a more complicated birth is past, parents may be delighted and proud of producing two babies after only one pregnancy and labor.

VENOUS THROMBOEMBOLISM AND PHLEBITIS

Venous thromboembolism is the medical term for a blood clot *(thrombosis)* in a vein and its consequences, the passage of a detached fragment of the clot through the veins to other organs, usually the lungs. The piece of clot that has broken free is called an *embolus*, and the carrying downstream of an embolus by the blood current to a distant site is called an *embolism*. The most common site of thrombosis in pregnancy is the deep veins of the legs, where the blood clot is called a *deep venous thrombosis*, or *DVT*. A current estimate is that DVT occurs once in 1,000 to 2,000 pregnancies. Seventy-five percent of DVTs take place before birth, and 66 percent of emboli to the lungs (pulmonary emboli) occur after birth. DVT can occur without an embolus. Without treatment, as many as 24 percent of women with DVT will have a pulmonary embolism, and 15 percent of these will die as a result. With treatment, pulmonary embolus occurs in only 4.5 percent of women and mortality is reduced to less than 1 percent.

DVT is heralded by swelling and pain of the leg, usually the left calf, a condition known as *phlebitis*, or inflammation of the vein with clotting of blood within it. Recognition of phlebitis is made difficult by the common swelling and discomfort of the legs experienced by pregnant women. The diagnosis is confirmed primarily by ultrasound, and the treatment is anticoagulation with the drug *heparin*, given initially by vein and later by injection. An anticoagulant is a drug that interferes with blood clotting, arresting the enlargement and extension of a clot through the interior of a vein and the splitting off of fragments that can travel to the lungs. Heparin treatment is continued throughout pregnancy and into the period after birth. Heparin is also used preventively in women at increased risk for thrombosis.

The symptoms of pulmonary embolus depend on the size and location of the clot or clots that have lodged in veins of the lung. They include shortness of breath, chest pain, cough, rapid heart and breathing rates, fever, and shock. A lung scan using a radioactive chemical (not harmful to the fetus) is the most common diagnostic test. Treatment is with heparin. Life-threatening embolus may require surgery for removal of the clot or at-the-site treatment with a drug to dissolve it. Women with a personal history of previous thromboembolism, whether during pregnancy or not, and women with a strong family history of this disorder are candidates for testing regarding preventive treatment with heparin throughout pregnancy.

The risk of venous thromboembolism in a pregnant woman is five times higher than it is in a nonpregnant woman of the same age. Known contributors to this increased risk are pregnancy-associated changes in the veins of the legs and in the blood-clotting system. The leg veins of the pregnant woman are more distensible and the flow of blood through them is more sluggish, largely as a result of pressure exerted by the uterus on the large vein in the abdomen that drains blood from the legs and pelvis. This pooling and slowing of flow is the perfect condition for clotting. Further adding to the predisposition to clotting is the marked increase in pregnancy of the proteins responsible for formation of a clot.

Several gene mutations are known to affect blood-clotting proteins and increase the risk for thrombosis. These mutations may be hereditary or occur spontaneously. They should be looked for if there is a family history of thromboembolism. Women with antiphospholipid syndrome (see p. 300) are also at increased risk.

In 1999, Michael Kupferminc and his colleagues in Israel reported an association between gene mutations known to promote blood clotting and serious obstetrical complications, including severe preeclampsia (see 307), placental abruption (see 304), intrauterine growth retardation (see 296), and stillbirth (see 284), all conditions involving abnormalities of the placenta. These findings point to a promising line of research into these vexing disorders. It remains to be seen whether anticoagulants will be preventive in the treatment of women identified as prone to blood clotting.

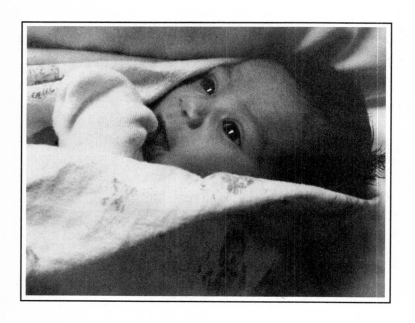

APPENDIX:
FURTHER READING AND
REFERENCE

PREGNANCY CARE

Balaskas, Jane. *Preparing for Birth with Yoga.* New York: Element Books, Inc., 1994.

Blumenthal, M., et al., eds. *The Complete German Commission E Monographs: Therapeutic Guide to Herbal Medicines.* Austin, TX: American Botanical Council, 1998.

Boston Women's Health Book Collective, *The New Our Bodies, Ourselves.* New York: Touchstone, 1998.

Brasner, Shari, M.D. *Advice from a Pregnant Obstetrician: An Insider's Guide.* New York: Hyperion, 1998.

Enkin, Murray W., Marc J. N. C. Keirse, Mary J. Renfrew, and Jamea P. Neilson. *A Guide to Effective Care in Pregnancy and Childbirth.* 3d ed. New York and Oxford: Oxford University Press, 2000.

Information published on the Internet by the National Institutes of Health on dietary supplements, including herbal products: *http://www.nal.usda.gov/fnic/IBIDS/*.

http://www.med.uc.edu/embryology/
Animations of major stages of fetal development.

Nilsson, Lennart. *A Child Is Born.* A Merloyd Lawrence Book. New York: Dell Publishing, 1990.

Noble, Elizabeth. *Essential Exercises for the Childbearing Year.* 3d ed. Boston: Houghton Mifflin, 1995.

Physicians Desk Reference for Herbal Medicines, Montvale, NJ: Medical Economics, 2000.

Pregnancy Today: *http://pregnancytoday.com.* Articles, interviews with experts, and lively chat site for expectant women. Run by Nancy Price of Walnut Creek, CA. Also runs similar site for parenting: Babies Today, at *http://babiestoday.com.*

Spencer, Paula. *Parenting Guide to Pregnancy and Childbirth.* New York: Ballantine, 1998.

tylerforlife.com and neogenscreening.com. Explains reason for testing all newborns for metabolic diseases, identifies deficiencies in existing mandated programs state-by-state, and provides information on how to arrange for private testing.

LABOR AND BIRTH

Born in the U.S.A., a video by Marsha Jarmel and Ken Schneider, Fanlight Productions, 4196 Washington St. Suite 2, Boston MA 02131, 800-937-4113 *www.fanlight.com.* A documentary video which portrays labor and birth occurring in different settings (hospital, birthing center, and home) as well as attendants from different disciplines (physician, nurse, midwife, and lay midwife).

Klaus, Marshall H., John H. Kennell, and Phyllis H. Klaus. *Mothering the Mother: How a Doula Can Help You Have a Shorter, Easier, and Healthier Birth.* Photographs by Suzanne Arms. A Merloyd Lawrence Book. Cambridge, MA: Perseus Publishing, 1993.

Korte, Diana, *The VBAC Companion*, Boston: The Harvard Common Press, 1997.

O'Driscoll, Kieran, and Declan Meagher, with Peter Boylan. *Active Management of Labor: The Dublin Experience.* St. Louis, MO: Mosby-Year Book Europe Limited, 1993.

Roan, Sharon L. *Postpartum Depression: Every Woman's Guide to Diagnosis, Treatment, and Prevention.* Holbrook, MA: Adams Media Corporation, 1997.

Rooks, Judith P. *Midwifery and Childbirth in America.* Philadelphia: Temple University Press, 1997.

THE NEWBORN

Brazelton, T. Berry, *On Becoming a Family.* New York: Delacorte Press, 1981.

Brazelton, T. Berry, M.D. *Touchpoints: Your Child's Emotional and Behavioral Development.* A Merloyd Lawrence Book. Cambridge, MA: Perseus Publishing, 1992.

Brazelton, T. Berry, and Cramer, Bertrand G., *The Earlier Relationship.* Cambridge, MA: Perseus Books, 1990.

Klaus, Marshall H., Kennell, John H., and Klaus, Phyllis H., *Bonding: Building the Foundation of Secure Attachment and Independence*. Cambridge, MA: Perseus Books, 1995.

Klaus, Marshall H., M.D., and Phyllis H. Klaus, C.S.W., M.E.C.C. *Your Amazing Newborn*. A Merloyd Lawrence Book, Cambridge, MA: Perseus Publishing, 1998.

Maurer, Daphne, and Charles Maurer. *The World of the Newborn*. New York: Basic Books, 1989.

BREAST-FEEDING

Huggins, Kathleen. *The Nursing Mother's Companion*. Revised. Boston: Harvard Common Press, 1999.

La Leche League International. *The Womanly Art of Breastfeeding*. Franklin Park, IL. The classic reference on the topic. Practical and complete.

Riordan, Jan, and Kathleen Auerbach. *Breastfeeding and Human Lactation*. 2d ed. Sudbury, MA: Jones and Bartlett, 1998. A scholarly textbook on the topic but also full of practical advice.

http://www.breastfeeding.com

ORGANIZATIONS

American Academy of Family Physicians (AAFP)
11400 Tomahawk Creek Parkway
Leawood, KS 66211–2672
Tel.: 913–906–6000
fp@aafp.org
http://www.aafp.org

American Academy of Pediatrics (AAP)
141 Northwest Point Blvd.
Elk Grove Village, Illinois 60007–1098
Tel.: 847–434–4000; Fax: 847–434–8000
kidsdocs@aap.org
http://www.aap.org

American Board of Family Practice (ABFP)
2228 Young Drive
Lexington, KY 40505
Tel.: 1–888–995–5700; Fax: 859–335–7501
general@abfp.org
http://www.abfp.org

American College of Nurse-Midwives (ACNM)
818 Connecticut Avenue NW, Suite 900
Washington, DC 20006

Tel.: 202–728–9860; Fax: 202–728–9897
For information on finding a midwife in your area,
    call 1–888-MIDWIFE
info@acnm.org
http://www.acnm.org

American College of Obstetricians and Gynecologists (ACOG)
409 12th Street SW
P.O. Box 96920
Washington, D.C. 20090–6920
http://www.acog.org

Battery Breast Pump 4850
White River Concepts
San Clemente, CA
Tel.: 1–800–342–3906
custsrc@whiteriver.com
http://www.whiteriver.com/
Low-cost pump ideal for part-time workers. Company also manufactures Breast-
    Feeding Success Nipples, designed to deliver bottled milk in the same way as the
    human breast.

Boston Women's Health Book Collective
P.O. Box 192
240a Elm Street
Somerville, MA 02144
Tel.: 617–625–0277; Fax: 617–625–0294
office@bwhbc.org
http://www.ourbodiesourselves.org

Breastfeeding National Network
Tel.: 1–800–835–5968
http://www.medela.com
The Medela Company provides information on where to rent its brand of breast pumps
    and find baby scales, nursing bras, and breastfeeding specialists in your area.

Citizens for Midwifery
P.O. Box 82227
Athens, GA 30608
Tel.: 1–888-CfM–4880
cfmidwifery@yahoo.com
http://www.cfmidwifery.org

Consumer Reports
Guide to Baby Products
P.O. Box 103637
Des Moines, IA 50336
Tel.: 515–237–4903; Fax: 515–237–4765
http://www.consumerreports.org

Cordblood Registry
Tel.: 1–888-CORDBLOOD (267–3256)
Outside U.S. Tel.: 650–635–1420
http://www.cordblood.com
Private company, currently the largest, that works with University of Arizona to freeze stem cells from cord blood for possible later use by the donor child and family. Arranges for collection and shipping.

Doulas of North America (DONA)
3513 North Grove Drive
Alpine, UT 84004
Tel.: 801–756–7331; Fax: 801–763–1847
AskDONA@aol.com
http://www.DONA.com

Global Maternal/Child Health Association, Inc.
P.O. Box 1400
Wilsonville, OR 97070
Tel.: 503–682–3600; Fax: 503–682–3434
waterbirth@aol.com
http://www.water birth.com
Advocates for water birth, founded by Barbara Harper, R.N. Provides names of hospitals and midwives who practice water birth. (See p. 193.)

International Childbirth Education Association, Inc.
P.O. Box 20048
Minneapolis, Minnesota 55420
Tel: 952–854–8660; Fax: 952–854–8772
info@icea.org
http://www.icea.org
Resource center for books, tapes, and videos, teacher's aids. Sponsors childbirth classes. Local chapters. Regularly updated catalogue is very complete (just about everything) on topics such as fathering, father's role in pregnancy, doulas, comfort measures, cesareans, child care. Offers training and curricula for childbirth educators, lactation consultants, and doulas.

International Lactation Consultants Association (ILCA)
4101 Lake Boone Trail, Suite 201
Raleigh, NC 27607
Tel: 919–787–5181; Fax: 919–787–4916
ilca@erols.com
http://www.ilca.org

La Leche League International, Inc.
1400 N. Meacham Road
Schaumberg, IL 60173–4048
Tel.:1–800-LA LECHE, 847–519–7730
http://www.lalecheleague.org

Advocacy group for breastfeeding. Resource list. Publishers of classic book, The Womanly Art of Breastfeeding. *Local chapters for support and lactation consultation.*

March of Dimes Birth Defects Foundation
1275 Mamaroneck Avenue
White Plains, NY 10605
Tel.: 914–428–7100
Resource Center Tel.: 1–888–663–4637
http://www.modimes.org

Midwives Alliance of North America (MANA)
Tel.: 1–888–923-MANA (6262)
MANAinfo@aol.com
http://www.mana.org

Mothers and Others for a Livable Planet
40 West 20ᵗʰ Street
New York, NY 10011
http://www.mothers.org
Education for safe and sustainable consumer choices.

National Association of Childbearing Centers (NACC)
3123 Gottschall Road
Perkiomenville, PA 18074
Tel.: 215–234–8068; Fax: 215–234–8829
http://www.birthcenters.org

National Committee for Quality Assurance (NCQA)
2000 L Street NW, Suite 500
Washington, DC 20036
Tel.: 202–955–3500
Tel.: 1–888–275–7585
http://www.ncqa.org
For "report cards" on HMOs.

National Maternal and Child Health Clearinghouse
Tel.: 1–888–434–4MCH
http://www.nmchc.org

National SIDS Resource Center
2070 Chain Bridge Road, Suite 450
Vienna, VA 22182–2536
Tel.: 703–821–8955; Fax: 703–821–2098
http:/www.circsol.com/mch

Organization of Teratology Information Services
Tel.: 801–328–2229
National referral: 1–888–285–3410
http://orpheus.ucsd.edu/otis/

For name of center nearest to you with information on the effects of drugs and chemi-
cals on the fetus.

SIDS: "Back to Sleep" Campaign

National Institute of Child Health & Human Development
National Institute of Health
http://156.40.88.3/sids/
Information on SIDS (Sudden Infant Death Syndrome—see p. 273) and the govern-
ment's efforts to prevent it.

World Institute on Disability (WID)

510 16th Street, Suite 100
Oakland, CA 94612–1500
Tel.: 510–763–4100; Fax: 510–763–4109
webmail@wid.org
http://www.wid.org

The Women's Institute for Childbearing Policy

c/o Jane Pincus
P.O. Box 72
Roxbury, VT 05669

INDEX

ABOUT THE AUTHOR

Richard I. Feinbloom, M.D., is a family practitioner and pediatrician. A native Philadelphian, he received his medical degree from the School of Medicine at the University of Pennsylvania. He has taught at Harvard Medical School and the State University of New York at Stony Brook, has been a consultant to the International Childbirth Education Association, and was a founding member of the Physicians for Social Responsibility. Dr. Feinbloom has had private practices in Cambridge, Massachusetts, and Cameron Park, California. He is the author and co-author of a number of books on pregnancy and child health. He currently is a member of the medical staff of The Permanente Medical Group (the physician component of the Kaiser Permanente Health Plan) in San Francisco.

pregnancybook.com

Because our knowledge about pregnancy is changing ever more rapidly, I am committed to keeping the book up-to-date using the internet website pregnancybook.com. The website contains instructions for contacting me.

Thank you.